Mastering Machine Learning with R
Third Edition

Advanced machine learning techniques for building smart applications with R 3.5

Cory Lesmeister

D1597141

BIRMINGHAM - MUMBAI

Mastering Machine Learning with R
Third Edition

Commissioning Editor: Sunith Shetty
Acquisition Editor: Devika Battike
Content Development Editor: Unnati Guha
Technical Editor: Dinesh Chaudhary
Copy Editor: Safis Editing
Project Coordinator: Manthan Patel
Proofreader: Safis Editing
Indexer: Priyanka Dhadke
Graphics: Jisha Chirayil
Production Coordinator: Jisha Chirayil

First published: October 2015
Second edition: April 2017
Third edition: January 2019

Production reference: 1310119

Published by Packt Publishing Ltd.
Livery Place
35 Livery Street
Birmingham
B3 2PB, UK.

ISBN 978-1-78961-800-6

www.packtpub.com

mapt.io

Mapt is an online digital library that gives you full access to over 5,000 books and videos, as well as industry leading tools to help you plan your personal development and advance your career. For more information, please visit our website.

Why subscribe?

- Spend less time learning and more time coding with practical eBooks and Videos from over 4,000 industry professionals

- Improve your learning with Skill Plans built especially for you

- Get a free eBook or video every month

- Mapt is fully searchable

- Copy and paste, print, and bookmark content

Packt.com

Did you know that Packt offers eBook versions of every book published, with PDF and ePub files available? You can upgrade to the eBook version at www.packt.com and as a print book customer, you are entitled to a discount on the eBook copy. Get in touch with us at customercare@packtpub.com for more details.

At www.packt.com, you can also read a collection of free technical articles, sign up for a range of free newsletters, and receive exclusive discounts and offers on Packt books and eBooks.

Contributors

About the author

Cory Lesmeister has over fourteen years of quantitative experience and is currently a senior data scientist for the Advanced Analytics team at Cummins, Inc. in Columbus, Indiana. Cory spent 16 years at Eli Lilly and Company in sales, market research, Lean Six Sigma, marketing analytics, and new product forecasting. He also has several years of experience in the insurance and banking industries, both as a consultant and as a manager of marketing analytics. A former US Army active duty and reserve officer, Cory was stationed in Baghdad, Iraq, in 2009 serving as the strategic advisor to the 29,000-person Iraqi Oil Police, succeeding where others failed by acquiring and delivering promised equipment to help the country secure and protect its oil infrastructure. Cory has a BBA in Aviation Administration from the University of North Dakota and a commercial helicopter license.

About the reviewers

Subhash Shah works as a head of technology at AIMDek Technologies Pvt. Ltd. He is an experienced solutions architect with over 12 years of experience. He holds a degree in information technology from a reputable university. He is an advocate of open source development and its use in solving critical business problems at a reduced cost. His interests include microservices, data analysis, machine learning, artificial intelligence, and databases. He is an admirer of quality code and TDD. His technical skills include translating business requirements into scalable architecture, designing sustainable solutions, and project delivery. He is a co-author of *MySQL 8 Administrator's Guide* and *Hands-on High Performance with Spring 5*.

Doug Ortiz is an experienced enterprise cloud, big data, data analytics, and solutions architect who has architected, designed, developed, re-engineered, and integrated enterprise solutions. His other expertise includes Amazon Web Services, Azure, Google Cloud Platform, business intelligence, Hadoop, Spark, NoSQL databases, and SharePoint. He is the founder of Illustris.

Packt is searching for authors like you

If you're interested in becoming an author for Packt, please visit `authors.packtpub.com` and apply today. We have worked with thousands of developers and tech professionals, just like you, to help them share their insight with the global tech community. You can make a general application, apply for a specific hot topic that we are recruiting an author for, or submit your own idea.

Table of Contents

Preface

Given the growing popularity of the R-zero-cost statistical programming environment, there has never been a better time to start applying **machine learning (ML)** to your data. This book will teach you advanced techniques in ML, using the latest code in R 3.5. You will delve into various complex features of supervised learning, unsupervised learning, and reinforcement learning algorithms to design efficient and powerful ML models.

This newly updated edition is packed with fresh examples covering a range of tasks from different domains. *Mastering Machine Learning with R* starts by showing you how to quickly manipulate data and prepare it for analysis. You will explore simple and complex models and understand how to compare them. You'll also learn to use the latest library support, such as TensorFlow and Keras-R, for performing advanced computations. Additionally, you'll explore complex topics such as **natural language processing (NLP)**, time series analysis, and clustering, which will further refine your skills in developing applications. Each chapter will help you implement advanced ML algorithms using real-world examples. You'll even be introduced to reinforcement learning, along with its various use cases and models. In the concluding chapters, you'll get a glimpse into how some of these black box models can be diagnosed and understood.

By the end of this book, you'll be equipped with the skills to deploy ML techniques in your own projects or at work.

Who this book is for

This book is designed for data science professionals, statisticians, data analysts, or anyone with a working knowledge of R who now wants to take their analytical skills to the next level and become an expert in the field. Not only do they want to learn the methods, but they also want to know how they can put them into practice, making a difference in the real world. The book has interesting datasets and covers the latest techniques for gleaning insights from that data.

What this book covers

Here is a list of changes compared with the second edition by chapter.

Chapter 1, *Preparing and Understanding Data*, covers the loading of data and demonstrates how to obtain an understanding of its structure and dimensions, as well as how to install the necessary packages.

Chapter 2, *Linear Regression,* contains improved code, and superior charts have been provided; other than that, it remains relatively close to the original.

Chapter 3, *Logistic Regression,* contains improved and streamlined code. One of my favorite techniques, multivariate adaptive regression splines, has been added. This technique performs well, handles non-linearity, and is easy to explain. It is my base model.

Chapter 4, *Advanced Feature Selection in Linear Models,* includes techniques not only for regression, but also for a classification problem.

Chapter 5, *K-Nearest Neighbors and Support Vector Machines,* includes streamlined and simplified code.

Chapter 6, *Tree-Based Classification,* is augmented by the addition of the very popular techniques provided by the XGBOOST package. Additionally, the technique of using a random forest as a feature selection tool is incorporated.

Chapter 7, *Neural Networks and Deep Learning,* has been updated with additional information on deep learning methods and includes improved code for the H2O package, including hyperparameter search.

Chapter 8, *Creating Ensembles and Multiclass Methods,* has completely new content, involving the utilization of several great packages.

Chapter 9, *Cluster Analysis,* includes the methodology for executing unsupervised learning with random forests added.

Chapter 10, *Principal Component Analysis,* uses a different dataset, while an out-of-sample prediction has been added.

Chapter 11, *Association Analysis,* explains association analysis, and applies not only to making recommendations, product placement, and promotional pricing, but can also be used in manufacturing, web usage, and healthcare.

Chapter 12, *Time Series and Causality,* includes a couple of additional years of climate data, along with a demonstration of different causality test methods.

Chapter 13, *Text Mining,* includes additional data and improved code.

Appendix, *Creating a Package,* includes additional data packages.

To get the most out of this book

Assuming the reader has a working knowledge of R and of basic statistics, this book will provide the skills and tools required to get the reader up and running with R and ML as quickly and painlessly as possible. There will probably always be detractors who complain that it does not offer enough math or does not do this, or that, or the other thing, but my answer to that is that these books already exist! Why duplicate what has already been done, and very well, for that matter? Again, I have sought to provide something different, something to hold the reader's attention, and allow them to succeed in this competitive and rapidly changing field.

Download the example code files

You can download the example code files for this book from your account at www.packt.com. If you purchased this book elsewhere, you can visit www.packt.com/support and register to have the files emailed directly to you.

You can download the code files by following these steps:

1. Log in or register at www.packt.com.
2. Select the **SUPPORT** tab.
3. Click on **Code Downloads & Errata**.
4. Enter the name of the book in the **Search** box and follow the onscreen instructions.

Once the file is downloaded, please make sure that you unzip or extract the folder using the latest version of:

- WinRAR/7-Zip for Windows
- Zipeg/iZip/UnRarX for Mac
- 7-Zip/PeaZip for Linux

The code bundle for the book is also hosted on GitHub at https://github.com/PacktPublishing/Mastering-Machine-Learning-with-R-Third-Edition. In case there's an update to the code, it will be updated on the existing GitHub repository.

We also have other code bundles from our rich catalog of books and videos available at https://github.com/PacktPublishing/. Check them out!

Download the color images

We also provide a PDF file that has color images of the screenshots/diagrams used in this book. You can download it here: http://www.packtpub.com/sites/default/files/downloads/9781789618006_ColorImages.pdf.

Conventions used

There are a number of text conventions used throughout this book.

CodeInText: Indicates code words in text, database table names, folder names, filenames, file extensions, pathnames, dummy URLs, user input, and Twitter handles. Here is an example: "Mount the downloaded WebStorm-10*.dmg disk image file as another disk in your system."

A block of code is set as follows:

```
html, body, #map {
  height: 100%;
  margin: 0;
  padding: 0
}
```

When we wish to draw your attention to a particular part of a code block, the relevant lines or items are set in bold:

```
[default]
exten => s,1,Dial(Zap/1|30)
exten => s,2,Voicemail(u100)
exten => s,102,Voicemail(b100)
exten => i,1,Voicemail(s0)
```

Any command-line input or output is written as follows:

```
$ mkdir css
$ cd css
```

Bold: Indicates a new term, an important word, or words that you see onscreen. For example, words in menus or dialog boxes appear in the text like this. Here is an example: "Select **System info** from the **Administration** panel."

 Warnings or important notes appear like this.

Tips and tricks appear like this.

Get in touch

Feedback from our readers is always welcome.

General feedback: If you have questions about any aspect of this book, mention the book title in the subject of your message and email us at customercare@packtpub.com.

Errata: Although we have taken every care to ensure the accuracy of our content, mistakes do happen. If you have found a mistake in this book, we would be grateful if you would report this to us. Please visit www.packt.com/submit-errata, selecting your book, clicking on the Errata Submission Form link, and entering the details.

Piracy: If you come across any illegal copies of our works in any form on the Internet, we would be grateful if you would provide us with the location address or website name. Please contact us at copyright@packt.com with a link to the material.

If you are interested in becoming an author: If there is a topic that you have expertise in and you are interested in either writing or contributing to a book, please visit authors.packtpub.com.

Reviews

Please leave a review. Once you have read and used this book, why not leave a review on the site that you purchased it from? Potential readers can then see and use your unbiased opinion to make purchase decisions, we at Packt can understand what you think about our products, and our authors can see your feedback on their book. Thank you!

For more information about Packt, please visit packt.com.

Preparing and Understanding Data

1

"We've got to use every piece of data and piece of information, and hopefully that will help us be accurate with our player evaluation. For us, that's our lifeblood."

– *Billy Beane, General Manager Oakland Athletics, subject of the book Moneyball*

Research consistently shows that machine learning and data science practitioners spend most of their time manipulating data and preparing it for analysis. Indeed, many find it the most tedious and least enjoyable part of their work. Numerous companies are offering solutions to the problem but, in my opinion, results at this point are varied. Therefore, in this first chapter, I shall endeavor to provide a way of tackling the problem that will ease the burden of getting your data ready for machine learning. The methodology introduced in this chapter will serve as the foundation for data preparation and for understanding many of the subsequent chapters. I propose that once you become comfortable with this tried and true process, it may very well become your favorite part of machine learning—as it is for me.

The following are the topics that we'll cover in this chapter:

- Overview
- Reading the data
- Handling duplicate observations
- Descriptive statistics
- Exploring categorical variables
- Handling missing values
- Zero and near-zero variance features
- Treating the data
- Correlation and linearity

Overview

If you haven't been exposed to large, messy datasets, then be patient, for it's only a matter of time. If you've encountered such data, has it been in a domain where you have little subject matter expertise? If not, then once again I proffer that it's only a matter of time. Some of the common problems that make up this term *messy* data include the following:

- Missing or invalid values
- Novel levels in a categorical feature that show up in algorithm production
- High cardinality in categorical features such as zip codes
- High dimensionality
- Duplicate observations

So this begs the question *what are we to do?* Well, first we need to look at what are the critical tasks that need to be performed during this phase of the process. The following tasks serve as the foundation for building a learning algorithm. They're from the paper by SPSS, *CRISP-DM 1.0*, a step-by-step data-mining guide available at `https://the-modeling-agency.com/crisp-dm.pdf`:

- Data understanding:
    1. Collect
    2. Describe
    3. Explore
    4. Verify
- Data preparation:
    1. Select
    2. Clean
    3. Construct
    4. Integrate
    5. Format

Certainly this is an excellent enumeration of the process, but what do we really need to do? I propose that, in practical terms we can all relate to, the following *must be done* once the data is joined and loaded into your machine, cloud, or whatever you use:

- Understand the data structure
- Dedupe observations
- Eliminate zero variance features and low variance features as desired
- Handle missing values

- Create dummy features (one-hot encoding)
- Examine and deal with highly correlated features and those with perfect linear relationships
- Scale as necessary
- Create other features as desired

Many feel that this is a daunting task. I don't and, in fact, I quite enjoy it. If done correctly and with a judicious application of judgment, it should reduce the amount of time spent at this first stage of a project and facilitate training your learning algorithm. None of the previous steps are challenging, but it can take quite a bit of time to write the code to perform each task.

Well, that's the benefit of this chapter. The example to follow will walk you through the tasks and the R code that accomplishes it. The code is flexible enough that you should be able to apply it to your projects. Additionally, it will help you gain an understanding of the data at a point you can intelligently discuss it with **Subject Matter Experts (SMEs)** if, in fact, they're available.

In the practical exercise that follows, we'll work with a small dataset. However, it suffers from all of the problems described earlier. Don't let the small size fool you, as we'll take what we learn here and use it for the more massive datasets to come in subsequent chapters.

As background, the data we'll use I put together painstakingly by hand. It's the Order of Battle for the opposing armies at the Battle of Gettysburg, fought during the American Civil War, July 1st-3rd, 1863, and the casualties reported by the end of the day on July 3rd. I purposely chose this data because I'm reasonably sure you know very little about it. Don't worry, I'm the SME on the battle here and will walk you through it every step of the way. The one thing that we won't cover in this chapter is dealing with large volumes of textual features, which we'll discuss later in this book. Enough said already; let's get started!

The source used in the creation of the dataset is *The Gettysburg Campaign in Numbers and Losses: Synopses, Orders of Battle, Strengths, Casualties, and Maps, June 9-July 14, 1863*, by J. David Petruzzi and Steven A. Stanley.

Reading the data

This first task will load the data and show how to get a how level understanding of its structure and dimensions as well as install the necessary packages.

You have two ways to access the data, which resides on GitHub. You can download `gettysburg.csv` directly from the site at this link: `https://github.com/datameister66/MMLR3rd`, or you can use the RCurl package. An example of how to use the package is available here: `https://github.com/opetchey/RREEBES/wiki/Reading-data-and-code-from-an-online-github-repository`.

Let's assume you have the file in your working directory, so let's begin by installing the necessary packages:

```
install.packages("caret")
install.packages("janitor")
install.packages("readr")
install.packages("sjmisc")
install.packages("skimr")
install.packages("tidyverse")
install.packages("vtreat")
```

Let me make a quick note about how I've learned (the hard way) about how to correctly write code. With the packages installed, we could now specifically call the libraries into the R environment. However, it's a best practice and necessary when putting code into production that a function that isn't in base R be specified. First, this helps you and unfortunate others to read your code with an understanding of which library is mapped to a specific function. It also eliminates potential errors because different packages call different functions the same thing. The example that comes to my mind is the `tsoutliers()` function. The function is available in the `forecast` package and was in the `tsoutliers` package during earlier versions. Now I know this extra typing might seem unwieldy and unnecessary, but once you discipline yourself to do it, you'll find that it's well worth the effort.

There's one library we'll call and that's `magrittr`, which allows the use of a pipe-operator, `%>%`, to chain code together:

```
library(magrittr)
```

We're now ready to load the `.csv` file. In doing so, let's utilize the `read_csv()` function from `readr` as it's faster than base R and creates a tibble dataframe. In most cases, using tibbles in a `tidyverse` style is easier to write and understand. If you want to learn all the benefits of `tidyverse`, check out their website: `tidyverse.org`.

The only thing we need to specify in the function is our filename:

```
gettysburg <- read_csv("~/gettysburg.csv")
```

Here's a look at the column (feature) names:

```
colnames(gettysburg)
[1]  "type"          "state"          "regiment_or_battery" "brigade"
[5]  "division"      "corps"          "army"
"july1_Commander"
[9]  "Cdr_casualty"  "men"            "killed"              "wounded"
[13] "captured"      "missing"        "total_casualties"    "3inch_rifles"
[17] "4.5inch_rifles" "10lb_parrots"  "12lb_howitzers"
"12lb_napoleons"
[21] "6lb_howitzers"  "24lb_howitzers" "20lb_parrots"
"12lb_whitworths"
[25] "14lb_rifles"    "total_guns"
```

We have 26 features in this data, and some of you're asking yourself things like, *what the heck is a 20 pound parrot?* If you put it in a search engine, you'll probably end up with the bird and not the 20 pound Parrot rifled artillery gun. You can see the dimensions of the data in RStudio in your Global Environment view, or you can dig on your own to see there're 590 observations:

```
dim(gettysburg)
[1] 590 26
```

In RStudio, you can click on the tibble name in the Global Environment or run the `View(tibblename)` code and it'll open a spreadsheet of all of the data.

So we have `590` observations of `26` features, but this data suffers from the issues that permeate large and complex data. Next, we'll explore if there're any duplicate observations and how to deal with them efficiently.

Handling duplicate observations

The easiest way to get started is to use the base R `duplicated()` function to create a vector of logical values that match the data observations. These values will consist of either TRUE or FALSE where TRUE indicates a duplicate. Then, we'll create a table of those values and their counts and identify which of the rows are dupes:

```
dupes <- duplicated(gettysburg)

table(dupes)
dupes
FALSE TRUE
```

```
    587      3
```

```
which(dupes == "TRUE")
[1] 588 589
```

 If you want to see the actual rows and even put them into a tibble dataframe, the janitor package has the `get_dupes()` function. The code for that would be simply: `df_dupes <- janitor::get_dupes(gettysburg)`.

To rid ourselves of these duplicate rows, we put the `distinct()` function for the `dplyr` package to good use, specifying `.keep_all = TRUE` to make sure we return all of the features into the new tibble. Note that `.keep_all` defaults to `FALSE`:

```
gettysburg <- dplyr::distinct(gettysburg, .keep_all = TRUE)
```

Notice that, in the Global Environment, the tibble is now a dimension of 587 observations of 26 variables/features.

With the duplicate observations out of the way, it's time to start drilling down into the data and understand its structure a little better by exploring the descriptive statistics of the quantitative features.

Descriptive statistics

Traditionally, we could use the base R `summary()` function to identify some basic statistics. Now, and recently I might add, I like to use the package `sjmisc` and its `descr()` function. It produces a more readable output, and you can assign that output to a dataframe. What works well is to create that dataframe, save it as a `.csv`, and explore it at your leisure. It automatically selects numeric features only. It also fits well with `tidyverse` so that you can incorporate `dplyr` functions such as `group_by()` and `filter()`. Here's an example in our case where we examine the descriptive stats for the infantry of the Confederate Army. The output will consist of the following:

- `var`: feature name
- `type`: integer
- `n`: number of observations
- `NA.prc`: percent of missing values
- `mean`
- `sd`: standard deviation
- `se`: standard error

- `md`: median
- `trimmed`: trimmed mean
- `range`
- `skew`

```
gettysburg %>%
  dplyr::filter(army == "Confederate" & type == "Infantry") %>%
  sjmisc::descr() -> descr_stats

readr::write_csv(descr_stats, 'descr_stats.csv')
```

The following is abbreviated output from the preceding code saved to a spreadsheet:

var	n	NA.prc	mean	sd	se	md	trimmed	range	skew
men	171	-	335.26	104.01	7.95	316.00	325.76	708 (135-843)	1.24
killed	171	-	26.27	22.79	1.74	19.00	23.07	172 (0-172)	2.35
wounded	171	-	69.53	52.86	4.04	61.00	62.80	440 (3-443)	2.62
captured	170	0.58	-	-	-	-	-	0 (0-0)	NaN
missing	160	6.43	34.16	30.25	2.39	26.00	29.77	158 (0-158)	1.46
total_casualties	170	0.58	127.34	88.30	6.77	106.50	117.82	680 (7-687)	2.05

In this one table, we can discern some rather interesting tidbits. In particular is the percent of missing values per feature. If you modify the precious code to examine the Union Army, you'll find that there're no missing values. The reason the usurpers from the South had missing values is based on a couple of factors; either shoddy staff work in compiling the numbers on July 3rd or the records were lost over the years. Note that, for the number of men captured, if you remove the missing value, all other values are zero, so we could just replace the missing value with it. The Rebels did not report troops as captured, but rather as missing, in contrast with the Union.

Once you feel comfortable with the descriptive statistics, move on to exploring the categorical features in the next section.

Exploring categorical variables

When it comes to an understanding of your categorical variables, there're many different ways to go about it. We can easily use the base R `table()` function on a feature. If you just want to see how many distinct levels are in a feature, then `dplyr` works well. In this example, we examine `type`, which has three unique levels:

```
dplyr::count(gettysburg, dplyr::n_distinct(type))
```

The output of the preceding code is as follows:

```
# A tibble: 1 x 2
    `dplyr::n_distinct(type)`            n
                                    <int>  <int>
                                        3     587
```

Let's now look at a way to explore all of the categorical features utilizing `tidyverse` principles. Doing it this way always allows you to save the tibble and examine the results in depth as needed. Here is a way of putting all categorical features into a separate tibble:

```
gettysburg_cat <-
  gettysburg[, sapply(gettysburg, class) == 'character']
```

Using `dplyr`, you can now summarize all of the features and the number of distinct levels in each:

```
gettysburg_cat %>%
  dplyr::summarise_all(dplyr::funs(dplyr::n_distinct(.)))
```

The output of the preceding code is as follows:

```
# A tibble: 1 x 9
   type  state regiment_or_battery brigade division corps  army
july1_Commander  Cdr_casualty
 <int> <int>                        <int>    <int>      <int>
 <int> <int>                <int>               <int>
        3     30                                  275        124
38      14          2                     586
6
```

Notice that there're `586` distinct values to `july1_Commander`. This means that two of the unit Commanders have the same rank and last name. We can also surmise that this feature will be of no value to any further analysis, but we'll deal with that issue in a couple of sections ahead.

Suppose we're interested in the number of observations for each of the levels for the `Cdr_casualty` feature. Yes, we could use `table()`, but how about producing the output as a tibble as discussed before? Give this code a try:

```
gettysburg_cat %>%
  dplyr::group_by(Cdr_casualty) %>%
  dplyr::summarize(num_rows = n())
```

The output of the preceding code is as follows:

```
# A tibble: 6 x 2
 Cdr_casualty                    num_rows
    <chr>                           <int>
1 captured                             6
2 killed                              29
3 mortally wounded                    24
4 no                                 405
5 wounded                            104
6 wounded-captured                    19
```

Speaking of tables, let's look at a tibble-friendly way of producing one using two features. This code takes the idea of comparing commander casualties by army:

```
gettysburg_cat %>%
   janitor::tabyl(army, Cdr_casualty)
```

The output of the preceding code is as follows:

army	captured	killed	mortally wounded	no	wounded	wounded-captured
Confederate	2	15	13	165	44	17
Union	4	14	11	240	60	2

Explore the data on your own and, once you're comfortable with the categorical variables, let's tackle the issue of missing values.

Handling missing values

Dealing with missing values can be a little tricky as there's a number of ways to approach the task. We've already seen in the section on descriptive statistics that there're missing values. First of all, let's get a full accounting of the missing quantity by feature, then we shall discuss how to deal with them. What I'm going to demonstrate in the following is how to put the count by feature into a dataframe that we can explore within RStudio:

```
na_count <-
  sapply(gettysburg, function(y)
    sum(length(which(is.na(
      y
    )))))

na_df <- data.frame(na_count)

View(na_df)
```

The following is a screenshot produced by the preceding code, after sorting the dataframe by descending count:

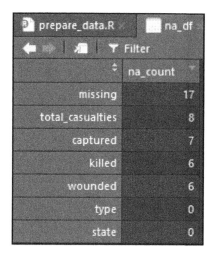

You can clearly see the count of missing by feature with the most missing is ironically named missing with a total of 17 observations.

So what should we do here or, more appropriately, what can we do here? There're several choices:

- **Do nothing**: However, some R functions will omit NAs and some functions will fail and produce an error.
- **Omit all observations with NAs**: In massive datasets, they may make sense, but we run the risk of losing information.
- **Impute values**: They could be something as simple as substituting the median value for the missing one or creating an algorithm to impute the values.
- **Dummy coding**: Turn the missing into a value such as 0 or -999, and code a dummy feature where if the feature for a specific observation is missing, the dummy is coded 1, otherwise, it's coded 0.

I could devote an entire chapter, indeed a whole book on the subject, delving into *missing at random* and others, but I was trained—and, in fact, shall insist—on the latter method. It's never failed me and the others can be a bit problematic. The benefit of dummy coding—or indicator coding, if you prefer—is that you don't lose information. In fact, missing-ness might be an essential feature in and of itself.

For a full discussion on the handling of missing values, you can reference the following articles: http://www.stat.columbia.edu/~gelman/arm/missing.pdf and https://pdfs.semanticscholar.org/4172/f558219b94f850c6567f93fa60dee7e65139.pdf.

So, here's an example of how I manually code a dummy feature and turn the NAs into zeroes:

```
gettysburg$missing_isNA <-
   ifelse(is.na(gettysburg$missing), 1, 0)

gettysburg$missing[is.na(gettysburg$missing)] <- 0
```

The first iteration of code creates a dummy feature for the missing feature and the second changes any NAs in missing to zero. In the upcoming section, where the dataset is fully processed (treated), the other missing values will be imputed.

Zero and near-zero variance features

Before moving on to dataset treatment, it's an easy task to eliminate features that have either one unique value (zero variance) or a high ratio of the most common value to the next most common value such that there're few unique values (near-zero variance). To do this, we'll lean on the caret package and the nearZeroVar() function. We get started by creating a dataframe and using the function's defaults except for saveMetrics = TRUE. We need to make that specification to return the dataframe:

```
feature_variance <- caret::nearZeroVar(gettysburg, saveMetrics = TRUE)
```

To understand the default settings of the nearZeroVar() function and determine how to customize it to your needs, just use the R help function by typing ?nearZeroVar in the Console.

The output is quite interesting, so let's peek at the first six rows of what we produced:

```
head(feature_variance)
```

The output of the preceding code is as follows:

	freqRatio	percentUnique	zeroVar	nzv
type	3.186047	0.5110733	FALSE	FALSE
state	1.094118	5.1107325	FALSE	FALSE
regiment_or_battery	1.105263	46.8483816	FALSE	FALSE
brigade	1.111111	21.1243612	FALSE	FALSE
division	1.423077	6.4735945	FALSE	FALSE
corps	1.080000	2.3850085	FALSE	FALSE

The two key columns are zeroVar and nzv. They act as an indicator of whether or not that feature is zero variance or near-zero variance; TRUE indicates yes and FALSE not so surprisingly indicates no. The other columns must be defined:

- freqRatio: This is the ratio of the percentage frequency for the most common value over the second most common value.
- percentUnique: This is the number of unique values divided by the total number of samples multiplied by 100.

Let me explain that with the data we're using. For the type feature, the most common value is Infantry, which is roughly three times more common than Artillery. For percentUnique, the lower the percentage, the lower the number of unique values. You can explore this dataframe and adjust the function to determine your relevant cut points. For this example, we'll see whether we have any zero variance features by running this code:

```
which(feature_variance$zeroVar == 'TRUE')
```

The output of the preceding code is as follows:

```
[1] 17
```

Alas, we see that row 17 (feature 17) has zero variance. Let's see what that could be:

```
row.names(feature_variance[17, ])
```

The output of the preceding code is as follows:

```
[1] "4.5inch_rifles"
```

This is quite strange to me. What it means is that I failed to record the number of the artillery piece in the one Confederate unit that brought them to the battle. An egregious error on my part discovered using an elegant function from the caret package. Oh well, let's create a new tibble with this filtered out for demonstration purposes:

```
gettysburg_fltrd <- gettysburg[, feature_variance$zeroVar == 'FALSE']
```

This code eliminates the zero variance feature. If we wanted also to eliminate near-zero variance as well, just run the code and substitute `feature_variance$zerVar` with `feature_variance$nzv`.

We're now ready to perform the real magic of this process and `treat` our data.

Treating the data

What do I mean when I say let's treat the data? I learned the term from the authors of the `vtreat` package, Nina Zumel, and John Mount. You can read their excellent paper on the subject at this link: `https://arxiv.org/pdf/1611.09477.pdf`.

The definition they provide is: *processor or conditioner that prepares real-world data for predictive modeling in a statistically sound manner*. In treating your data, you'll rid yourself of many of the data preparation headaches discussed earlier. The example with our current dataset will provide an excellent introduction into the benefits of this method and how you can tailor it to your needs. I kind of like to think that treating your data is a smarter version of one-hot encoding.

The package offers three different functions to treat data, but I only use one and that is `designTreatmentsZ()`, which treats the features without regard to an outcome or response. The functions `designTreatmentsC()` and `designTreatmentsN()` functions build dataframes based on categorical and numeric outcomes respectively. Those functions provide a method to prune features in a univariate fashion. I'll provide other ways of conducting feature selection, so that's why I use that specific function. I encourage you to experiment on your own.

The function we use in the following will produce an object that you can apply to training, validation, testing, and even production data. In later chapters, we'll focus on training and testing, but here let's treat the entire data without considerations of any splits for simplicity. There're a number of arguments in the function you can change, but the defaults are usually sufficient. We'll specify the input data, the feature names to include, and `minFraction`, which is defined by the package as the optional minimum frequency a categorical level must have to be converted into an indicator column. I've chosen 5% and the minimum frequency. In real-world data, I've seen this number altered many times to find the right level of occurrence:

```
my_treatment <- vtreat::designTreatmentsZ(
  dframe = gettysburg_fltrd,
  varlist = colnames(gettysburg_fltrd),
  minFraction = 0.05
)
```

We now have an object with a stored treatment plan. Now we just use the `prepare()` function to apply that treatment to a dataframe or tibble, and it'll give us a treated dataframe:

```
gettysburg_treated <- vtreat::prepare(my_treatment, gettysburg_fltrd)

dim(gettysburg_treated)
```

The output of the preceding code is as follows:

```
[1]    587       54
```

We now have 54 features. Let's take a look at their names:

```
colnames(gettysburg_treated)
```

The abbreviated output of the preceding code is as follows:

```
[1]     "type_catP"        "state_catP"        "regiment_or_battery_catP"
[4]   "brigade_catP"    "division_catP"                  "corps_catP"
```

As you explore the names, you'll notice that we have features ending in `catP`, `clean`, and `isBAD` and others with `_lev_x_` in them. Let's cover each in detail. As for `catP` features, the function creates a feature that's the frequency for the categorical level in that observation. What does that mean? Let's see a table for `type_catP`:

```
table(gettysburg_treated$type_catP)
```

The output of the preceding code is as follows:

```
 0.080068143100     0.21976149914     0.70017035775
             47               129               411
```

This tells us that `47` rows are of category level *x* (in this case, Cavalry), and this is 8% of the total observations. As such, 22% are Artillery and 70% Infantry. This can be helpful in further exploring your data and to help adjust the minimum frequency in your category levels. I've heard it discussed that these values could help in the creation of a distance or similarity matrix.

The next is `clean`. These are our numeric features that have had missing values imputed, which is the feature mean, and outliers winsorized or collared if you specified the argument in the `prepare()` function. We didn't, so only missing values were imputed.

Here's an interesting blog post of the merits of winsorizing from SAS: `https://blogs.sas.com/content/iml/2017/02/08/winsorization-good-bad-and-ugly.html`.

Speaking of missing values, this brings us to `isBAD`. This feature is the 1 for missing and 0 if not missing we talked about where I manually coded it.

Finally, `lev_x` is the dummy feature coding for a specific categorical level. If you go through the levels that were hot-encoded for `states`, you'll find features for Georgia, New York, North Carolina, Pennsylvania, US (this is US Regular Army units), and Virginia.

My preference is to remove the `catP` features and remove the `clean` from the feature name, and change `isBAD` to `isNA`. This a simple task with these lines of code:

```
gettysburg_treated <-
  gettysburg_treated %>%
  dplyr::select(-dplyr::contains('_catP'))

colnames(gettysburg_treated) <-
  sub('_clean', "", colnames(gettysburg_treated))

colnames(gettysburg_treated) <-
  sub('_isBAD', "_isNA", colnames(gettysburg_treated))
```

Are we ready to start building learning algorithms? Well, not quite yet. In the next section, we'll deal with highly correlated and linearly related features.

Correlation and linearity

For this task, we return to our old friend the `caret` package. We'll start by creating a correlation matrix, using the Spearman Rank method, then apply the `findCorrelation()` function for all correlations above `0.9`:

```
df_corr <- cor(gettysburg_treated, method = "spearman")

high_corr <- caret::findCorrelation(df_corr, cutoff = 0.9)
```

Why Spearman versus Pearson correlation? Spearman is free from any distribution assumptions and is robust enough for any task at hand: `http://www.statisticssolutions.com/correlation-pearson-kendall-spearman/`.

The `high_corr` object is a list of integers that correspond to feature column numbers. Let's dig deeper into this:

```
high_corr
```

The output of the preceding code is as follows:

```
[1]    9    4    22    43    3    5
```

The column indices refer to the following feature names:

```
colnames(gettysburg_treated)[c(9, 4, 22, 43, 3, 5)]
```

The output of the preceding code is as follows:

```
[1]                          "total_casualties"      "wounded"
"type_lev_x_Artillery"
 [4] "army_lev_x_Confederate" "killed_isNA"               "wounded_isNA"
```

We saw the features that're highly correlated to some other feature. For instance, `army_lev_x_Confederate` is perfectly and negatively correlation with `army_lev_x_Union`. After all, you can only two armies here, and Colonel Fremantle of the British Coldstream Guards was merely an observer. To delete these features, just filter your dataframe by the list we created:

```
gettysburg_noHighCorr <- gettysburg_treated[, -high_corr]
```

There you go, they're now gone. But wait! That seems a little too clinical, and maybe we should apply our judgment or the judgment of an SME to the problem? As before, let's create a tibble for further exploration:

```
df_corr <- data.frame(df_corr)

df_corr$feature1 <- row.names(df_corr)

gettysburg_corr <-
  tidyr::gather(data = df_corr,
                key = "feature2",
                value = "correlation",
                -feature1)

gettysburg_corr <-
  gettysburg_corr %>%
  dplyr::filter(feature1 != feature2)
```

What just happened? First of all, the correlation matrix was turned into a dataframe. Then, the row names became the values for the first feature. Using `tidyr`, the code created the second feature and placed the appropriate value with an observation, and we cleaned it up to get unique pairs. This screenshot shows the results. You can see that the Confederate and Union armies have a perfect negative correlation:

	feature1	feature2	correlation
1933	army_lev_x_Union	army_lev_x_Confederate	-1.0000000
1978	army_lev_x_Confederate	army_lev_x_Union	-1.0000000
968	type_lev_x_Infantry	type_lev_x_Artillery	-0.8110109
1057	type_lev_x_Artillery	type_lev_x_Infantry	-0.8110109
878	type_lev_x_Infantry	total_guns	-0.8006141
1055	total_guns	type_lev_x_Infantry	-0.8006141
2025	Cdr_casualty_lev_x_wounded	Cdr_casualty_lev_x_no	-0.6922053
2070	Cdr_casualty_lev_x_no	Cdr_casualty_lev_x_wounded	-0.6922053

You can see that it would be safe to dedupe on correlation as we did earlier. I like to save this to a spreadsheet and work with SMEs to understand what features we can drop or combine and so on.

After handling the correlations, I recommend exploring and removing as needed linear combinations. Dealing with these combinations is a similar methodology to high correlations:

```
linear_combos <- caret::findLinearCombos(gettysburg_noHighCorr)

linear_combos
```

The output of the preceding code is as follows:

```
$`linearCombos`
$`linearCombos`[[1]]
 [1] 16 7 8 9 10 11 12 13 14 15

$remove
[1] 16
```

The output tells us that feature column `16` is linearly related to those others, and we can solve the problem by removing it. What are these feature names? Let's have a look:

```
colnames(gettysburg_noHighCorr)[c(16, 7, 8, 9, 10, 11, 12, 13, 14, 15)]
```

The output of the preceding code is as follows:

```
[1]             "total_guns"         "X3inch_rifles" "X10lb_parrots"
"X12lb_howitzers" "X12lb_napoleons"
 [6] "X6lb_howitzers" "X24lb_howitzers" "X20lb_parrots" "X12lb_whitworths"
"X14lb_rifles"
```

Removing the feature on the number of `"total_guns"` will solve the problem. This makes total sense since it's the number of guns in an artillery battery. Most batteries, especially in the Union, had only one type of gun. Even with multiple linear combinations, it's an easy task with this bit of code to get rid of the necessary features:

```
linear_remove <- colnames(gettysburg_noHighCorr[16])

df <- gettysburg_noHighCorr[, !(colnames(gettysburg_noHighCorr) %in%
linear_remove)]

dim(df)
```

The output of the preceding code is as follows:

```
[1] 587    39
```

There you have it, a nice clean dataframe of 587 observations and 39 features. Now depending on the modeling, you may have to scale this data or perform other transformations, but this data, in this format, makes all of that easier. Regardless of your prior knowledge or interest of one of the most important battles in history, and the bloodiest on American soil, you've developed a workable understanding of the Order of Battle, and the casualties at the regimental or battery level. Start treating your data, not next week or next month, but right now!

 If you desire, you can learn more about the battle here: `https://www.battlefields.org/learn/civil-war/battles/gettysburg`.

Summary

This chapter looked at the common problems in large, messy datasets common in machine learning projects. These include, but are not limited to the following:

- Missing or invalid values
- Novel levels in a categorical feature that show up in algorithm production
- High cardinality in categorical features such as zip code
- High dimensionality
- Duplicate observations

This chapter provided a disciplined approach to dealing with these problems by showing how to explore the data, treat it, and create a dataframe that you can use for developing your learning algorithm. It's also flexible enough that you can modify the code to suit your circumstances. This methodology should make what many feels is the most arduous, time-consuming, and least enjoyable part of the job an easy task.

With this task behind us, we can now get started on our first modeling task using linear regression in the following chapter.

Linear Regression

2

"An approximate answer to the right problem is worth a good deal more than an exact answer to an approximate problem."

– John Tukey

It's essential that we get started with a simple yet extremely effective technique that's been used for a long time: **linear regression**. Albert Einstein is believed to have remarked at one time or another that things should be made as simple as possible, but no simpler. This is sage advice and a good rule of thumb in the development of algorithms for machine learning. Considering the other techniques that we'll discuss later, there's no simpler model than tried and tested linear regression, which uses the **least squares approach** to predict a quantitative outcome. We can consider it to be the foundation of all the methods that we'll discuss later, many of which are mere extensions. If you can master the linear regression method, well then quite frankly I believe you can master the rest of this book. Therefore, let's consider this as a good starting point for our journey towards becoming a machine learning guru.

This chapter covers introductory material and an expert in this subject can skip ahead to the next topic. Otherwise, ensure that you thoroughly understand this topic before venturing to other, more complex learning methods. I believe you'll discover that many of your projects can be addressed by just applying what's discussed in the following sections. Linear regression is probably the most straightforward model to explain to your customers, most of whom will have at least a cursory understanding of **R-squared**. Many of them will have been exposed to it at great depth and hence will be comfortable with variable contribution, collinearity, and the like.

The following are the topics that we'll be covering in this chapter:

- Univariate linear regression
- Multivariate linear regression

Univariate linear regression

We begin by looking at a simple way to predict a quantitative response, Y, with one predictor variable, x, assuming that Y has a linear relationship with x. The model for this can be written as follows:

$$Y = B_o + B_1x + e$$

We can state it as the expected value of Y is a function of the parameters B_o (the intercept) plus B_1 (the slope) times x, plus an error term e. The least squares approach chooses the model parameters that minimize the **Residual Sum of Squares (RSS)** of the predicted y values versus the actual Y values. For a simple example, let's say we have the actual values of $Y1$ and $Y2$ equal to 10 and 20 respectively, along with the predictions of $y1$ and $y2$ as *12* and *18*. To calculate RSS, we add the squared differences:

$$RSS = (Y1 - y1)^2 + (Y2 - y2)^2$$

This, with simple substitution, yields the following:

$$(10 - 12)^2 + (20 - 18)^2 = 8$$

Before we begin with an application, I want to point out that if you read the headlines of various research breakthroughs, you should do so with a jaded eye and a skeptical mind as the conclusion put forth by the media may not be valid. As we shall see, R—and any other software, for that matter—will give us a solution regardless of the input. However, just because the math makes sense and a high correlation or R-squared statistic is reported doesn't mean that the conclusion is valid.

To drive this point home, let's have a look at the famous `Anscombe` dataset, which is available in R. The statistician Francis Anscombe produced this set to highlight the importance of data visualization and outliers when analyzing data. It consists of four pairs of X and Y variables that have the same statistical properties but when plotted show something very different. I've used the data to train colleagues and to educate business partners on the hazards of fixating on statistics without exploring the data and checking assumptions. I think this is an excellent place to start should you have a similar need. It's a brief digression before moving on to serious modeling:

```
> #call up and explore the data

> data(anscombe)

> attach(anscombe)
```

```
> anscombe
   x1 x2 x3 x4    y1   y2    y3    y4
1  10 10 10  8  8.04 9.14  7.46  6.58
2   8  8  8  8  6.95 8.14  6.77  5.76
3  13 13 13  8  7.58 8.74 12.74  7.71
4   9  9  9  8  8.81 8.77  7.11  8.84
5  11 11 11  8  8.33 9.26  7.81  8.47
6  14 14 14  8  9.96 8.10  8.84  7.04
7   6  6  6  8  7.24 6.13  6.08  5.25
8   4  4  4 19  4.26 3.10  5.39 12.50
9  12 12 12  8 10.84 9.13  8.15  5.56
10  7  7  7  8  4.82 7.26  6.42  7.91
11  5  5  5  8  5.68 4.74  5.73  6.89
```

As we shall see, each of the pairs has the same correlation coefficient: `0.816`. The first two are as follows:

```
> cor(x1, y1) #correlation of x1 and y1
[1] 0.8164205

> cor(x2, y1) #correlation of x2 and y2

[1] 0.8164205
```

The real insight here, as `Anscombe` intended, is when we plot all four pairs together, as follows:

```
> par(mfrow = c(2,2)) #create a 2x2 grid for plotting

> plot(x1, y1, main = "Plot 1")

> plot(x2, y2, main = "Plot 2")

> plot(x3, y3, main = "Plot 3")

> plot(x4, y4, main = "Plot 4")
```

Downloading the example code
You can download the example code files for all Packt books you've purchased from your account at http://www.packtpub.com. If you bought this book elsewhere, you can visit http://www.packtpub.com/support and register to have the files emailed directly to you.

The output of the preceding code is as follows:

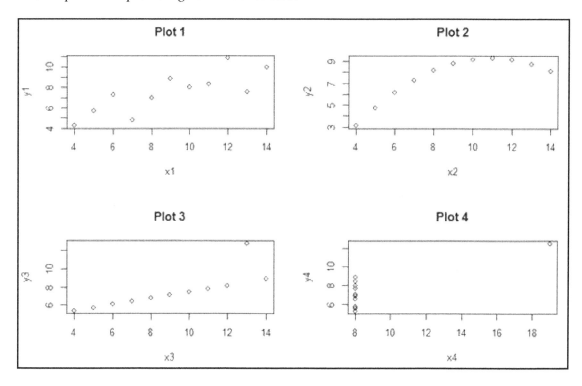

We can see the following:

- **Plot 1** appears to have a true linear relationship
- **Plot 2** is curvilinear, **Plot 3** has a dangerous outlier
- **Plot 4** is driven by one outlier

There you have it: a cautionary tale about the dangers of solely relying on correlation.

Building a univariate model

Our first case focuses on the goal of predicting the water yield (in inches) of the Snake River Watershed in Wyoming, USA, as a function of the water content of the year's snowfall. This forecast will be useful in managing the water flow and reservoir levels, as the Snake River provides much-needed irrigation water for the farms and ranches of several western states. The snake dataset is available in the alr3 package (note that alr stands for applied linear regression):

```
> install.packages("alr3")
> library(alr3)
> data(snake)
> dim(snake)
[1] 17  2
> head(snake)
     X    Y
1 23.1 10.5
2 32.8 16.7
3 31.8 18.2
4 32.0 17.0
5 30.4 16.3
6 24.0 10.5
```

Now that we have 17 observations, data exploration can begin. But first, let's change X and Y to meaningful variable names, as follows:

```
> names(snake) <- c("content", "yield")
> attach(snake) # attach data with new names
> head(snake)

  content yield
1    23.1  10.5
2    32.8  16.7
3    31.8  18.2
4    32.0  17.0
5    30.4  16.3
6    24.0  10.5

> plot(content,
       yield, main = "Scatterplot of Snow vs. Yield",
       xlab = "water content of snow",
       ylab = "water yield")
```

The output of the preceding code is as follows:

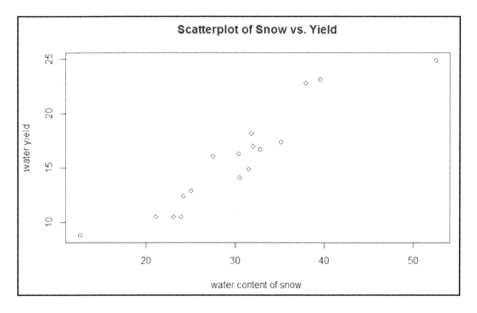

This is an intriguing plot as the data is linear and has a slight curvilinear shape driven by two potential outliers at both ends of the extreme.

To perform a linear regression in R, we use the `lm()` function to create a model in the standard form of *fit = lm(Y ~ X)*. You can then test your assumptions using various functions on your fitted model by using the following code:

```
> yield_fit <- lm(yield ~ content)

> summary(yield_fit)

Call:
lm(formula = yield ~ content)

Residuals:
       Min       1Q   Median       3Q      Max
-2.1793  -1.5149  -0.3624   1.6276   3.1973

Coefficients: Estimate Std. Error t value Pr(>|t|)
(Intercept)  0.72538    1.54882   0.468    0.646
content      0.49808    0.04952  10.058 4.63e-08
    ***
---
Signif. codes:  0 '***' 0.001 '**' 0.01 '*' 0.05
```

```
        '.' 0.1 ' ' 1

 Residual standard error: 1.743 on 15 degrees of
       freedom
 Multiple R-squared:  0.8709,    Adjusted R-squared:
       0.8623
 F-statistic: 101.2 on 1 and 15 DF,  p-value:
       4.632e-08
```

With the `summary()` function, we can examine some items, including the model specification, descriptive statistics about the residuals, the coefficients, codes to model significance, and a summary of the model error and fit. Right now, let's focus on the parameter coefficient estimates, and see whether our predictor variable has a significant `p-value` and whether the overall model F-test has a significant `p-value`. Looking at the parameter estimates, the model tells us that `yield` is equal to `0.72538` plus `0.49808` times `content`. We can state that for every one unit change in the content, the yield will increase by `0.49808` units. `F-statistic` is used to test the null hypothesis that the model coefficients are all zero.

Since `p-value` is highly significant, we can reject the null and move on to the t-test for content, which tests the null hypothesis that it's zero. Again, we can reject the null. Additionally, we can see the `Multiple R-squared` and `Adjusted R-squared` values. `Adjusted R-squared` will be covered under the multivariate regression topic, so let's zero in on `Multiple R-squared`; here, we see that it's `0.8709`. In theory, it can range from zero to one and is a measure of the strength of the association between *X* and *Y*. The interpretation, in this case, is that the water content of snow can explain 87 percent of the variation in the water yield. On a side note, R-squared is nothing more than the correlation coefficient of *[X, Y]* squared.

We can recall our scatter plot and now add the best fit line produced by our model using the following code:

```
> plot(content, yield)
```

```
> abline(yield_fit, lwd = 3, col = "red")
```

The output of the preceding code is as follows:

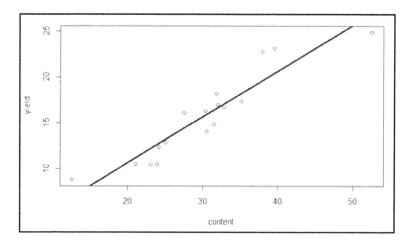

Reviewing model assumptions

A linear regression model is only as good as the validity of its assumptions, which can be summarized as follows:

- **Linearity**: This is a linear relationship between the predictor and the response variables. If this relationship is not explicitly present, transformations (log, polynomial, exponent, and so on) of X or Y may solve the problem.
- **Non-correlation of errors**: This is a common problem in time series and panel data where $e_n = beta_{n-1}$; if the errors are correlated, you run the risk of creating a poorly specified model.
- **Homoscedasticity**: This refers to normally distributed and constant variance of errors, which means that the variance of errors is constant across different input values. Violations of this assumption don't create biased coefficient estimates, but because of improper standard errors for the coefficients can lead to statistical tests for significance that can be either too high or too low, leading to wrong conclusions. This violation is also called **heteroscedasticity**.
- **No collinearity**: No linear relationship should exist between two predictor variables, which is to say that there should be no correlation between the features. This issue can lead to incorrect statistical tests for the coefficients.

- **Presence of outliers**: Outliers can severely skew the estimation, and they must be examined and handled via removal or transformation while fitting a model using linear regression; as we saw in the Anscombe example, outliers can lead to a biased estimate.

A simple way to initially check the assumptions is by producing plots. The `plot()` function, when combined with a linear model fit, will automatically generate four plots, allowing you to examine the assumptions. R produces the plots one at a time, and you advance through them by hitting the *Enter* key. It's best to explore all four simultaneously, and we can do so in the following manner:

```
> par(mfrow = c(2,2))

> plot(yield_fit)
```

The output of the preceding code is as follows:

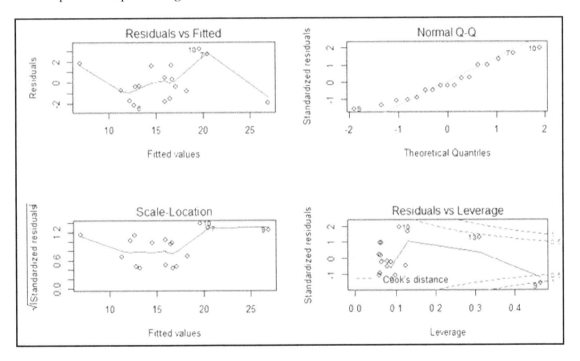

The two plots on the left allow us to examine the homoscedasticity of errors and non-linearity. What we're looking for is some pattern or, more importantly, that no pattern exists. Given the sample size of only 17 observations, nothing visible exists. Common heteroscedastic errors will appear to be u-shaped, inverted u-shaped, or clustered close together on the left of the plot. They'll become wider as the fitted values increase (a funnel shape). It's safe to conclude that no violation of homoscedasticity is apparent in our model.

The **Normal Q-Q** plot in the upper-right corner helps us to determine whether the residuals are normally distributed. The **Quantile-Quantile (Q-Q)** represents the quantile values of one variable plotted against the quantile values of another. It appears that the outliers (observations **7**, **9**, and **10**) may be causing a violation of the assumption. The **Residuals vs Leverage** plot can tell us what observations, if any, are unduly influencing the model; in other words, if there are any outliers we should be concerned about. The statistic is **Cook's distance** or **Cook's D**, and it's generally accepted that a value greater than one should be worthy of further inspection.

What exactly is further inspection? This is where art meets science. The easy way out would be to delete the observation, in this case number **9**, and redo the model. However, a better option may be to transform the predictor and/or the response variables. If we just delete observation **9**, then maybe observations **10** and **13** would fall outside the band for greater than one. In this simple example, I believe that this is where domain expertise can be critical. More times than I can count, I've found that exploring and understanding outliers can yield valuable insights. When we first examined the previous scatter plot, I pointed out the potential outliers and these happen to be observations number **9** and number **13**. It seems important to discuss with the appropriate subject matter experts to understand why this is the case. Is it a measurement error? Is there a logical explanation for these observations? I certainly don't know, but this is an opportunity to increase the value that you bring to an organization.

Let's leave this simple case behind us and move on to a supervised learning case involving multivariate linear regression.

Multivariate linear regression

In the case study that follows, we're going to look at the application of some exciting methods on an interesting dataset. Like in the previous chapter, once the data is loaded we'll *treat* it, but unlike the previous example, we'll split it into training and testing sets. Given the dimensionality of the data, feature reduction and selection are critical.

We'll explore the oft-maligned stepwise selection, then move on to one of my favorite methodologies, which is **Multivariate Adaptive Regression Splines** (**MARS**). If you're not using MARS, I highly recommend it. I've been told, but cannot verify it, that Max Kuhn stated in a conference that it's his starting procedure. I'm not surprised if it's true. I learned the technique from a former Senior Director of Analytics at one of the largest banks in the world and haven't looked back since.

Loading and preparing the data

To get the data into your working directory, you can find it on my GitHub at this link: https://github.com/datameister66/MMLR3rd.

The file we're using is ames.csv. This data is from the sales of homes sold in Ames, Iowa, which is the location of Iowa State University, and I believe has a population of around 70,000. I downloaded the data from Kaggle.com, and the response we're trying to predict is the final sales price. It's a nice size to practice machine learning methods with 1,460 observations of 84 features, and many of the features are categorical.

Before we load the data, if not already done, load the necessary packages, call the magrittr library, and, if you so choose, update the options. I prefer not to have scientific number notation and want to round the values to four decimals:

```
library(magrittr)
options(scipen = 999)
options(digits = 4)
# install.packages("caret")
# install.packages("ggthemes")
# install.packages("janitor")
# install.packages("leaps")
# install.packages("plm")
# install.packages("readr")
# install.packages("sjmisc")
# install.packages("tidyverse")
# install.packages("vtreat")
```

Now, load the data and confirm the dimensions:

```
> ames <- readr::read_csv(~/ames.csv")

> dim(ames)

[1] 1460    84
```

I don't believe there are any duplicate observations, but let's confirm:

```
> dupes <- duplicated(ames)

> table(dupes)
dupes
FALSE
 1460
```

Excellent! There are no duplicates. Here, we create a tibble of the descriptive statistics. Open the data in RStudio and explore it by feature to get a feel for it:

```
> ames %>%
    sjmisc::descr() -> ames_descr

> View(ames_descr)
```

There are some thought-provoking features but focus first on Id. Notice that this has a unique value for all of the observations. Hence, we can remove it as it has no value in predictions:

```
> range(ames$Id)
[1]  1 1460

> ames <- ames[, -1]
```

Three other features are interesting as they are the year that an event happened. Instead of the year as the value of the feature, how about we create a feature of years since the event? This is easy to do by taking YrSold and subtracting in sequence YearBuilt, YearRemodAdd, and GarageYrBuilt just like this:

```
 > ames %>%
    dplyr::mutate(yearsOld = YrSold - YearBuilt) -> ames

> ames %>%
    dplyr::mutate(yearsRemodel = YrSold - YearRemodAdd) -> ames

> ames %>%
    dplyr::mutate(yearsGarage = YrSold - GarageYrBlt) -> ames
```

Another thing of interest when you look at the descriptive stats is the fact that GarageYrBlt has roughly 5.5% missing values. So, yearsGarage will have a corresponding amount of missing values. As is my standard procedure, I want us to code a dummy feature that indicates missing values and changes those missing values to zero.

I'm not sure that any imputation here would add value:

```
> ames$yearsGarage_isNA <-
    ifelse(is.na(ames$yearsGarage), 1, 0)

> ames$yearsGarage[is.na(ames$yearsGarage)] <- 0
```

Let's remove those unnecessary features given that we created a new feature of years since the event:

```
> ames <- ames[, c(-19, -20, -59)]
```

Another feature of interest is `MoSold`. This is a numeric that corresponds to the month it was sold, so 1 = January, 2 = February, and so on. This is probably better conditioned as a character feature and will end up as dummy features during one-hot encoding:

```
> ames$MoSold <- as.character(ames$MoSold)
```

The one plot we should look at is of the response, which is `SalesPrice`. I like to try out different plot themes, so I'll use different themes for different plots for illustration purposes, which should help you discover your favorite ones:

```
> ggplot2::ggplot(ames, ggplot2::aes(x = SalePrice)) +
    ggplot2::geom_histogram() +
    ggthemes::theme_few()
```

The output of the preceding code is as follows:

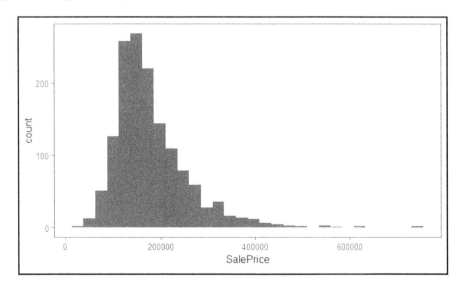

The histogram shows the data is skewed to the right. In non-linear methods, this may not be a problem, but in linear models, you can usually count on biased estimates and/or severe problems with outliers in your residuals. It seems like a good idea to transform this using the natural log:

```
> ames %>%
    dplyr::mutate(logSales = log(SalePrice)) -> ames

> ggplot2::ggplot(ames, ggplot2::aes(x = logSales)) +
    ggplot2::geom_histogram() +
    ggthemes::theme_economist_white()
```

The output of the preceding code is as follows:

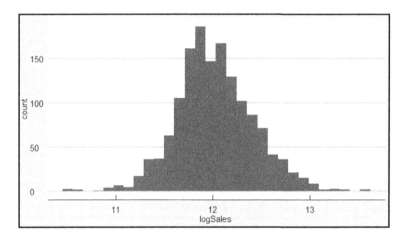

We now have a much more normal distribution but can see some potentially problematic outliers of homes selling at meager and very high prices.

My usual next step is to finalize any missing values in features of interest. Again, we code a dummy feature and turn the missing values into zero:

```
> ames$LotFrontage_isNA <-
    ifelse(is.na(ames$LotFrontage), 1, 0)

> ames$LotFrontage[is.na(ames$LotFrontage)] <- 0

> ames$MasVnrArea_isNA <-
    ifelse(is.na(ames$MasVnrArea), 1, 0)

> ames$MasVnrArea[is.na(ames$MasVnrArea)] <- 0
```

I don't believe we have any zero variance features (we removed `Id`) but let's double-check:

```
> feature_variance <- caret::nearZeroVar(ames, saveMetrics = TRUE)

> table(feature_variance$zeroVar)

FALSE
   84
```

All good! We now come to the point where we can safely split the data into training and testing sets. I guess you could call the training set a validation set, as the real test data is a separate file that you would submit to Kaggle for evaluation. That is out of scope here; hence, I call our holdout sample `test`.

In this example, let's use an 80/20 split:

```
> set.seed(1944)

> ames %>%
    dplyr::sample_frac(.8) -> train

> ames %>%
    dplyr::anti_join(train) -> test
```

If you look in the **Global Environment** tab of RStudio, you'll see that `train` has 1,168 observations and `test` 292 observations.

We now come to the point where we're almost ready to treat the training data. However, let's create an object called `varlist`, which we'll feed into the treat function, which is the predictor features, and generate response variables:

```
> varlist = colnames(ames[, !colnames(ames) %in% c('SalePrice',
'logSales')])

> train_y <- train$SalePrice
> train_logy <- train$logSales
> test_y <- test$SalePrice
> test_logy <- test$logSales
```

Now you can design a treatment scheme. Do this by only treating the training data, so you don't bias your model building. As you'll see, you can apply that treatment scheme to the test data or any currently unseen data for that matter. We'll just specify our training data, `varlist`, and set `minFraction` for coding character feature levels to 10%:

```
> df_treatment <- vtreat::designTreatmentsZ(
    dframe = train,
    varlist = varlist,
```

```
    minFraction = 0.10
  )
```

 For a further discussion on designing data treatment strategies, refer to `Chapter 1`, *Preparing and Understanding Data*.

Now, apply the treatment to both train and test datasets:

```
> trained <- vtreat::prepare(df_treatment, train)

> tested <- vtreat::prepare(df_treatment, test)
```

Notice that we now have 155 features in each of these treated datasets. Feel free to explore them, keeping in mind how the features are renamed as discussed in `Chapter 1`, *Preparing and Understanding Data*.

As I stated in the previous chapter, we can drop the `_catP` features and rename the others as in the following code:

```
> trained <-
    trained %>%
    dplyr::select(-dplyr::contains('_catP'))

> tested <-
    tested %>%
    dplyr::select(-dplyr::contains('_catP'))

> colnames(trained) <-
    sub('_clean', "", colnames(trained))

> colnames(tested) <-
    sub('_clean', "", colnames(tested))

> colnames(trained) <-
    sub('_isBAD', "_isNA", colnames(trained))

> colnames(tested) <-
    sub('_isBAD', "_isNA", colnames(tested))
```

Just removing the category percentage features reduced the number of them to `114`. The final step before moving on to model creation is to remove highly correlated pairs of features and verify there are no linear dependencies. In linear models, this is critical to sort out. During one-hot encoding, if you create as many indicator/dummy features as levels in the parent categorical feature, you would fall into the dummy variable trap, which results in perfect multicollinearity. The classic example is a feature with levels of only male or female. One-hot would give us two features, whereas it should be encoded to one feature with, say, female = 1 and male = 0. Then, in the linear regression, the expectation for male would just be the intercept *B0*, while for female it would be *B0 + B1x*.

As for correlation, we could explore the various relationships in depth, as discussed in `Chapter 1`, *Preparing and Understanding Data*. Given the size of this data, let's identify and remove those pairs with correlation greater than `0.79`. I encourage you to experiment with this specification:

```
> df_corr <- cor(trained)

> high_corr <- caret::findCorrelation(df_corr, cutoff = 0.79)

> length(high_corr)
[1] 19
```

There are 19 features we can eliminate. As I stated, you can examine this problem in more depth, but let's proceed by merely removing them:

```
trained <- trained[, -high_corr]
```

For linear dependencies, the `caret` package comes in handy again. To be sure, I like to double check with the `detect_lin_dep()` function:

```
> caret::findLinearCombos(trained)
$`linearCombos`
list()

$`remove`
NULL

> # linear dependency
> plm::detect_lin_dep(trained)
[1] "No linear dependent column(s) detected."
```

The results from the `caret` package tell us there are no features to remove since no dependency exists, and the `plm` package confirms this.

We'll now move on to training our model. This should be interesting!

Modeling and evaluation – stepwise regression

The model we're looking to create will consist of the following form:

$$Y = B0 + B1x1 + \ldots Bnxn + e$$

In this formula, the predictor variables (features) can be from 1 to n.

One of the critical elements that we'll cover here is the vital task of feature selection. Later chapters will include more advanced techniques.

Forward selection starts with a model that has zero features; it then iteratively adds features one at a time until achieving the best fit based on say the reduction in residual sum of squares or overall model AIC. This iteration continues until a stopping rule is satisfied for example, setting maximum p-values for features in the model at 0.05.

Backward selection begins with all of the features in the model and removes the least useful, one at a time.

Stepwise selection is a hybrid approach where the features are added through forward stepwise regression, but the algorithm then examines whether any features that no longer improve the model fit can be removed.

It's important to add here that stepwise techniques can suffer from serious issues. You can perform a forward stepwise on a dataset then a backward stepwise and end up with two completely conflicting models. The bottom line is that stepwise can produce biased regression coefficients; in other words, they're too large and the confidence intervals are too narrow (Tibshirani, 1996).

Best subsets regression can be a satisfactory alternative to the stepwise methods for feature selection. In best subsets regression, the algorithm fits a model for all of the possible feature combinations; so, if you have three features, seven models are created. As you might've guessed, if your dataset has many features like the one we're analyzing here, this can be a heavy computational burden. A possible solution you can try is to use forward, backward, or stepwise selection to reduce your features to a point where best subset regression becomes practical. A key point to remember is that we still need to focus on our holdout sample performance as best subsets are no guarantee of producing the best results.

For both of the stepwise models, we'll use cross-validation `k` = 3 folds. We can specify this in an object using the `caret` package function, `trainControl()`, then pass that to our model for training:

```
> step_control <-
    caret::trainControl(method = "cv",
    number = 3,
    returnResamp = "final")
```

The method for training the model is based on forward feature selection from the leaps package.

This code gets us our results and, using `trace` = `FALSE`, we suppress messages on training progress. I'm also constraining the minimum and the maximum number of features to consider as 10 and 25. You can experiment with that parameter as you desire, but I am compelled to advise that you can end up with dozens of features and easily overfit the model:

```
> set.seed(1984)

> step_fit <-
    caret::train(trained, train_logy, method = "leapForward",
    tuneGrid = data.frame(nvmax = 10:25),
    trControl = step_control,
    trace = FALSE)
```

You can see all of the resulting metrics for each number of features using `step_fit$results`. However, let's just identify the best model:

```
> step_fit$bestTune
   nvmax
11    20
```

The output shows up that the model with the lowest **Root Mean Square Error (RMSE)** is with 20 features included, which corresponds to model number 11. To understand more about the specific model and its corresponding coefficients, it's quite helpful to put the features into a dataframe or, in this case, a tibble:

```
> broom::tidy(coef(step_fit$finalModel, 20)) -> step_coef

> View(step_coef)
```

The abbreviated output of the preceding code is as follows:

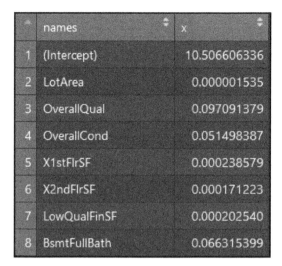

	names	x
1	(Intercept)	10.506606336
2	LotArea	0.000001535
3	OverallQual	0.097091379
4	OverallCond	0.051498387
5	X1stFlrSF	0.000238579
6	X2ndFlrSF	0.000171223
7	LowQualFinSF	0.000202540
8	BsmtFullBath	0.066315399

As you can see, it includes the intercept term. You can explore this data further and see if it makes sense.

We should build a separate model with these features, test out of sample performance, and explore the assumptions. An easy way to do this is to drop the intercept from the tibble then paste together a formula of the names:

```
> step_coef <- step_coef[-1, ]

> lm_formula <- as.formula(paste("y ~ ",paste(step_coef$names,
collapse="+"), sep = ""))
```

Now, build a linear model, incorporating the response in the dataframe:

```
> trained$y <- train_logy

> step_lm <- lm(lm_formula, data = trained)
```

You can examine the results the old fashioned way using `summary()`. However, let's stay in the `tidyverse` format, putting the coefficients into a tibble with `tidy()` and using `glance()` to see how the entire model performs:

```
> # summary(step_lm)

> # broom::tidy(step_lm)

> broom::glance(step_lm)
```

```
# A tibble: 1 x 11
  r.squared adj.r.squared sigma statistic p.value    df logLik   AIC
*     <dbl>         <dbl> <dbl>     <dbl>   <dbl> <int>  <dbl> <dbl>
1     0.862         0.860 0.151      359.       0    21   563. -1082.
# ... with 3 more variables: BIC <dbl>, deviance <dbl>, df.residual <int>
```

A quick *glance* shows us we have an adjusted R-squared value of `0.86` and a highly statistic p-value for the overall model. What about our assumptions? Let's take a look:

```
> par(mfrow = c(2,2))

> plot(step_lm)
```

The output of the preceding code snippet is as follows:

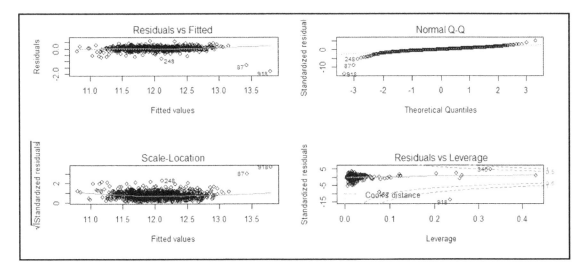

Even a brief examination shows we're having some issues with three observations: **87, 248,** and **918**. If you look at the Q-Q plot, you can see a pattern known as heavy-tailed. What's happening is the model isn't doing very well at predicting extreme values.

Recall the histogram plot of the log response and how it showed outlier values at the high and low ends of the distribution. We could truncate the response, but that may not help in out of sample predictions. In this case, let's drop those three observations noted and re-run the model:

```
> train_reduced <- trained[c(-87, -248, -918), ]

> step_lm2 <- lm(lm_formula, data = train_reduced)
```

Here, we just look at the Q-Q plot:

```
> car::qqPlot(step_lm2$residuals)
```

The output of the preceding code is as follows:

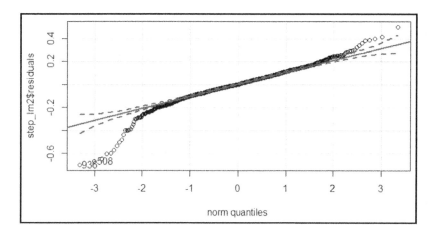

Clearly, we have some issues here where the residuals are negative (actual price-predicted price). What are the implications of our analysis? If we're producing *prediction intervals*, there could be problems since they're calculated on the assumption of normally distributed residuals. Also, with a dataset of this size, our other statistical tests are very robust to the problem of heteroscedasticity.

To investigate the issue of collinearity, one can call up the **Variance Inflation Factor** (**VIF**) statistic. VIF is the ratio of the variance of a feature's coefficient when fitting the full model, divided by the feature's coefficient variance when fitted by itself. The formula is as follows:

$$1/(1 - R_i^2)$$

In the preceding equation, R_i^2 is the R-squared for our feature of interest, *i*, being regressed by all the other features. The minimum value that the VIF can take is 1, which means no collinearity at all. There are no hard and fast rules, but in general, a VIF value that exceeds 5 (or some say 10) indicates a problematic amount of collinearity (James, p.101, 2013).

A precise value is difficult to select because there's no hard statistical cut-off point for when multi-collinearity makes your model unacceptable.

The `vif()` function in the `car` package is all that's needed to produce the values, as we can put them in a tibble and examine them:

```
> step_vif <- broom::tidy(car::vif(step_lm2))

> View(step_vif)
```

The abbreviated output of the preceding code is as follows:

	names	x
20	X2ndFlrSF	3.926
19	X1stFlrSF	3.917
18	yearsOld	3.850
17	TotRmsAbvGrd	3.574
16	OverallQual	2.755
15	yearsRemodel	2.172
14	GarageArea	1.891
13	GarageFinish_lev_x_Unf	1.550
12	OverallCond	1.540

I've sorted the view in descending order by VIF value. I believe we can conclude that there are no apparent problems with multicollinearity.

Finally, we have to see how we're doing out of sample, that is, on our test data. We make the model predictions and examine the results as follows:

```
> step_pred <- predict(step_lm2, tested)

> caret::postResample(pred = step_pred, obs = test_logy)
    RMSE Rsquared      MAE
 0.12978   0.89375 0.09492

> caret::postResample(step_lm2$fitted.values, train_reduced$y)
    RMSE Rsquared      MAE
 0.12688   0.90072 0.09241
```

We see the error increases only slightly: `0.12688` versus `0.12978` in the test data. I think we can do better with our MARS model. Let's not delay in finding out.

Modeling and evaluation – MARS

How would you like a modeling technique that provides all of the following:

- Offers the flexibility to build linear and nonlinear models for both regression and classification
- Can support variable interaction terms
- Is simple to understand and explain
- Requires little data processing
- Handles all types of data: numeric and categorical
- Performs well on unseen data, that is, it does well in a bias-variance trade-off

If that all sounds appealing, then I cannot recommend the use of MARS models enough. I've found them to perform exceptionally well. In fact, in a past classification problem of mine, they outperformed both a random forest and boosted trees on test/validation data.

To understand MARS is quite simple:

1. First, just start with a linear or generalized linear model like we discussed previously.
2. Then, to capture any nonlinear relationship, a hinge function is added. These hinges are simply points in the input feature that equate to a coefficient change. For example, say we have this:
$$Y = 12.5(our\ intercept) + 1.5(variable\ 1) + 3.3(variable\ 2)$$
   Where variables 1 and 2 are on a scale of 1 to 10.
3. Now, let's see how a hinge function for variable 2 could come into play:
$$Y = 11(new\ intercept) + 1.5(variable\ 1) + 4.26734(max(0, variable\ 2 - 5.5)$$

We read the `hinge` function as we take the maximum of either 0 or *variable 2-5.50*. So, whenever variable 2 has a value greater than 5.5, that value will be multiplied times the coefficient; otherwise, it will be zero. The method will accommodate multiple hinges for each variable and also interaction terms.

The other interesting thing about MARS is the automatic variable selection. This can be done with cross-validation, but the default is to build through a forward pass, much like forward selection, then a backward pass to prune the model, which after the forward pass is likely to overfit the data. This backward pass prunes input features and removes hinges based on **Generalized Cross Validation (GCV)**:

$GCV = RSS/(N * (1 - Effective\ Number\ of\ Parameters/N)2)Effective\ Number\ of\ Parameters = Number\ of\ Input\ Features + Penalty * (Number\ of\ Input\ Features - 1)/2$

In the `earth` package in R, `Penalty = 2` for an additive model and `3` for a multiplicative model. A multiplicative model is one with interaction terms. In `earth`, there are quite a few parameters you can tune. I'll demonstrate, in the example, a practical and straightforward way to implement the methodology. If you so desire, you can learn more about its flexibility in the excellent vignette on the `earth` package by Stephen Milborrow, available at this link: `http://www.milbo.org/doc/earth-notes.pdf`.

I'll specify a model selection of a five-fold cross-validation (`pmethod = `*cv* and `nfold = 5`) as an additive model only with no interactions (`degree = 1`) and only one hinge per input feature (`minspan = -1`). I also want to have a maximum of 25 features (`nprune = 25`). The code is as follows:

```
> set.seed(1988)
> earth_fit <-
    earth::earth(
      x = train_reduced[, -96],
      y = train_reduced[, 96],
      pmethod = 'cv',
      nfold = 5,
      degree = 1,
      minspan = -1,
      nprune = 25
    )
```

`summary()` of `earth_fit` is quite lengthy, so here's the abbreviated version:

```
> summary(earth_fit)

Selected 20 of 26 terms, and 13 of 95 predictors using pmethod="cv"
Termination condition: RSq changed by less than 0.001 at 26 terms
Importance: OverallQual, X1stFlrSF, X2ndFlrSF, yearsOld, ...
Number of terms at each degree of interaction: 1 19 (additive model)
GRSq 0.9052 RSq 0.9113 mean.oof.RSq 0.8979 (sd 0.0115)
```

What we can discern is that only 13 features were selected with a total of 20 terms, including hinged features. `mean.oof.RSq` is the average of the out of fold R-squared values (`0.8979`), and the full-model R-squared is `0.9113`. You can call feature importance as well:

```
> earth::evimp(earth_fit)
                  nsubsets   gcv    rss
OverallQual             19 100.0  100.0
X1stFlrSF               17  49.7   50.0
X2ndFlrSF               16  42.7   43.0
yearsOld                14  33.8   34.1
OverallCond             13  28.0   28.4
```

```
BsmtFinSF1                  11   22.6   23.1
LotArea                     10   19.1   19.7
Fireplaces                   7   12.7   13.4
yearsGarage_isNA             6   10.9   11.6
CentralAir_lev_x_Y           4    7.9    8.5
Functional_lev_x_Typ         3    6.3    6.9
Condition1_lev_x_Norm        2    5.1    5.6
ScreenPorch                  1    3.4    3.8
```

We see the feature name, *n* subsets, which is the number of model subsets that include the feature if we did the pruning pass instead of cross-validation, and the `gcv` and `rss` columns show the decrease in the respective value that the feature contributes (`gcv` and `rss` are scaled 0 to 100). Notice that the feature we created, `yearsGarage_isNA`, was selected by the model. You can ponder the hinge functions, but there's an excellent visual to see the various piecewise linear functions:

```
> plotmo::plotmo(earth_fit, nrug = TRUE, rug.col = "red")
```

The output of the preceding code is as follows:

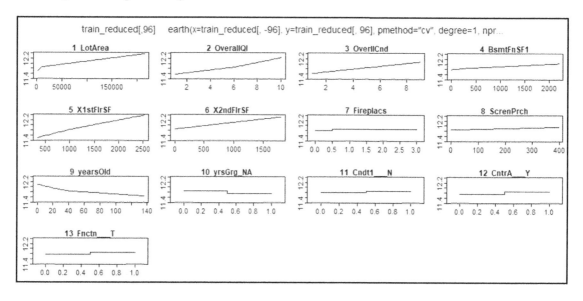

Notice in the plot that **LotArea** contains a hinge. Initially, as the size of the property increases, the increase is rather dramatic, then at a certain point, a new slope is applied from there to the maximum observed value. Contrast that with **OverallCond**, which has only one slope coefficient over all possible values. An excellent example of how MARS can capture linear and non-linear relationships in a piecewise fashion.

Now, we must see how it performs out of sample:

```
> earth_pred <- predict(earth_fit, tested)

> caret::postResample(earth_pred, test_logy)
    RMSE Rsquared      MAE
 0.12363  0.90120 0.08986
```

This is a superior RMSE than what we saw with simple linear regression! I'm curious how the residuals look on the test set:

```
> earth_residTest <- test_logy - earth_pred

> car::qqPlot(earth_residTest)
```

The output of the preceding code is as follows:

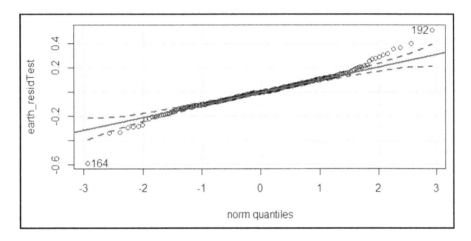

We still see a heavy-tailed distribution of the residuals. What this tells me is that we may have to resort to quantile regression (out-of-scope here) or create separate models for specific cuts of the response. Another option is to build an ensemble of models, but that's the subject of a later chapter.

Now, the issue I have here is that we predicted the natural log of sales price. How do we reverse transform to get actual sales price? I hear you saying, *just take the exponent*, correct? Well, maybe—or maybe not! I learned this painful lesson through experience, suffering the wrath of a PhD econometrician that just applying the exponent can lead to severe bias.

This is because the expected value of the response (sales price) is a function of the exponent of the predicted value plus an error term. If the error term isn't perfectly normal, then you have bias. The solution is **Duan's Smearing Estimator**. I shall address that with a custom function in the next section.

Should you desire to amuse yourself with the math behind all this, you can get started with Duan's paper:
Smearing Estimate: A Nonparametric Retransformation Method

Naihua Duan
Journal of the American Statistical Association
Vol. 78, No. 383 (Sep., 1983), pp. 605-610
Published by: Taylor & Francis, Ltd. on behalf of the American Statistical Association
DOI: 10.2307/2288126
https://www.jstor.org/stable/2288126?seq=1/subjects

Reverse transformation of natural log predictions

Now that you have read Duan's paper several times, here's how to apply to our work. I'm going to provide you with a user-defined function. It will do the following:

1. Exponentiate the residuals from the transformed model
2. Exponentiate the predicted values from the transformed model
3. Calculate the mean of the exponentiated residuals
4. Calculate the smeared predictions by multiplying the values in step 2 by the value in step 3
5. Return the results

Here's the function, which requires only two arguments:

```
> duan_smear <- function(pred, resid){
    expo_resid <- exp(resid)
    expo_pred <- exp(pred)
    avg_expo_resid <- mean(expo_resid)
    smear_predictions <- avg_expo_resid * expo_pred
    return(smear_predictions)
}
```

Next, we calculate the new predictions from the results of the MARS model:

```
> duan_pred <- duan_smear(pred = earth_pred, resid = earth_residTest)
```

We can now see how the model error plays out at the original sales price:

```
> caret::postResample(duan_pred, test_y)
      RMSE Rsquared         MAE
23483.5659    0.9356 16405.7395
```

We can say that the model is wrong, on average, by $16,406. How does that compare with not smearing? Let's see:

```
> exp_pred <- exp(earth_pred)
> caret::postResample(exp_pred, test_y)
      RMSE Rsquared         MAE
23106.1245    0.9356 16117.4235
```

The error is slightly less so, in this case, it just doesn't seem to be the wise choice to smear the estimate. I've seen examples where Duan's method, and others, are combined in an ensemble model. Again, more on ensembles later in this book.

Let's conclude the analysis by plotting the non-smeared predictions alongside the actual values. I'll show how to do this in ggplot fashion:

```
> results <- data.frame(exp_pred, test_y)

> colnames(results) <- c('predicted', 'actual')

> ggplot2::ggplot(results, ggplot2::aes(predicted, actual)) +
    ggplot2::geom_point(size=1) +
    ggplot2::geom_smooth() +
    ggthemes::theme_fivethirtyeight()
```

The output of the preceding code is as follows:

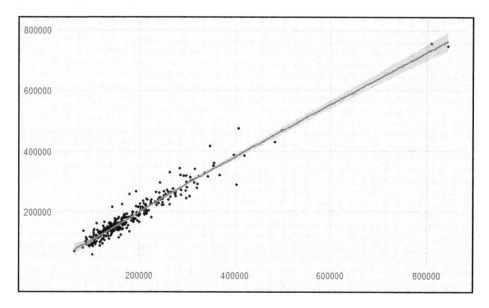

This is interesting as you can see that there's almost a subset of actual values that have higher sales prices than we predicted with their counterparts. There's some feature or interaction term that we could try and find to address that difference. We also see that, around the $400,000 sale price, there's considerable variation in the residuals—primarily, I would argue, because of the paucity of observations.

For starters, we have a pretty good model and serves as an excellent foundation for other modeling efforts as discussed. Additionally, we produced a model that's rather simple to interpret and explain, which in some cases may be more critical than some rather insignificant reduction in error. Hey, that's why you make big money. If it were easy, everyone would be doing it.

Summary

In the context of machine learning, we train a model and test it to predict an outcome. In this chapter, we had an in-depth look at the simple yet extremely effective methods of linear regression and MARS to predict a quantitative response. We also applied the data preparation paradigm put forth in Chapter 1, *Preparing and Understanding Data*, to quickly and efficiently get the data ready for modeling. We produced several simple plots to understand the response we were trying to predict, explore model assumptions, and model results.

Later chapters will cover more advanced techniques like Logistic regression, Support Vector Machines, Classification, Neural Networks, and Deep Learning but many of them are mere extensions of what we've learned in this chapter.

3
Logistic Regression

"The true logic of this world is the calculus of probabilities."

- *James Clerk Maxwell, Scottish physicist*

In the previous chapter, we took a look at using **Ordinary Least Squares** (**OLS**) to predict a quantitative outcome or, in other words, linear regression. It's now time to shift gears somewhat and examine how we can develop algorithms to predict qualitative outcomes. Such outcome variables could be binary (male versus female, purchase versus doesn't purchase, or a tumor is benign versus malignant) or multinomial categories (education level or eye color). Regardless of whether the outcome of interest is binary or multinomial, our task is to predict the probability of an observation belonging to a particular category of the outcome variable. In other words, we develop an algorithm to classify the observations.

To begin exploring classification problems, we'll discuss why applying the OLS linear regression isn't the correct technique and how the algorithms introduced in this chapter can solve these issues. We'll then look at the problem of predicting whether or not a banking customer is satisfied. To tackle this problem, we'll begin by building and interpreting a logistic regression model. We'll also start examining a univariate method to select features. Next, we'll turn to multivariate regression splines and discover ways to choose the best overall algorithm. This chapter will set the stage for more advanced machine learning methods in subsequent chapters.

We'll be covering the following topics in this chapter:

- Classification methods and linear regression
- Logistic regression
- Model training and evaluation

Classification methods and linear regression

So, why can't we use the least square regression method that we learned in the previous chapter for a qualitative outcome? Well, as it turns out, you can, but at your own risk. Let's assume for a second that you have an outcome that you're trying to predict and it has three different classes: mild, moderate, and severe. You and your colleagues also assume that the difference between mild and moderate and moderate and severe is an equivalent measure and a linear relationship. You can create a dummy variable where 0 is equal to mild, 1 is equal to moderate, and 2 is equal to severe. If you have reason to believe this, then linear regression might be an acceptable solution. However, qualitative labels such as the previous ones might lend themselves to a high level of measurement error that can bias the OLS. In most business problems, there's no scientifically acceptable way to convert a qualitative response into one that's quantitative. What if you have a response with two outcomes, say fail and pass? Again, using the dummy variable approach, we could code the fail outcome as 0 and the pass outcome as 1. Using linear regression, we could build a model where the predicted value is the probability of an observation of pass or fail. However, the estimates of Y in the model will most likely exceed the probability constraints of [0, 1] and hence be a bit difficult to interpret.

Logistic regression

As previously discussed, our classification problem is best modeled with the probabilities that are bound by 0 and 1. We can do this for all of our observations with some different functions, but here we'll focus on the logistic function. The logistic function used in logistic regression is as follows:

$$Probability\ of\ Y = e^{B0+B1x}/1 + e^{B0+B1x}$$

If you've ever placed a friendly wager on horse races or the World Cup, you may understand the concept better as odds. The logistic function can be turned to odds with the formulation of *Probability (Y) / 1 - Probability (Y)*. For instance, if the probability of Brazil winning the World Cup is 20 percent, then the odds are *0.2 / 1 - 0.2*, which is equal to *0.25*, translating to odds of one in four.

To translate the odds back to probability, take the odds and divide by one plus the odds. The World Cup example is hence *0.25 / 1 + 0.25*, which is equal to 20 percent. Additionally, let's consider the odds ratio. Assume that the odds of Germany winning the Cup are *0.18*. We can compare the odds of Brazil and Germany with the odds ratio. In this example, the odds ratio would be the odds of Brazil divided by the odds of Germany. We'll end up with an odds ratio equal to *0.25/0.18*, which is equal to *1.39*. Here, we'll say that Brazil is *1.39* times more likely than Germany to win the World Cup.

One way to look at the relationship of logistic regression with linear regression is to show logistic regression as the log odds or *log (P(Y)/1 - P(Y))* is equal to *Bo + B1x*. The coefficients are estimated using a maximum likelihood instead of the OLS. The intuition behind the maximum likelihood is that we're calculating the estimates for *Bo* and *B1*, which will create a predicted probability for an observation that's as close as possible to the actual observed outcome of *Y*, a so-called likelihood. The R language does what other software packages do for the maximum likelihood, which is to find the optimal combination of beta values that maximize the likelihood.

With these facts in mind, logistic regression is a potent technique to predict the problems involving classification and is often the starting point for model creation in such problems. Therefore, in this chapter, we'll attack the future problem with logistic regression first.

Model training and evaluation

As mentioned previously, we'll be predicting customer satisfaction. The data is based on a former online competition. I've taken the training portion of the data and cleaned it up for our use.

 A full description of the contest and the data is available at the following link: `https://www.kaggle.com/c/santander-customer-satisfaction/data`.

This is an excellent dataset for a classification problem for many reasons. Like so much customer data, it's very messy— especially before I removed a bunch of useless features (there was something like four dozen zero variance features). As discussed in the prior two chapters, I addressed missing values, linear dependencies, and highly correlated pairs. I also found the feature names lengthy and useless, so I coded them V1 through V142. The resulting data deals with what's usually a difficult thing to measure: satisfaction. Because of proprietary methods, no description or definition of satisfaction is given.

Having worked previously in the world of banking, I can assure you that it's a somewhat challenging proposition and fraught with measurement error. As such, there's quite a bit of noise relative to the signal and you can expect model performance to be rather poor. Also, the outcome of interest, *customer dissatisfaction*, is relatively rare when compared to customers not dissatisfied. The classic problem is that you end up with quite a few false positives when trying to classify the minority labels.

As always, you can find the data on GitHub: `https://github.com/datameister66/MMLR3rd/blob/master/santander_prepd.RData`.

So, let's start by first loading the data and training a logistic regression algorithm.

Training a logistic regression algorithm

Follow these simple steps to train a logistic regression algorithm:

1. The first step is to make sure we load our packages and call the `magrittr` library into our environment:

```
> library(magrittr)
> install.packages("caret")
> install.packages("classifierplots")
> install.packages("earth")
> install.packages("Information")
> install.packages("InformationValue")
> install.packages("Metrics")
> install.packages("tidyverse")
```

2. Here, we load the file then check the dimensions and examine a table of the customer labels:

```
> santander <- read.csv("~/santander_prepd.csv")

> dim(santander)
[1] 76020 143

> table(santander$y)

    0    1
73012 3008
```

We have 76,020 observations, but only 3,008 customers are labeled 1, which means dissatisfied. I'm going to use caret next to create training and test sets with an 80/20 split.

---

3. Within caret's `createDataPartition()` function, it automatically stratifies the sample based on the response, so we can rest assured about having a balanced percentage between the train and test sets:

```
> set.seed(1966)

> trainIndex <- caret::createDataPartition(santander$y, p = 0.8,
list = FALSE)

> train <- santander[trainIndex, ]

> test <- santander[-trainIndex, ]
```

4. Let's see how the response is balanced between the two datasets:

```
> table(train$y)

     0     1
58411  2405

> table(test$y)

     0     1
14601   603
```

There are roughly 4 percent in each set, so we can proceed. One interesting thing that can happen when you split the data is that you now end up with what was a near zero variance feature becoming a zero variance feature in your training set. When I treated this data, I only took out the zero variance features.

5. There were some low variance features, so let's see if we can eliminate some new zero variance ones:

```
> train_zero <- caret::nearZeroVar(train, saveMetrics = TRUE)

> table(train_zero$zeroVar)

FALSE TRUE
  142    1
```

6. OK, one feature is now zero variance because of the split, and we can remove it:

```
> train <- train[, train_zero$zeroVar == 'FALSE']
```

Our data frame now has 139 input features and the column of labeled customers. As we did with linear regression, for logistic regression to have meaningful results, which is to say not to overfit, you need to reduce the number of input features. We could press forward with stepwise selection or the like, as we did in the previous chapter. We could implement feature regularization methods as we'll discuss in the next chapter. However, I want to introduce a univariate feature reduction method using **Weight Of Evidence** (**WOE**) and **Information Value** (**IV**) and discuss how we can get an understanding of how to use it in a classification problem in conjunction with logistic regression.

Weight of evidence and information value

I stumbled into this method several years ago during consulting work. The team I was on was really into big datasets and constrained to using SAS statistical software. It was also a critical requirement that the customer teams could easily interpret the models.

Given the possibility of hundreds, even thousands, of possible features, I was privileged enough to learn the use of WOE and IV by a former rocket scientist. That's right: a person who actually worked on manned space flight. I became an eager pupil. Now, this method isn't a panacea. First of all, it's univariate, so features that are thrown out can become significant in a multivariate model and vice versa. I can say that it provides a nice complement to other methods, and you should keep it in your modeling toolbox. I believe it had its origins in the world of credit scoring, so if you work in the financial industry, you may already be familiar with it.

First, let's look at the formula for WOE:

$$WOE = ln(\frac{percentOfEvents}{percentOfNonEvents})$$

The WOE serves as a component in the IV. For numeric features, you would bin your data then calculate WOE separately for each bin. For categorical ones, or when one-hot encoded, bin for each level and calculate the WOE separately. Let's take an example and demonstrate in R.

Our data consists of one input feature coded as 0 or 1, so we'll have just two bins. For each bin, we calculate our WOE. In bin 1, or where values are equal to 0, there are four observations as events and 96 as non-events. Conversely, in bin 2, or where values are equal to 1, we have 12 observations as events and 88 as non-events. Let's see how to calculate the WOE for each bin:

```
> bin1events <- 4

> bin1nonEvents <- 96

> bin2events <- 12

> bin2nonEvents <- 88

> totalEvents <- bin1events + bin2events

> totalNonEvents <- bin1nonEvents + bin2nonEvents
# Now calculate the percentage per bin
> bin1percentE <- bin1events / totalEvents

> bin1percentNE <- bin1nonEvents / totalNonEvents

> bin2percentE <- bin2events / totalEvents

> bin2percentNE <- bin2nonEvents / totalNonEvents
# It's now possible to produce WOE
> bin1WOE <- log(bin1percentE / bin1percentNE)

> bin2WOE <- log(bin2percentE / bin2percentNE)
```

With completing this, you end up with the WOE for `bin1` and `bin2` of roughly -0.74 and 0.45 respectively. We now use that to calculate the IV per bin, then sum that up to arrive at an overall IV for the feature. The formula is as follows:

$$IV = \sum_{i=1}^{n}(Percent of Events - Percent of NonEvents) * WOE$$

Taking our current example; this is our feature IV:

```
> bin1IV <- (bin1percentE - bin1percentNE) * bin1WOE

> bin2IV <- (bin2percentE - bin2percentNE) * bin2WOE

> bin1IV + bin2IV
[1] 0.3221803
```

The IV for the feature is `0.322`. Now, what does that mean? The short answer is that it depends. There's a heuristic provided to help decide what IV threshold makes sense for inclusion in model development:

- < 0.02 not predictive
- 0.02 to 0.1 weak
- 0.1 to 0.3 medium
- 0.3 to 0.5 strong
- > 0.5 suspicious

Our following example will provide us with interesting decisions to make regarding where to draw the line.

Feature selection

What we're going to do now is use the `Information` package to calculate the IVs for our features. Then, I'll show you how to evaluate those values and run some plots as well. Since there are no hard and fast rules about thresholds for feature inclusion, I'll provide my judgment about where to draw the line. Of course, you can reject that and apply your own.

In this example, the code will create a series of tables you can use to explore the results. To get started, you only need to specify the data and the response or "y" variable:

```
IV <- Information::create_infotables(data = train, y = "y", parallel =
FALSE)
```

This will give us an IV summary of the top 25 features:

```
> knitr::kable(head(IV$Summary, 25))
```

```
|     |Variable |      IV|
|:---|:--------|------:|
|2   |V2       | 0.7006|
|102 |V103     | 0.5296|
|124 |V125     | 0.5281|
|45  |V45      | 0.5273|
|31  |V31      | 0.5213|
|125 |V126     | 0.4507|
|55  |V55      | 0.3135|
|140 |V141     | 0.0982|
|108 |V109     | 0.0711|
|130 |V131     | 0.0681|
|33  |V33      | 0.0672|
```

```
|104  |V105     |  0.0640|
|66   |V66      |  0.0519|
|92   |V93      |  0.0519|
|128  |V129     |  0.0499|
|121  |V122     |  0.0461|
|24   |V24      |  0.0417|
|131  |V132     |  0.0365|
|34   |V34      |  0.0323|
|47   |V47      |  0.0323|
|123  |V124     |  0.0289|
|129  |V130     |  0.0194|
|83   |V84      |  0.0189|
|19   |V19      |  0.0181|
|35   |V35      |  0.0181|
```

The results show us the feature column number, the feature name, and the `IV`. Notice that we have five features that are possibly suspicious. I'm all for taking any feature with an `IV` above `0.02`, which is the bottom of the weak predictors. That will give us 21 input features. The `V2` feature is interesting. If you look at the values and think about the data, it seems clear that it's the customer's age. Let's see how the data is binned, the `WOE` values, and the IVs:

```
> knitr::kable(IV$Tables$V2)
```

V2	N	Percent	WOE	IV
[5,22]	951	0.0156	0.0000	0.0000
[23,23]	16222	0.2667	−1.6601	0.3705
[24,24]	4953	0.0814	−1.2811	0.4481
[25,26]	6048	0.0994	−0.7895	0.4919
[27,31]	8088	0.1330	0.2261	0.4994
[32,36]	6037	0.0993	0.4923	0.5297
[37,42]	6302	0.1036	0.6876	0.5975
[43,51]	6095	0.1002	0.7328	0.6737
[52,105]	6120	0.1006	0.4636	0.7006

OK, you've got to be kidding me. Look at bin number 2, which I believe is customer age of 23 years. It constitutes almost 27 percent of the total observations and contributes over half of the IV. Suspicious indeed! How is any algorithm we produce on this data going to help if this feature is genuine AGE as I suspect? However, that's outside the scope of this endeavor and not worth wasting any more time or effort. Here we can quickly bring up a bar plot of the WOEs by bin:

```
> Information::plot_infotables(IV, "V2", show_values = TRUE)
```

The output of the preceding code is as follows:

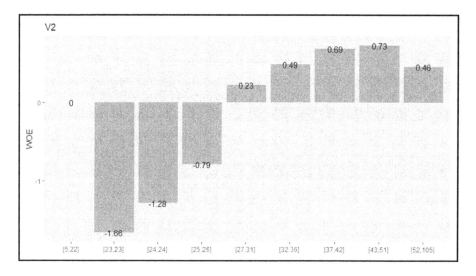

Interesting that there's a somewhat linear relationship between this feature and the response. What can be done is we can create features that turn the binned values into the WOE values. These new features would be linear and could be used in place of the original features. We shall forgo that because what method will do that for us? That's right, MARS in the next section can do that for us! Here is a grid plot of the top four features:

```
> Information::plot_infotables(IV, IV$Summary$Variable[1:4],
same_scales=TRUE)
```

The output of the preceding code is as follows:

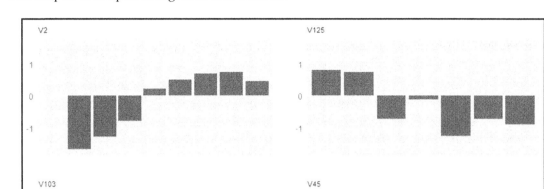

Now, given the cutoff point I picked previously, we can select those 21 features:

```
> features <- IV$Summary$Variable[1:21]

> train_reduced <- train[, colnames(train) %in% features]

> train_reduced$y <- train$y
```

There you go. We're now ready to begin training our algorithm.

Cross-validation and logistic regression

Our goal here is to build a model using 5-fold cross-validation. We'll utilize the `caret` package to establish our sampling scheme and to produce the final model. Start by building a separate `trainControl()` function:

```
> glm_control <-
    caret::trainControl(method = "cv",
    number = 5,
    returnResamp = "final")
```

This object is passed as an argument to train the algorithm. We now produce our input features, response variable (must be a factor for caret to train as logistic regression), set our random seed, and train the model. For the `train()` function, specify `glm` for **Generalized Linear Model (GLM)**:

```
> x <- train_reduced[, -22]

> y <- as.factor(train_reduced$y)

> set.seed(1988)

> glm_fit <-
    caret::train(x, y, method = "glm",
                trControl = glm_control,
                trace = FALSE)
```

When that's done *grinding away*, you can quickly check the results:

```
> glm_fit$results
  parameter Accuracy    Kappa AccuracySD  KappaSD
1      none   0.9602 0.0002369  0.0001591 0.001743
```

Look at that, 96 percent accuracy! I know that's entirely meaningless because if we just guessed that all labels in the response were zero, we would achieve 96 percent. That may seem obvious, but I've interviewed people with *Data Science degrees* that missed that fact. `Kappa` refers to what's known as Cohen's Kappa statistic. The Kappa statistic provides an insight into this problem by adjusting the accuracy scores, which is done by accounting for the model being entirely correct by mere chance. The formula for the statistic is as follows:

$$Kappa = (percent\ of\ agreement\ -\ percent\ of\ chance\ agreement)/(1\ -\ percent\ of\ chance\ agreement)$$

The *percent of agreement* is the rate that the model agreed on for the class (accuracy) and *percent of chance agreement* is the rate that the model randomly agreed. The higher the statistic, the better the performance is with the maximum agreement being one. So, with this Kappa score, the model is pathetic.

Well, Kappa would be useful with more balanced labels. We're now left to find other ways to examine model results. It's always a good idea to compare the probability distributions of the different classes with a density or box plot.

Here we produce an elegant and colorful density plot on the training data:

```
> glm_train_pred <- predict(glm_fit, train, type = "prob")

> colnames(glm_train_pred) <- c("zero", "one")

> classifierplots::density_plot(train_reduced$y, glm_train_pred$one)
```

The output of the preceding code is as follows:

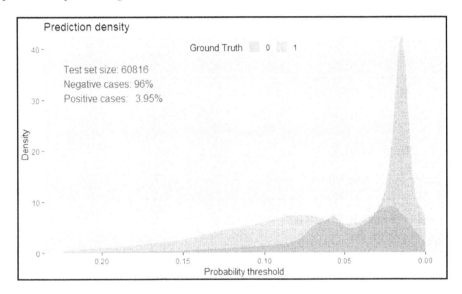

This gives us an interesting look at what the model's doing. We don't see any predictive power until we get around 7 percent. We can identify an optimal probability threshold to maximize our classification objective. There's an excellent function in the `InformationValue` package we'll apply later. It allows for the determination of four different thresholds:

- `misclasserror`: The default setting in the function, this identifies the threshold that minimizes a classification error
- `Ones`: This is the threshold that maximizes detection of 1s
- `Zeros`: This is the threshold that maximizes detection of 0s
- `Both`: This is the threshold that maximizes Youden's Index, which is *(sensitivity + specificity) - 1*

Sensitivity = True Positives / (True Positives + False Negatives): This is also called the True Positive Rate or Recall and is a measure of correctly identifying positive labels. *Specificity = True Negatives / (True Negatives + False Positives)*: Also called the True Negative Rate, this is a measure of correctly identifying negative labels.

In this case, we shall take a look at the threshold for `Both`. We'll also ask for all of the diagnostics:

```
> glm_cutoff <-
   InformationValue::optimalCutoff(
   train_reduced$y,
   glm_train_pred$one,
   optimiseFor = 'Both',
   returnDiagnostics = TRUE
   )
```

If you click on `glm_cutoff` in your global environment or run `View(glm_cutoff)`, you'll see a list of six different results:

- `optimalCutoff` = 0.0606
- A sensitivity table you can examine further on your own
- Misclassification error = 0.2006
- TPR = 0.6079
- FPR = 0.1927
- Specificity = 0.8073

If we select a cutoff of 0.0606, we'll achieve a **True Positive Rate (TPR)** of almost 61 percent. However, over 19 percent will be false positives.

Given the imbalance in the classes, that's a huge amount of customers. A confusion matrix can demonstrate that fact:

```
> InformationValue::confusionMatrix(train_reduced$y, glm_train_pred$one,
  threshold = 0.0607)
       0    1
0  47164  944
1  11247 1461
```

Of the training data, customers that were dissatisfied, a total of 2,405; if we correctly classify 1,461 of them, we'll incorrectly classify 11,247. So where we decide to put an optimal threshold depends on the needs of the business. We'll see how to portray that differently during model comparison.

Let's now see how the algorithm ranked variable importance:

```
> caret::varImp(glm_fit)
glm variable importance

only 20 most important variables shown (out of 21)

       Overall
V2     100.0000
V103   70.2840
V141   33.2809
V105   18.0160
V24    13.1048
V129   12.4327
V55    10.7379
V34     8.7920
V45     8.5681
V124    7.1968
V122    5.9959
V109    5.8668
V33     4.8295
V125    3.6369
V131    1.5439
V126    0.8383
V47     0.7430
V132    0.4286
V66     0.3133
V31     0.0912
```

Our `suspicious` variable is number one in overall importance. I would recommend you to try other models dropping `V2` from any consideration. But this is up to you as I'm of the mindset right now to see how performance is on the test data:

```
> glm_test_pred <- predict(glm_fit, test, type = "prob")

> colnames(glm_test_pred) <- c("zero", "one")

> classifierplots::density_plot(test$y, glm_test_pred$one)
```

The output of the preceding code is as follows:

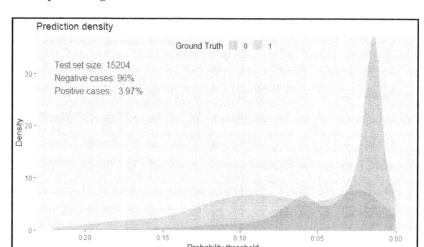

Very similar results on the test data. What about a confusion matrix given our threshold determined during training? Let's see:

```
> InformationValue::confusionMatrix(test$y, glm_test_pred$one, threshold =
0.0607)
        0    1
0 11710 227
1  2891 376
```

Consistent results! Now, let's examine this model's performance on the test data so that we can compare it to what the upcoming MARS model will produce. Two metrics should address the issue, **Area Under the Curve (AUC)**, and log-loss. The AUC provides you with a useful indicator of performance, and it can be shown that the AUC is equal to the probability that the observer will correctly identify the positive case when presented with a randomly chosen pair of cases in which one case is positive and one case is negative (Hanley JA & McNeil BJ, 1982). In our case, we'll switch the observer with our algorithm and evaluate accordingly. Log-loss is an effective metric as it takes into account the predicted probability and how much it deviates from the correct label. The following formula produces it:

$$logloss = -\frac{1}{n}\sum_{i=1}^{n}[y_i\,logy_i + (1 - y_i)log(1 - y_i)]$$

Like golf, a lower value is better with values between 0 and 1. A perfect model would have a value of 0. We can produce these values easily with the `Metrics` package:

```
> Metrics::auc(test$y, glm_test_pred$one)
[1] 0.7794

> Metrics::logLoss(test$y, glm_test_pred$one)
[1] 0.1499
```

Our AUC isn't that great, I would say. If the model were no better than a random guess, then AUC would be equal to 0.5, and if perfect, it would be 1. Our log-loss is only essential when comparing it to the next model.

Multivariate adaptive regression splines

In the prior chapter, we went through a discussion on MARS, how it works, why use it, and so on, so I won't duplicate that here; other than that, it can be applied in a classification problem as a generalized linear model. One of the key benefits is its power to conduct feature selection, so there's no need to run stepwise or IV—or even regularization, for that matter.

We'll train it with 5-fold cross-validation and set `nprune = 15` to limit the maximum number of features at 15. Recall from the previous chapter that more than 15 terms are possible as it fits piecewise splines.

This code will give us our `model` object. Be advised that this may take some time to complete:

```
> set.seed(1972)

> earth_fit <-
    earth::earth(
    x = train[, -142],
    y = train[, 142],
    pmethod = 'cv',
    nfold = 5,
    degree = 1,
    minspan = -1,
    nprune = 15,
    glm = list(family = binomial)
    )
```

Here's the model summary:

```
> summary(earth_fit)
Call: earth(x=train[,-142], y=train[,142], pmethod="cv",
            glm=list(family=binomial), degree=1, nprune=15, nfold=5,
            minspan=-1)

GLM coefficients
                             y
(Intercept)         -3.4407
V23                 -6.6750
V24                 -1.3539
V105                -0.8200
h(28-V2)            -0.4769
h(V2-28)             0.0071
h(1-V31)             1.4876
h(V31-1)             0.0947
h(106449-V141)       0.0000
h(V141-106449)       0.0000

Earth selected 10 of 10 terms, and 6 of 141 predictors using pmethod="cv"
```

As you can see in the summary, the model ended up with six total predictive features and a total of ten terms, including a `hinge` function on `V2`. By standard protocol, the paired hinge terms can be read first predictor less than the hinge value, and then predictor greater than or equal to hinge. For instance, for `V31`, a value less than 1 has a coefficient of 1.4876, otherwise 0.0947.

We can plot the linear interactions with respect to predicted probability. Setting `ylim` to `NA` helps to show changes in *y* (predicted probability) versus changes in feature values:

```
> plotmo::plotmo(earth_fit, ylim = NA)
```

The output of the preceding code is as follows:

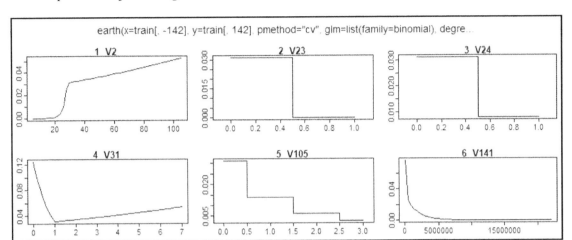

Notice how, for V31, values equal to zero have one coefficient else another one as described previously. Feature importance is trivial to produce:

```
> earth::evimp(earth_fit)
      nsubsets    gcv    rss
V31          9  100.0  100.0
V2           8   74.8   75.0
V141         7   40.2   41.1
V105         6   31.5   32.5
V23          5   26.8   27.8
V24          4   20.7   21.8
```

The nsubsets criterion counts the number of model subsets that include the feature. Features that included in more subsets are considered more important. These subsets are of the terms generated by earth's pruning pass.

Now, we specified cross-validation, but earth concurrently does forward and backward feature selection and elimination, using **Generalized Cross-Validation (GCV)** as discussed in the previous chapter. So, GCV and rss results for a feature are normalized from 0 to 100 for comparison purposes.

Like we did previously, a plot of the probability densities is useful, and `earth` comes with its own `plotd()` function:

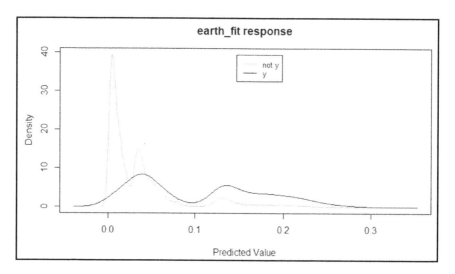

I like how the predicted values are reversed compared to the prior plots. Other than that, it's hard to discern anything meaningful with the exception that the densities are quite similar. Let's get the `cutoff` value:

```
> mars_cutoff <-
    InformationValue::optimalCutoff(
    train$y,
    pred,
    optimiseFor = 'Both',
    returnDiagnostics = TRUE
    )
```

Examination of the object provides the following:

- Optimal cutoff = 0.04976
- TPR = 0.6449
- FPR = 0.208

In comparison with logistic regression, we have a higher rate of finding true positives at the expense of a slightly higher rate of false positives.

Let's move on to evaluating performance on the test set:

```
> test_pred <- predict(earth_fit, test, type = 'response')

> Metrics::auc(test$y, test_pred)
[1] 0.8079

> Metrics::logLoss(test$y, test_pred)
[1] 0.1406
```

What do we see here? A slight improvement in AUC, and a lower (better) log-loss. While not dramatic, it may be of value. We can now turn to visually comparing the two models to confirm that MARS is indeed the preferred algorithm.

Model comparison

A useful tool for a classification model comparison is the **Receiver Operating Characteristic (ROC)** chart. ROC is a technique for visualizing, organizing, and selecting classifiers based on their performance (Fawcett, 2006). On the ROC chart, the y axis is the **True Positive Rate (TPR)**, and the x axis is the **False Positive Rate (FPR)**.

To create a ROC chart in R, you can use the ROCR package. I think this is a great package and allows you to build a chart in just three lines of code. The package also has an excellent companion website (with examples and a presentation) that can be found at the following link: http://rocr.bioinf.mpi-sb.mpg.de/.

For each model, you create a prediction object of the actual labels and the predicted probabilities, then create a performance object that embeds TPR and FPR, and finally plot it:

```
> pred.glm <- ROCR::prediction(glm_test_pred$one, test$y)

> perf.glm <- ROCR::performance(pred.glm, "tpr", "fpr")

> ROCR::plot(perf.glm, main = "ROC", col = 1)
```

That gives us the plot for the GLM (logistic regression). Now, we'll superimpose the MARS model on the same plot and create a legend:

```
> pred.earth <- ROCR::prediction(test_pred, test$y)

> perf.earth <- ROCR::performance(pred.earth, "tpr", "fpr")

> ROCR::plot(perf.earth, col = 2, add = TRUE)

> legend(0.6, 0.6, c("GLM", "MARS"), 1:2)
```

The output of the preceding code is as follows:

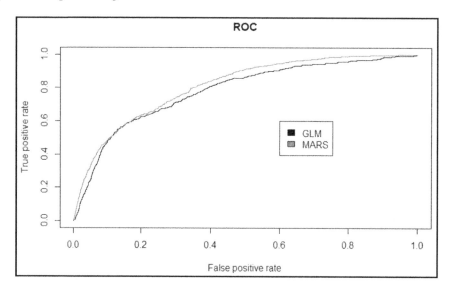

The area under the ROC curves corresponds to the prior calculated AUCs. The MARs model had a higher AUC; hence, its curve is slightly higher than the GLM model. It's noteworthy that around a TPR of 0.5, they have almost the same FPR. The bottom line though is the MARS model with fewer input features outperformed logistic regression albeit just slightly.

In a problem such as that which this data provides, there are quite a few things we could do to increase performance. You could further explore the data to try and add custom features. You could also use more advanced methods, creating more models for comparison, or even build several models and create an ensemble. As for advanced techniques and building ensembles, we'll cover those in subsequent chapters. Let your imaginations run wild!

Summary

In this chapter, we looked at using probabilistic linear models to predict a qualitative response with two generalized linear model methods: logistic regression, and multivariate adaptive regression splines. We explored using the weight of information and information value as a technique to do univariate feature selection. We covered the concept of finding the proper probability threshold to minimize classification error. Additionally, we began the process of using various performance metrics such as AUC, log-loss, and ROC charts to explore model selection visually and statistically. These metrics proved to be more informative than just pure accuracy, especially in a situation where class labels are highly imbalanced. In the next chapter, we'll cover regularization methods for feature selection, and how it can be used in training your algorithms. We'll see how we can create a dataset. We'll know about ridge regression and dive deeper in feature selection.

4
Advanced Feature Selection in Linear Models

"There is nothing permanent except change."

– Heraclitus

So far, we've examined the usage of linear models for both quantitative and qualitative outcomes with an eye on the techniques of feature selection, that is, the methods and techniques that exclude useless or unwanted predictor variables. We saw that linear models can be quite useful in machine learning problems, how piece-wise linear models can capture non-linear relationships as multivariate adaptive regression splines. Additional techniques have been developed and refined in the last couple of decades that can improve predictive ability and interpretability above and beyond the linear models that we discussed in the preceding chapters. In this day and age, many datasets, such as those in the two prior chapters, have numerous features. It isn't unreasonable to have datasets with thousands of potential features.

The methods in this chapter might prove to be a better way to approach feature reduction and selection. In this chapter, we'll look at the concept of regularization where the coefficients are constrained or shrunk towards zero. There're many methods and permutations to these methods of regularization, but we'll focus on ridge regression, **Least Absolute Shrinkage and Selection Operator (LASSO)**, and, finally, elastic net, which combines the benefits of both techniques into one.

The following are the topics we'll cover in this chapter:

- Overview of regularization
- Dataset creation
- Ridge regression
- LASSO
- Elastic net

Regularization overview

You may recall that our linear model follows the form: $Y = B0 + B_1x_1 + ... B_nx_n + e$, and that the best fit tries to minimize the RSS, which is the sum of the squared errors of the actual minus the estimate, or $e_1^2 + e_2^2 + ... e_n^2$.

With regularization, we'll apply what is known as a **shrinkage penalty** in conjunction with RSS minimization. This penalty consists of a lambda (symbol λ), along with the normalization of the beta coefficients and weights. How these weights are normalized differs in terms of techniques, and we'll discuss them accordingly. Quite simply, in our model, we're minimizing *(RSS + λ (normalized coefficients))*. We'll select λ, which is known as the tuning parameter, in our model building process. Please note that if lambda is equal to 0, then our model is equivalent to OLS, as it cancels out the normalization term. As we work through this chapter, the methods can be applied to a classification problem.

So what does regularization do for us and why does it work? First of all, regularization methods are very computationally efficient. In a best subsets of features, we're searching 2^p **models** and, in large datasets, it isn't feasible to attempt this. In the techniques that follow, we only fit one model to each value of lambda and, as you can imagine this, is far less computationally demanding. Another reason goes back to our bias-variance trade-off, discussed in the preface. In the linear model, where the relationship between the response and the predictors is close to linear, the least squares estimates will have low bias but may have high variance. This means that a small change in the training data can cause a significant change in the least squares coefficient estimates (James, 2013). Regularization through the proper selection of lambda and normalization may help you improve the model fit by optimizing the bias-variance trade-off. Finally, the regularization of coefficients may work to solve multicollinearity problems as we shall see.

Ridge regression

Let's begin by exploring what ridge regression is and what it can and can't do for you. With ridge regression, the normalization term is the sum of the squared weights, referred to as an **L2-norm**. Our model is trying to minimize $RSS + \lambda(sum\ Bj^2)$. As lambda increases, the coefficients shrinks toward zero but never become zero. The benefit may be an improved predictive accuracy but, as it doesn't zero out the weights for any of your features, it could lead to issues in the model's interpretation and communication. To help with this problem, we can turn to LASSO.

LASSO

LASSO applies the **L1-norm** instead of the L2-norm as in ridge regression, which is the sum of the absolute value of the feature weights and so minimizes $RSS + \lambda(sum\ |Bj|)$. This shrinkage penalty will indeed force a feature weight to zero. This is a clear advantage over ridge regression, as it may improve the model interpretability.

The mathematics behind the reason that the L1-norm allows the weights/coefficients to become zero is beyond the scope of this book (refer to Tibsharini, 1996 for further details).

If LASSO is so great, then ridge regression must be obsolete in machine learning. Not so fast! In a situation of high collinearity or high pairwise correlations, LASSO may force a predictive feature to zero, hence you can lose the predictive ability; that is, if both feature A and B should be in your model, LASSO may shrink one of their coefficients to zero. The following quote sums up this issue nicely:

> *"One might expect the lasso to perform better in a setting where a relatively small number of predictors have substantial coefficients, and the remaining predictors have coefficients that are very small or that equal zero. Ridge regression will perform better when the response is a function of many predictors, all with coefficients of roughly equal size."*

> *– James, 2013*

There is the possibility of achieving the best of both worlds and that leads us to the next topic, elastic net.

Elastic net

The power of elastic net is that it performs feature extraction, unlike ridge regression, and it'll group the features that LASSO fails to do. Again, LASSO will tend to select one feature from a group of correlated ones and ignore the rest. Elastic net does this by including a mixing parameter, alpha, in conjunction with lambda. Alpha will be between 0 and 1, and as before, lambda will regulate the size of the penalty. Please note that an alpha of zero is equal to ridge regression and an alpha of 1 is equivalent to LASSO. Essentially, we're blending the L1 and L2 penalties by including a second tuning parameter with a quadratic (squared) term of the beta coefficients. We'll end up with the goal of minimizing *(RSS + λ[(1-alpha) (sum|Bj|^2)/2 + alpha (sum |Bj|)])/N)*.

Let's put these techniques to the test. We'll utilize a dataset I created to demonstrate the methods. In the next section, I'll discuss how I created the dataset with a few predictive features and some noise features, including those with high correlation. I recommend that, once you feel comfortable with this chapter's content, you go back and apply them to the data examined in the prior two chapters, comparing performance.

Data creation

In this section, I'll discuss how I created the dataset used for this chapter and provide insight into the features and the class labels we'll endeavor to predict. The data is available on GitHub at `https://github.com/datameister66/MMLR3rd/blob/master/sim_df.csv`:

1. Let's get our libraries and data loaded:

```
> library(magrittr)

> install.packages("glmnet")

> install.packages("caret")

> install.packages("classifierplots")

> install.packages("DataExplorer")

> install.packages("InformationValue")
```

```
> install.packages("Metrics")

> install.packages("ROCR")

> install.packages("tidyverse")

> options(scipen=999)

> sim_df <- readr::read_csv('sim_df.csv')
```

The dataframe is 10,000 observations of 17 variables, consisting of 16 input features and 1 response. I created this dataset using the `twoClassSim()` function from the `caret` package. The full code with seeds is available in the online code, allowing you to make changes and create whatever data you would like to explore. A full explanation of your options in creating your own set is available in the function's help.

2. Now, let me go over the column names and tell you what this is all about:

```
> colnames(sim_df)
 [1] "TwoFactor1" "TwoFactor2" "Linear1" "Linear2" "Linear3"
"Linear4"
 [7] "Linear5" "Linear6" "Nonlinear1" "Nonlinear2" "Nonlinear3"
"Noise1"
[13] "Noise2" "Noise3" "Noise4" "Class" "random1"
```

First of all, the `TwoFactor` features are correlated with each other and slightly predictive of the response, y. Five of the six linear features, the three non-linear features, and the feature named `random1` might have some predictive power. The four noise features should have absolutely no predictive power unless by pure chance. Also, the `Linear5` and `Linear6` features are highly correlated. I created that relationship to help point out how the different methods will handle it.

3. The y labels are somewhat imbalanced, roughly 70/30:

```
> table(sim_df$y)

    0    1
 7072 2928
```

4. The data isn't too wide to include all of it in a correlation plot:

```
> DataExplorer::plot_correlation(sim_df)
```

The output of the preceding code is as follows:

Features	TwoFactor1	TwoFactor2	Linear1	Linear2	Linear3	Linear4	Linear5	Linear6	Nonlinear1	Nonlinear2	Nonlinear3	Noise1	Noise2	Noise3	Noise4	random1	y
y	-0.18	0.17	0	-0.25	0.22	-0.16	0.11	0.09	0.1	0.04	0.04	-0.01	0.01	0.01	0.02	-0.12	1
random1	0.01	-0.03	0	0.02	-0.01	0.03	-0.02	-0.02	-0.02	0	-0.02	-0.01	0.01	0	-0.01	1	-0.12
Noise4	-0.02	-0.01	0.02	0	0	-0.01	0.01	0.01	-0.01	0	0.01	0.01	-0.03	0.01	1	-0.01	0.02
Noise3	0	-0.01	0.01	0	0.01	-0.01	0.01	0.01	0	-0.01	-0.02	0	-0.01	1	0.01	0	0.01
Noise2	0	0	0.01	0.01	-0.01	-0.02	0.01	0.01	0.02	-0.01	0	-0.01	1	-0.01	-0.03	0.01	0.01
Noise1	0	0	0	0.01	0	0	0	-0.01	0.01	0	0	1	-0.01	0	0.01	-0.01	-0.01
Nonlinear3	-0.02	-0.01	0	0.01	-0.01	-0.01	-0.01	-0.01	-0.01	-0.02	1	0	0	-0.02	0.01	-0.02	0.04
Nonlinear2	0.01	0.01	0	-0.01	0.01	-0.01	-0.02	-0.01	-0.01	1	-0.02	0	-0.01	-0.01	0	0	0.04
Nonlinear1	0.01	0.02	0.01	0.01	-0.01	0	0.01	0	1	-0.01	-0.01	0.01	0.02	0	-0.01	-0.02	0.1
Linear6	0	-0.01	-0.01	-0.01	-0.01	-0.01	0.89	1	0	-0.01	-0.01	-0.01	0.01	0.01	0.01	-0.02	0.09
Linear5	-0.01	-0.02	-0.02	0	-0.02	0	1	0.89	0.01	-0.02	-0.01	0	0.01	0.01	0.01	-0.02	0.11
Linear4	0	0	0.01	0	0.01	1	0	-0.01	0	-0.01	-0.01	0	-0.02	-0.01	-0.01	0.03	-0.16
Linear3	0.01	0	-0.01	-0.02	1	0.01	-0.02	-0.01	-0.01	0.01	-0.01	0	-0.01	0.01	0	-0.01	0.22
Linear2	0	0.01	0	1	-0.02	0	0	-0.01	0.01	-0.01	0.01	0.01	0.01	0	0	0.02	-0.25
Linear1	-0.01	-0.01	1	0	0.01	0.01	-0.02	-0.01	-0.01	0	0	0	0.01	0.01	0.02	0	0
TwoFactor2	0.64	1	-0.01	0.01	0	0	-0.02	-0.01	0.02	0.01	-0.01	0	0	-0.01	-0.01	-0.03	0.17
TwoFactor1	1	0.64	-0.01	0	0.01	0	-0.01	0	0.01	0.01	-0.02	0	0	0	-0.02	0.01	-0.18

Features

Correlation Meter
-1.0 -0.5 0.0 0.5 1.0

The plot confirms visually what I described previously. The highest correlation is between **Linear5** and **Linear6**. What we can do is eliminate one of the pairs of highly correlated features, which I did in `Chapter 2`, *Linear Regression*. In this instance, we'll keep both in and let the algorithms handle it.

This data is fully prepared for modeling in this chapter, so let's begin.

Modeling and evaluation

We'll begin the modeling process of developing a classification algorithm to predict *y*. We'll conduct, in sequence, ridge regression, LASSO, and elastic net models, evaluating their performance as we go using the area under the curve and log-loss.

Ridge regression

The package we're using will be `glmnet`. I like it because it has a built-in cross-validation function, standardizes the input features, and returns coefficients on their original scale, so it's quite easy to implement. If you standardize your features yourself, you can specify `standardize = FALSE` in the function. Either way, don't run features that aren't standardized as the results will be undesirable as the regularization won't be applied evenly. If you do standardize on your own, I recommend utilizing the `vtreat` package functions as we did in *Chapter 2, Linear Regression*, specifying `scale = TRUE` in the `prepare()` function. This will help us apply the centering and scaling values from your training data to the test/validation sets.

I'll let `glmnet` handle the standardizing, and we can begin with a 70/30 train/test split:

```
> set.seed(1066)

> index <- caret::createDataPartition(sim_df$y, p = 0.7, list = F)

> train <- sim_df[index, ]

> test <- sim_df[-index, ]
```

Now, `glmnet` requires that your features are input as a matrix, and if you're doing a classification problem, the response is a factor. This code handles the requirement:

```
> x <- as.matrix(train[, -17])

> y <- as.factor(train$y)
```

For the function to train the algorithm, there're a couple of things you can specify. Here, I'll execute five-fold cross-validation—the loss function for training, which in the case of classification can be `class` for misclassification errors or `auc` for the area under the curve. I'll go with `auc`, and leave it up to you to assess. Since this is ridge regression, our alpha will be equal to 0.

Accordingly, we'll set the `family` argument to `binomial`. This makes the function run a logistic regression instead of its standard linear regression. The following is the code to train the ridge regression algorithm:

```
> set.seed(1999)

> ridge <- glmnet::cv.glmnet(
    x,
    y,
    nfolds = 5,
    type.measure = "auc",
    alpha = 0,
    family = "binomial"
  )
```

To begin, `glmnet` offers a number of different plots. The default plot shows the relationship of the log of the lambda values searched and its relation to the loss function, in our case `auc`:

```
> plot(ridge)
```

The output of the preceding code is as follows:

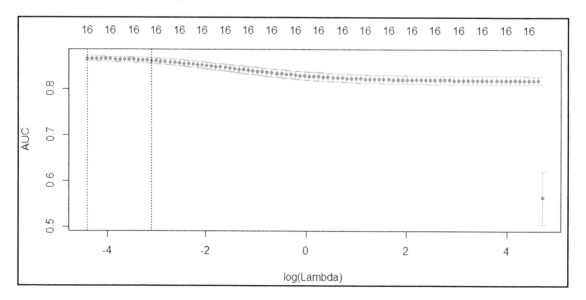

We see **log(Lambda)** on the *x* axis and **AUC** on the *y* axis. At the top of the plot is a series of the value 16. This tracks the number of non-zero coefficients corresponding to **log(Lamda)**. We'll see how that changes with LASSO. The two dotted vertical lines show the **log(Lambda)** value with the maximum **AUC** and the **log(Lamda)** value with the maximum **AUC** within one standard error of the maximum, for the left and right lines respectively.

Let's review what those actual lambda values are:

```
> ridge$lambda.min
[1] 0.01216653

> ridge$lambda.1se
[1] 0.04475312
```

Recall that, if lambda were equal to zero, there would be no regularization penalty at all.

To see the coefficients, run this code:

```
> coef(ridge, s = "lambda.1se")
17 x 1 sparse Matrix of class "dgCMatrix"
                        1
(Intercept) 0.535798579
TwoFactor1  -0.541881256
TwoFactor2   0.530637287
Linear1     -0.005472570
Linear2     -0.506143897
Linear3      0.454702486
Linear4     -0.316847306
Linear5      0.182733133
Linear6      0.070036471
Nonlinear1   0.354214422
Nonlinear2   0.238778841
Nonlinear3   0.322499067
Noise1      -0.028226796
Noise2       0.002973271
Noise3       0.014767631
Noise4       0.038038078
random1     -0.237527142
```

To convert the logistic regression coefficients, called **logits**, into a probability, do the following:

1. Calculate the odds by exponentiation, for example, exp(coef)
2. Calculate the probability with the formula, *probability = odds / 1+ odds*

Notice that the `noise` features and `Linear1`, which are irrelevant to making a prediction, are close, but not equal to, zero. The algorithm puts a larger coefficient on `Linear5` versus `Linear6`. By the way, those features are on the same scale, so a direct comparison is possible. To predict the probabilities with a `glmnet` model, be sure to specify `type = "response"` and which lambda value to use. I recommend starting with using the `lambda.1se` value to prevent overfitting. But you can experiment accordingly:

```
> ridge_pred <-
    data.frame(predict(ridge, newx = x, type = "response", s =
"lambda.1se"))
```

Like in the previous chapter on logistic regression, a plot of the probability distributions by class is in order:

```
> classifierplots::density_plot(y, ridge_pred$X1)
```

The output of the preceding code is as follows:

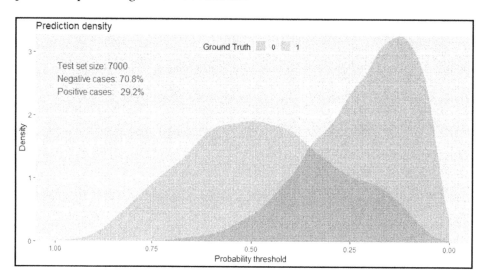

There seems to be an excellent separation in the probabilities above 50%.

Let's see the AUC:

```
> Metrics::auc(y, ridge_pred$X1)
[1] 0.8632982
```

The AUC is above `0.86`. This brings us to the question of whether or not this will remain consistent on the test data:

```
> ridge_test <-
    data.frame(predict(ridge, newx = as.matrix(test[, -17]),
    type = 'response'), s = "lambda.1se")

> Metrics::auc(test$y, ridge_test$X1)
[1] 0.8706708

> Metrics::logLoss(test$y, ridge_test$X1)
[1] 0.4307592

> classifierplots::density_plot(test$y, ridge_test$X1)
```

The output of the preceding code is as follows:

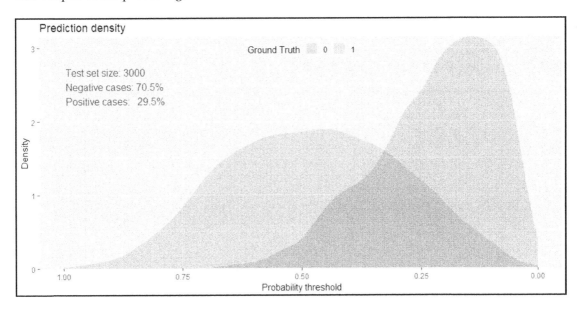

There's very consistent performance between the train and test data. The AUC is now above 0.87, and we have a benchmark log-loss of 0.4307592. You can try different k-folds, a different loss function, and even different random seeds to see how the model changes. For now, we need to move on to the next algorithm, LASSO.

LASSO

It's a simple matter to update the code we used for ridge regression to accommodate LASSO. I'm going to change just two things: the random `seed` and I'll set `alpha` to `1`:

```
> set.seed(1876)

> lasso <- glmnet::cv.glmnet(
    x,
    y,
    nfolds = 5,
    type.measure = "auc",
    alpha = 1,
    family = "binomial"
 )
```

The plot of the model is quite interesting:

```
> plot(lasso)
```

The output of the preceding code is as follows:

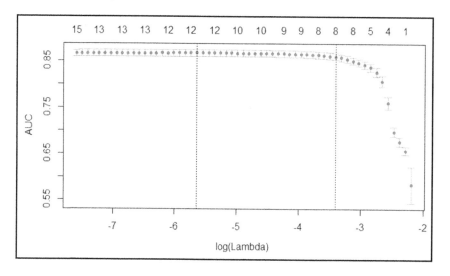

You can now see the number of non-zero features as the Lambda changes. The number of features included at one standard error is just eight!

Let's have a gander at those coefficients:

```
> coef(lasso, s = "lambda.1se")
17 x 1 sparse Matrix of class "dgCMatrix"
                           1
(Intercept) -0.30046007
TwoFactor1  -0.53307368
TwoFactor2   0.52110703
Linear1         .
Linear2     -0.42669146
Linear3      0.35514853
Linear4     -0.20726177
Linear5      0.10381320
Linear6         .
Nonlinear1   0.10478862
Nonlinear2      .
Nonlinear3      .
Noise1          .
Noise2          .
Noise3          .
Noise4          .
random1     -0.06581589
```

Now, this looks much better. LASSO threw out those nonsense noise features and `Linear1`. However, before we start congratulating ourselves, look at how `Linear6` was constrained to zero. Does it need to be in the model or not? We could undoubtedly adjust the lambda value and see where it enters and what effect it makes.

It's time to check how it does on the training data:

```
> lasso_pred <-
    data.frame(predict(
    lasso,
    newx = x,
    type = "response",
    s = "lambda.1se"
  ))

> Metrics::auc(y, lasso_pred$X1)
[1] 0.8621664

> classifierplots::density_plot(y, lasso_pred$X1)
```

The output of the preceding code is as follows:

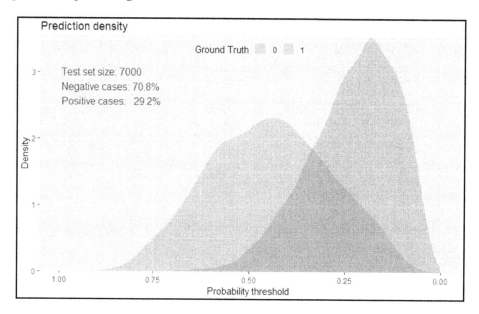

These are quite similar results to those with ridge regression. Correct evaluation, however, is done on the test data:

```
> lasso_test <-
    data.frame(predict(lasso, newx = as.matrix(test[, -17]), type =
'response'),
    s = "lambda.1se")

> Metrics::auc(test$y, lasso_test$X1)
[1] 0.8684276

> Metrics::logLoss(test$y, lasso_test$X1)
[1] 0.4512764

> classifierplots::density_plot(test$y, lasso_test$X1)
```

The output of the preceding code is as follows:

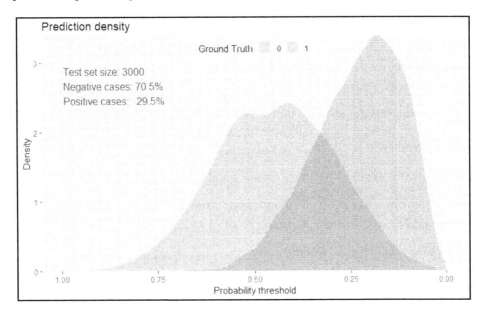

The LASSO model does have a slightly lower AUC and marginally higher log-loss (0.45 versus 0.43). In the real world, I'm not sure that would be meaningful given that we have a more parsimonious model with LASSO. I guess that's another dimension alongside bias-variance, *predictive power versus complexity*.

Speaking of complexity, let's move on to elastic net.

Elastic net

For our purposes here, we want to focus on finding the optimal mix of lambda and our elastic net mixing parameter, `alpha`. This is done using the following simple three-step process:

1. Use the `expand.grid()` function in base R to create a vector of all of the possible combinations of `alpha` and `lambda` that we want to investigate.
2. Use the `trainControl()` function from the `caret` package to determine the resampling method; we'll use 5-fold cross-validation again.

3. Train a model to select our `alpha` and `lambda` parameters using `glmnet()` in caret's `train()` function.

Once we've selected our parameters, we'll apply them to the `test` data in the same way as we did with ridge regression and LASSO.

 Our grid of combinations should be large enough to capture the best model but not so large that it becomes computationally unfeasible. That won't be a problem with this big a dataset, but keep this in mind for future reference.

The following are the hyperparameters values we'll try:

- Alpha from 0 to 1 by 0.2 increments; remember that this is bound by 0 and 1
- Lambda from 0.01 to 0.03 in steps of 0.002

You can create this matrix by using the `expand.grid()` function and building a sequence of numbers that the `caret` package will automatically use. The `caret` package will take the values for `alpha` and `lambda` with the following code:

```
> grid <-
    expand.grid(.alpha = seq(0, 1, by = .2),
    .lambda = seq(0.01, 0.03, by = 0.002))

> head(grid)
  .alpha .lambda
1    0.0    0.01
2    0.2    0.01
3    0.4    0.01
4    0.6    0.01
5    0.8    0.01
6    1.0    0.01
```

There are 66 different models to be built, compared, and selected. The preceding list shows the various combinations with all of the possible alpha parameters for a lambda of 0.01. Now, we set up an object to specify we want to do 5-fold cross-validation:

```
> control <- caret::trainControl(method = 'cv', number = 5)
```

Training the model with `caret` in this instance requires *y* to be a factor, which we've already done. It also requires the specification of train control or passing an object as we just did. There're a couple of different selection metrics you can choose from for a classification problem: accuracy or Kappa. Well, we covered this in the previous chapter, in a class imbalance situation; I think Kappa is preferred. Refer to the previous chapter if you need to refresh your understanding of Kappa. The following is the relevant code:

```
> set.seed(2222)
> enet <- caret::train(x,
                       y,
                       method = "glmnet",
                       trControl = control,
                       tuneGrid = grid,
                       metric = "Kappa")
```

To find the best overall model according to Kappa, we call the best-tuned version:

```
> enet$bestTune
   alpha lambda
23   0.4   0.01
```

The best model is alpha `0.4` and lambda `0.01`. To see how it affects the coefficients (logits), we will run them through `glmnet` without cross-validation:

```
> best_enet <- glmnet::glmnet(x,
    y,
    alpha = 0.4,
    lambda = 0.01,
    family = "binomial")

> coef(best_enet)
17 x 1 sparse Matrix of class "dgCMatrix"
                      s0
(Intercept)   1.310419410
TwoFactor1   -0.933300729
TwoFactor2    0.917877320
Linear1           .
Linear2      -0.689547039
Linear3       0.619432149
Linear4      -0.416603510
Linear5       0.315207408
Linear6       0.002005802
Nonlinear1    0.454620511
Nonlinear2    0.224564104
Nonlinear3    0.343687158
Noise1       -0.009290811
Noise2            .
```

```
Noise3          .
Noise4       0.014674805
random1     -0.261039240
```

With alpha at 0.4, three features are forced to zero. Examining the metrics on training data comes next:

```
> enet_pred <- predict(enet, train, type = "prob")

> Metrics::auc(y, enet_pred$`1`)
[1] 0.8684076

> classifierplots::density_plot(y, enet_pred$`1`)
```

The output of the preceding code is as follows:

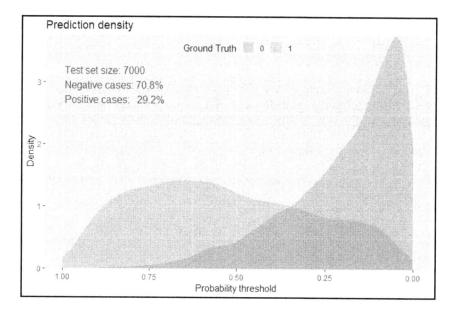

The probability skew for labels of 1 seems higher than the previous models as well as for labels of 0. The AUC is in line with the other models as well. The proof will lie in predicting the test data:

```
> enet_test <-
    predict(enet, test, type = "prob")

> Metrics::auc(test$y, enet_test$`1`)
[1] 0.8748963

> Metrics::logLoss(test$y, enet_test$`1`)
```

```
[1] 0.3977438

> classifierplots::density_plot(test$y, enet_test$`1`)
```

The output of the preceding code is as follows:

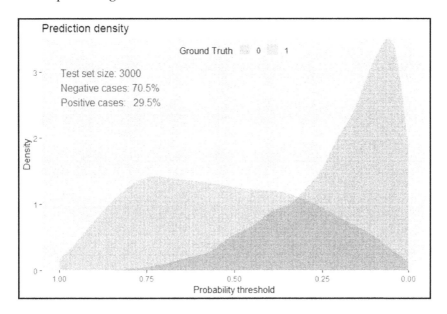

There's a consistent skew in the distributions and a superior AUC and log-loss versus the other two models, so it seems our elastic net version is the *best*. We can confirm this by looking at the ROC plots of all three models, using a similar technique to evaluate the classifiers visually, as in the previous chapter:

```
pred.ridge <- ROCR::prediction(ridge_test$X1, test$y)

perf.ridge <- ROCR::performance(pred.ridge, "tpr", "fpr")

ROCR::plot(perf.ridge, main = "ROC", col = 1)

pred.lasso <- ROCR::prediction(lasso_test$X1, test$y)

perf.lasso <- ROCR::performance(pred.lasso, "tpr", "fpr")

ROCR::plot(perf.lasso, col = 2, add = TRUE)

pred.enet <- ROCR::prediction(enet_test$'1', test$y)

perf.enet <- ROCR::performance(pred.enet, "tpr", "fpr")
```

```
ROCR::plot(perf.enet, col = 3, add = TRUE)

legend(0.6, 0.6, c("Ridge", "LASSO", "ENET"), 1:3)
```

The output of the preceding code is as follows:

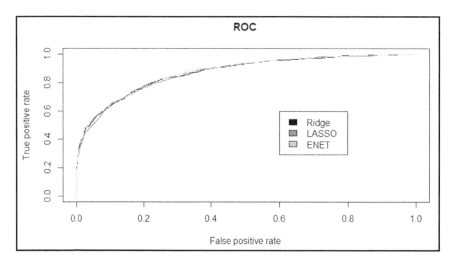

I think, as we would expect, the elastic net is just ever so slightly better than the other two. Which model goes into production is a matter for you and your business partners to decide as you balance complexity and performance.

Summary

In this chapter, the goal was to use a simulated dataset to provide an introduction to learning how to apply advanced feature selection for linear and generalized linear models. We used the `glmnet` package to predict class probabilities for a binary classification problem using logistic regression. These methods can be adapted to linear regression and multinomial classifications. An introduction to regularization and the three techniques that incorporate it was provided and utilized to build and compare models. Regularization is a powerful technique to improve computational efficiency and to possibly extract more meaningful features when compared to the other modeling techniques. We saw how to use various performance metrics to compare and select the most appropriate model.

Up to this point, we've been purely talking about linear and generalized linear models. In the next couple of chapters, we'll begin to use more complex nonlinear models for both classification and regression problems we'll encounter in further chapters.

K-Nearest Neighbors and Support Vector Machines

"Statistical thinking will one day be as necessary for efficient citizenship as the ability to read and write."

–H.G. Wells

In `Chapter 3`, *Logistic Regression*, we discussed using generalized linear models to determine the probability that a predicted observation belongs to a categorical response what we refer to as a classification problem. That was just the beginning of classification methods, with many techniques that we can use to try and improve our predictions.

In this chapter, we'll delve into two nonlinear techniques: **K-Nearest Neighbors** (**KNN**) and **Support Vector Machines** (**SVMs**). These techniques are more sophisticated than those we discussed earlier because the assumptions on linearity can be relaxed, which means a linear combination of the features to define the decision boundary isn't needed. Be forewarned, though, that this doesn't always equal superior predictive ability. Additionally, these models can be a bit problematic to interpret for business partners, and they can be computationally inefficient. When used wisely, they provide a powerful complement to the other tools and techniques discussed in this book. They can be used for continuous outcomes in addition to classification problems; however, for this chapter, we'll focus only on the latter.

After a high-level background on the techniques, we'll put both of them to the test, starting with KNN.

Following are the topics that we'll be covering in this chapter:

- K-nearest neighbors
- Support vector machines
- Manipulating data
- Modeling and evaluation

K-nearest neighbors

In our previous efforts, we built models that had coefficients or, to put it in another way, parameter estimates for each of our included features. With KNN, we have no parameters as the learning method is so-called instance-based learning. In short, *labeled examples (inputs and corresponding output labels) are stored, and no action is taken until a new input pattern demands an output value* (Battiti and Brunato, 2014, p. 11). This method is commonly called **lazy learning**, as no specific model parameters are produced. The `train` instances themselves represent the knowledge. For the prediction of any new instance (a new data point), the `training` data is searched for an instance that most resembles the new instance in question. KNN does this for a classification problem by looking at the closest points—the nearest neighbors—to determine the proper class. The *k* comes into play by deciding how many neighbors should be examined by the algorithm, so if *k=5*, it will consider the five nearest points. A weakness of this method is that all five points are given equal weight in the algorithm even if they're less relevant in learning. We'll look at methods using R and try to alleviate this issue.

The best way to understand how this works is with a simple visual example of a binary classification learning problem. In the following screenshot, we have a plot showing whether a tumor is **benign** or **malignant** based on two predictive features. The **X** in the plot indicates a new observation that we would like to predict. If our algorithm considers **K=3**, the circle encompasses the three observations that are nearest to the one that we want to score. As the most commonly occurring classifications are **malignant**, the **X** data point is classified as **malignant,** as shown in the following screenshot:

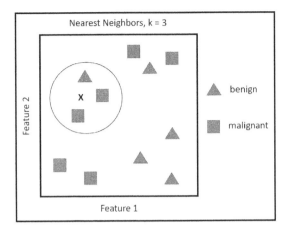

Even from this simple example, it's clear that the selection of *k* for the nearest neighbors is critical. If *k* is too small, you may have a high variance on the `test` set observations even though you have a low bias. On the other hand, as *k* grows, you may decrease your variance, but the bias may be unacceptable. Cross-validation is necessary to determine the proper *k*.

It's also important to point out the calculation of the distance or the nearness of the data points in our feature space. The default distance is **Euclidean distance**. This is merely the straight-line distance from point A to point B—as the crow flies—or you can utilize the formula that states it's equivalent to the square root of the sum of the squared differences between the corresponding points. The formula for Euclidean distance, given point A and B with coordinates p1, p2, ... pn and q1, q2, ... qn respectively, would be as follows:

$$\text{Euclidean Distance (A, B)} = \sqrt{\sum_{i=1}^{n}(pi - qi)^2}$$

This distance is highly dependent on the scale that the features were measured on, so it's critical to standardize them. Other distance calculations as well as weights can be used, depending on the distance. We'll explore this in the upcoming example.

Support vector machines

The first time I heard of support vector machines, I have to admit that I was scratching my head, thinking that this was some form of academic obfuscation or inside joke. However, my fair review of SVM has replaced this natural skepticism with a healthy respect for the technique.

SVMs have been shown to perform well in a variety of settings and are often considered one of the best out-of-the-box classifiers (James, G., 2013). To get a practical grasp of the subject, let's look at another simple visual example. In the following screenshot, you'll see that the classification task is linearly separable. However, the dotted line and solid line are just two among an infinite number of possible linear solutions.

You would have separating hyperplanes in a problem that has more than two dimensions:

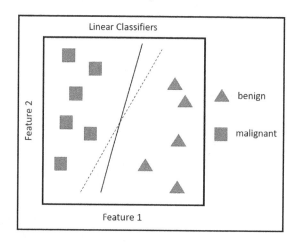

So many solutions can be problematic for generalization because, whatever solution you choose, any new observation to the right of the line will be classified as **benign**, and to the left of the line, it'll be classified as **malignant**. Therefore, either line has no bias on the train data but may have a widely divergent error on any data to test. This is where the support vectors come into play. The probability that a point falls on the wrong side of the linear separator is higher for the dotted line than the solid line, which means that the solid line has a higher margin of safety for classification. Therefore, as Battiti and Brunato say, *SVMs are linear separators with the largest possible margin and the support vectors the ones touching the safety margin region on both sides.*

The following screenshot illustrates this idea. The thin solid line is the optimal linear separator to create the aforementioned largest possible margin, hence increasing the probability that a new observation will fall on the correct side of the separator. The thicker black lines correspond to the safety margin, and the shaded data points constitute the support vectors. If the support vectors were to move, then the margin and, subsequently, the decision boundary would change. The distance between the separators is known as the **margin**:

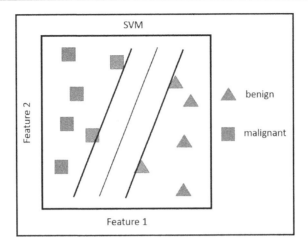

This is all fine and dandy, but real-world problems aren't so clear-cut.

 In data that isn't linearly separable, many observations will fall on the wrong side of the margin (these are so-called slack variables), which is a misclassification. The key to building an SVM algorithm is to solve for the optimal number of support vectors via cross-validation. Any observation that lies directly on the wrong side of the margin for its class is known as a **support vector**.

If the tuning parameter for the number of errors is too large, which means that you have many support vectors, you'll suffer from a high bias and low variance. On the other hand, if the tuning parameter is too small, the opposite might occur. According to James et al., who refer to the tuning parameter as C, as C decreases, the tolerance for observations being on the wrong side of the margin decreases and the margin narrows. This C, or rather, the cost function, allows for observations to be on the wrong side of the margin. If C were set to zero, then we would prohibit a solution where any observation violates the margin. This is a hyperparameter you can tune to optimize bias/variance.

Another essential aspect of SVM is the ability to model nonlinearity with quadratic or higher order polynomials of the input features. In SVMs, this is known as the **kernel trick**. These can be estimated and selected with cross-validation. In the example, we'll look at the alternatives.

As with any model, you can expand the number of features using polynomials to various degrees, interaction terms, or other derivations. In large datasets, the possibilities can quickly get out of control. The kernel trick with SVMs allows us to efficiently expand the feature space, with the goal that you achieve an approximate linear separation.

To check out how this is done, let's first look at the SVM optimization problem and its constraints. We're trying to achieve the following:

- Creating weights that maximize the margin
- Subject to the constraints, no (or as few as possible) data points should lie within that margin

Now, unlike linear regression, where each observation is multiplied by a weight, in SVM, the weights are applied to the inner products of just the support vector observations.

What does this mean? Well, an inner product for two vectors is just the sum of the paired observations' product. For example, if vector one is *3, 4*, and *2* and vector two is *1, 2*, and *3*, then you end up with *(3x1) + (4x2) + (2x3)* or *17*. With SVMs, if we take a possibility that an inner product of each observation has an inner product of every other observation, this amounts to the formula that there would be *n(n-1)/2* combinations, where *n* is the number of observations. With just *10* observations, we end up with *45* inner products. However, SVM only concerns itself with the support vectors' observations and their corresponding weights. For a linear SVM classifier, the formula is as follows:

$$f(x) = \beta o + \sum_{i=1}^{n} a(x, xi)$$

Here, (x, xi) are the inner products of the support vectors, as α is non-zero only when an observation is a support vector.

This leads to far fewer terms in the classification algorithm and allows the use of the `kernel` function, commonly referred to as the kernel trick.

The trick in this is that the `kernel` function mathematically summarizes the transformation of the features in higher dimensions instead of creating them explicitly. In a simplistic sense, a kernel function computes a dot product between two vectors. This has the benefit of creating the higher dimensional, nonlinear space, and decision boundary while keeping the optimization problem computationally efficient. The `kernel` functions compute the inner product in a higher dimensional space without transforming them into the higher dimensional space.

The notation for popular kernels is expressed as the inner (dot) product of the features, with x_i and x_j representing vectors, gamma, and `c` parameters, as follows:

- linear, no transformation, $K(x_i, x_j) = x_i \bullet x_j$

- polynomial, where d = degree of polynomial, $K(x_i, x_j) = (\gamma x_i \bullet x_j + c)^d$

- radial basis function, $K(x_i, x_j) = e(-\gamma|x_i - x_j|^2)$

- sigmoid function, $K(x_i, x_j) = \tanh(\gamma x_i \bullet x_j + c)$

As for the selection of the nonlinear techniques, they require some trial and error, but we'll walk through the various selection techniques.

Manipulating data

In the upcoming case study, we'll apply KNN and SVM to the same dataset. This will allow us to compare R code and learning methods on the same problem, starting with KNN. We'll also spend time drilling down into new ways of comparing different classifiers on the same data.

Dataset creation

The data we use in this chapter can be downloaded from any source on the internet or from GitHub at this link: `https://github.com/datameister66/MMLR3rd/blob/master/chapter5`.

I found this data on a website dedicated to providing datasets for support vector machine analysis. You can follow the following link to find numerous sets to test your learning methods: `https://www.csie.ntu.edu.tw/~cjlin/libsvmtools/datasets/`.

The authors have asked to cite their work, which I will abide by:

Chih-Chung Chang and Chih-Jen Lin, LIBSVM: a library for support vector machines. ACM Transactions on Intelligent Systems and Technology, 2:27:1--27:27, 2011

The data we're using is named `a5a`, consisting of the training data with 6414 observations. This is a sufficient size dataset for the interest of facilitating learning, and not causing computational speed issues. Also, when doing KNN or SVM, you need to center/scale or normalize your data to 0/1 if the input features are of different scales. Well, this data's input features are of just two levels, 0 or 1, so we can forgo any normalization efforts.

I'll show you how to load this data into R, and you can replicate that process on any data you desire to use.

While we're at it, we may as well load all of the packages needed for this chapter:

```
> library(magrittr)

> install.packages("ggthemes")

> install.packages("caret")

> install.packages("classifierplots")

> install.packages("DataExplorer")

> install.packages("e1071")

> install.packages("InformationValue")

> install.packages("kknn")

> install.packages("Matrix")

> install.packages("Metrics")

> install.packages("plm")

> install.packages("ROCR")

> install.packages("tidyverse")

> options(scipen=999)
```

It's a simple matter to access this data using R's `download.file()` function. You need to provide the link and give the file a name:

```
>
download.file('https://www.csie.ntu.edu.tw/~cjlin/libsvmtools/datasets/binary/
  a5a', 'chap5')
```

What's rather interesting now is that you can put this downloaded file into a usable format with a function created explicitly for this data from the `e1071` library:

```
> df <- e1071::read.matrix.csr("chap5")
```

The `df` object is now an extensive list of input features, and the response labels structured as a factor with two levels (-1 and +1). This list is what is saved on GitHub in an R data file like this:

```
> saveRDS(df, file = "chapter5")
```

Let's look at how to turn this list into something usable, assuming we need to start by loading it into your environment:

```
> df <- readRDS("chapter5")
```

We'll create the classification labels in an object called `y`, and turn -1 into 0, and +1 into 1:

```
> y <- df$y

> y <- ifelse(y == "+1", 1, 0)

> table(y)
y
   0    1
4845 1569
```

The table shows us that just under 25% of the labels are considered an `event`. What event? It doesn't matter for our purposes, so we can move on and produce a dataframe of the predictors called *x*. I tried a number of ways to put the sparse matrix into a dataframe, and it seems that the following code is the easiest, using a function from the `Matrix` package:

```
> x <- Matrix::as.matrix(df$x)

> x <- as.data.frame(x)

> dim(x)
[1] 6414 122
```

We now have our dataframe of 6,414 observations and 122 input features. Next, we'll create train/test sets and explore the features.

Data preparation

What we should do now is create our training and test data using a 70/30 split. Then, we should subject it to the standard feature exploration we started discussing in Chapter 1, *Preparing and Understanding Data*, with these tasks in mind:

- Eliminate low variance features
- Identify and remove linear dependencies
- Explore highly correlated features

The first thing then is for us to turn the numeric outcome into a factor to be used for creating a stratified data index, like so:

```
> y_factor <- as.factor(y)

> set.seed(1492)

> index <- caret::createDataPartition(y_factor, p = 0.7, list = F)
```

Using the index, we create train/test input features and labels:

```
> train <- x[index, ]

> train_y <- y_factor[index]

> test <- x[-index, ]

> test_y <- y_factor[-index]
```

With our training data in hand, let's find and eliminate the low variance features, which I can state in advance are quite a few:

```
> train_NZV <- caret::nearZeroVar(train, saveMetrics = TRUE)

> table(train_NZV$nzv)

FALSE  TRUE
   48    74

> table(train_NZV$zeroVar)

FALSE  TRUE
  121     1
```

We see that 74 features are low variance, and one of those is zero variance. Let's rid ourselves of these pesky features:

```
> train_r <- train[train_NZV$nzv == FALSE]
```

Given our new dataframe of reduced features, we now identify and eliminate linear dependency combinations:

```
> linear_combos <- caret::findLinearCombos(x = train_r)

> linear_combos
$`linearCombos`
$`linearCombos`[[1]]
 [1] 13 1 2 3 4 5 9 10 11 12

$`linearCombos`[[2]]
[1] 19 16

$`linearCombos`[[3]]
[1] 20 15

$`linearCombos`[[4]]
 [1] 22 1 2 3 4 5 15 16 18 21

$`linearCombos`[[5]]
[1] 40 1 2 3 4 5 39

$`linearCombos`[[6]]
[1] 42 1 2 3 4 5 41

$`linearCombos`[[7]]
 [1] 47 1 2 3 4 5 43 44 45 46

$remove
[1] 13 19 20 22 40 42 47
```

The output provides a list of 7 linear dependencies and recommends the removal of 7 features. The number in $remove corresponds to the column index number in the dataframe. For example, in combination number 2, the indices would be indicative of the column names, V36 and V22. Here's a table of these two features for demonstration purposes:

```
> table(train_r$V36, train_r$V22)
        0    1
  0 3032    0
  1    0 1459
```

It's clear these two features are measuring the same thing. We'll remove those recommended, but there's one more thing to discuss. When doing cross-validation during the modeling process, you may run into warnings that linear dependencies exist even though you ran this methodology. I found that to be the case with this dataset in the modeling exercises that follow. After some exploration of features V1 through V5, I found that, by dropping V5, this was no longer a problem. Let's proceed with that in mind:

```
> train_r <- train_r[, -linear_combos$remove]

> train_r <- train_r[, -5]

> plm::detect_lin_dep(train_r)
[1] "No linear dependent column(s) detected."
```

Here we can check if there're any correlations over 0.7, and remove a feature if it's highly correlated with another:

```
> high_corr <- caret::findCorrelation(my_data_cor, cutoff = 0.7)

> high_corr
[1] 29

> train_df <- train_r[, -high_corr]
```

The code found and removed the feature with a column index of 30 and 34. We now have a dataframe ready for modeling. If you want to look at a correlation heatmap, then run this handy function from the DataExplorer package:

```
> DataExplorer::plot_correlation(train_df)
```

The output of the preceding code is as follows:

Notice that features **V67** and **V71** are highly correlated. In a real-world setting, this would probably warrant further investigation, but we'll feed both into our learning algorithms, as no subject matter expert can tell us otherwise.

We can now proceed with our model training, starting with KNN, then SVM, and comparing their performance.

Modeling and evaluation

Now we'll discuss various aspects of modeling and assessment. In both the KNN and SVM cases, we'll do feature selection using a technique known as **Recursive Feature Elimination (RFE)** in conjunction with cross-validation. As with all feature reduction and selection, this will help to prevent overfitting the model.

KNN modeling

As stated previously, we'll begin with feature selection. The `caret` package helps out in this matter. In RFE, a model is built using all features, and a feature importance value is assigned. Then the features are recursively pruned and an optimal number of features selected based on a performance metric such as accuracy. In short, it's a type of backward feature elimination.

To do this, we'll need to set the random seed, specify the cross-validation method in caret's `rfeControl()` function, perform a recursive feature selection with the `rfe()` function, and then test how the model performs on the `test` set. In `rfeControl()`, you'll need to specify the function based on the model being used. There are several different functions that you can use. Here we'll need `lrFuncs`. To see a list of the available functions, your best bet is to explore the documentation with `?rfeControl` and `?caretFuncs`. The metric we'll use is **Cohen's Kappa statistic**, which we used and explained in a prior chapter.

To recap, the `Kappa` statistic is commonly used to provide a measure of how well two evaluators can classify an observation correctly. It gives an insight into this problem by adjusting the accuracy scores, which is done by accounting for the evaluators being entirely correct by mere chance. The formula for the statistic is: *Kappa = (percent of agreement - percent of chance agreement) / (1 - percent of chance agreement)*.

The *percent of agreement* is the rate that the evaluators agreed on for the class (accuracy), and *percent of chance agreement* is the rate that the evaluators randomly agreed on. The higher the statistic, the better they performed, with the maximum agreement being one.

Altman (1991) provides a heuristic to assist us in the interpretation of the statistic, which is shown in the following table:

Value of *K*	Strength of Agreement
<0.20	Poor
0.21-0.40	Fair
0.41-0.60	Moderate
0.61-0.80	Good
0.81-1.00	Very good

The following code gets our control function established:

```
> ctrl <- caret::rfeControl(
    functions = caret::lrFuncs,
    method = "cv",
    number = 10,
    verbose = TRUE
  )
```

I now specify the number of feature subsets for consideration between 25 and 35. After setting the random seed, we can run the RFE using a KNN algorithm. With `verbose = TRUE`, the status of training is displayed in the console. Of course, setting that to `FALSE` will hide it:

```
> subsets <- c(25:35)

> set.seed(1863)

> knnProfile <- caret::rfe(
    train_df,
    train_y,
    sizes = subsets,
    rfeControl = ctrl,
    method = "knn",
    metric = "Kappa"
  )
```

Calling the `knnProfile` object tells us what we need to know:

```
> knnProfile #33

Recursive feature selection
Outer resampling method: Cross-Validated (10 fold)
Resampling performance over subset size:

 Variables Accuracy  Kappa AccuracySD KappaSD Selected
        25   0.8377 0.5265    0.01524 0.05107
```

```
26    0.8383 0.5276    0.01594 0.05359 *
27    0.8377 0.5271    0.01616 0.05462
28    0.8375 0.5257    0.01612 0.05416
29    0.8370 0.5247    0.01668 0.05503
30    0.8370 0.5241    0.01654 0.05464
31    0.8381 0.5272    0.01649 0.05465
32    0.8368 0.5233    0.01727 0.05623
33    0.8361 0.5212    0.01623 0.05393
34    0.8366 0.5231    0.01676 0.05525
35    0.8361 0.5218    0.01644 0.05487
39    0.8361 0.5217    0.01705 0.05660

The top 5 variables (out of 26):
   V74, V35, V22, V78, V20
```

The results state that 26 features provide the highest Kappa statistic of 0.5276 (moderate strength), and it offers the highest accuracy rate of 83.83%. The output also gives us the top 5 features based on importance score. If you want, you can plot the results by putting it into a dataframe and passing it to ggplot:

```
> knn_results <- knnProfile$results

> ggplot2::ggplot(knn_results, aes(Variables, Kappa)) +
    ggplot2::geom_line(color = 'darkred', size = 2) +
    ggthemes::theme_economist()
```

The output of the preceding code is as follows:

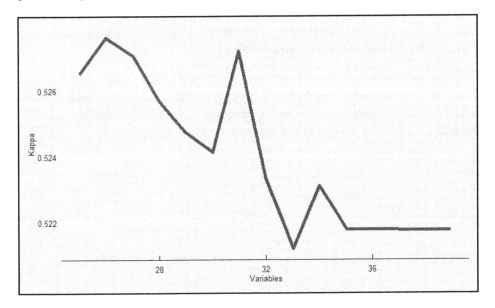

Let's select those 26 features in a new dataframe, then add to the dataframe the response, `train_y`. This will get our data ready for training the KNN model:

```
> vars <- knnProfile$optVariables

> x_selected <-
    train_df[, (colnames(train_df) %in% vars)]

> knn_df <- cbind(x_selected, train_y)
```

What I like to do is use the `train.kknn()` function from the `kknn` package. We use cross-validation again within the `train.kknn()` function to select the best parameters for the optimal `k` neighbors and a `kernel` function.

The kernel function allows you to specify an unweighted `k` neighbors algorithm using the Euclidian distance and weighted functions for distance.

For the weighting of the distances, many different methods are available. For our purpose, the package that we'll use has ten different weighting schemas, which includes unweighted. They're rectangular (unweighted), triangular, Epanechnikov, biweight, triweight, cosine, inversion, Gaussian, rank, and optimal. A full discussion of these weighting techniques is available in *Hechenbichler K.* and *Schliep K.P.* (2004).

For simplicity, let's focus on just two: `triangular` and `epanechnikov`. Before having the weights assigned, the algorithm standardizes all of the distances so that they're between zero and one. The triangular weighting method multiplies the observation distance by one minus the distance. With Epanechnikov, the distance is multiplied by ¾ times (one minus the distance). For our problem, we'll incorporate these weighting methods along with the standard unweighted version for comparison purposes.

After specifying a random seed, we'll create the `train` set object with `kknn()`. This function asks for the maximum number of k-nearest neighbor values (`kmax`), `distance` (one is equal to Euclidean and two is equal to absolute), `kcv` for the number of k-fold cross-validation, and `kernel`. For this model, `kmax` will be set to `25` and `distance` will be `1`:

```
> knn_fit <-
    kknn::train.kknn(
    train_y ~ .,
    data = knn_df,
    distance = 1,
    kmax = 25,
    kcv = 10,
    kernel = c("rectangular", "triangular", "epanechnikov")
  )
```

A nice feature of the package is the ability to plot and compare the results, as follows:

```
> plot(knn_fit)
```

The following is the output of the preceding command:

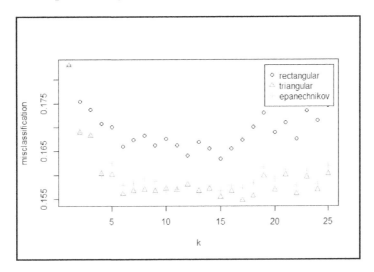

This plot shows **k** on the *x* axis and the percentage of misclassified observations by the `kernel` on the *y* axis. The weighted (triangular) version at `k: 17` performs the best. You can also call the object to see what the classification error and the best parameter are in the following way:

```
> knn_fit

Call:
kknn::train.kknn(formula = train_y ~ ., data = knn_df, kmax = 25, distance
= 1, kernel = c("rectangular", "triangular", "epanechnikov"), kcv = 10)

Type of response variable: nominal
Minimal misclassification: 0.154754
Best kernel: triangular
Best k: 17
```

With the model object created, it's time to see how it performs, starting with the predicted probabilities on the training data:

```
> knn_pred_train <-
    data.frame(predict(knn_fit, newdata = knn_df, type = "prob"))

> classifierplots::density_plot(train_y, knn_pred_train$X1)
```

The output of the preceding code is as follows:

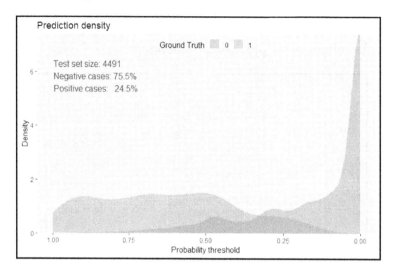

The plot shows quality separation between the probability densities for events versus non-events. This should have a high area under the curve value:

```
> Metrics::auc(train_y, knn_pred_train$X1)
[1] 0.9460519
```

Almost 0.95! Well, let me say that it's quite good, but I sense that we've overfitted and will see this low bias on train turn into a miss on the test set. Let's have a look, but also determine the probability cut point to minimize misclassification error:

```
> InformationValue::optimalCutoff(train_y, knn_pred_train$X1)
[1] 0.48
```

So, `0.48` minimizes error on the training data. This will help us produce a confusion matrix, but first, here's the density plot and AUC for test data:

```
> knn_pred_test <-
    data.frame(predict(knn_fit, newdata = test, type = "prob"))

> classifierplots::density_plot(test_y, knn_pred_test$X1)
```

The output of the preceding code is as follows:

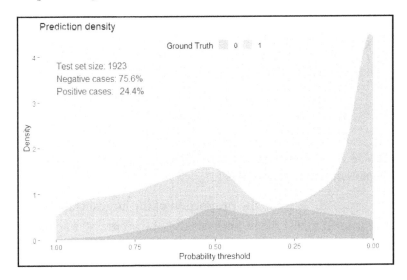

Given the different skews in the density plots from before, it sure does look like we lost some predictive power on the test data:

```
> Metrics::auc(test_y, knn_pred_test$X1)
[1] 0.8592589
```

Indeed, our area under the curve has fallen from 0.95 to 0.86. We can drill down further into this model's performance with a confusion matrix and associated results. We'll use the `caret` package and the `confusionMatrix()` function. This version provides a considerable amount of detail, and it will produce all of the statistics that we need to evaluate and select the best model. You need to specify your predictions as a factor, not probability, and the actual values need to be structured as a factor. I recommend you specify the positive class—in other words, our events:

```
> pred_class <- as.factor(ifelse(knn_pred_test$X1 >= 0.48, "1", "0"))
> caret::confusionMatrix(data = pred_class, reference = test_y, positive =
"1")
Confusion Matrix and Statistics
          Reference
Prediction    0    1
         0 1262  178
         1  191  292

               Accuracy : 0.8081
                 95% CI : (0.7898, 0.8255)
    No Information Rate : 0.7556
    P-Value [Acc > NIR] : 0.00000002214
```

```
                  Kappa : 0.4853
   Mcnemar's Test P-Value : 0.5322
           Sensitivity : 0.6213
           Specificity : 0.8685
         Pos Pred Value : 0.6046
         Neg Pred Value : 0.8764
             Prevalence : 0.2444
         Detection Rate : 0.1518
   Detection Prevalence : 0.2512
      Balanced Accuracy : 0.7449
         'Positive' Class : 1
```

The function produces some items that we already covered such as `Accuracy` and `Kappa`. Here are the other statistics that it provides:

- `No Information Rate` is the proportion of the largest class: 76 % of no events.
- `P-Value` is used to test the hypothesis that the accuracy is actually better than `No Information Rate`.
- We'll not concern ourselves with `Mcnemar's Test`, which is used for the analysis of matched pairs, primarily in epidemiology studies.
- `Sensitivity` is the true positive rate.
- `Specificity` is the true negative rate.
- The positive predictive value (`Pos Pred Value`) is the probability of an observation being classified as being an event and it truly is an event. The following formula is used:

$$PPV = \frac{sensitivity * prevalence}{(sensitivity * prevalence) + (1 - specificity) * (1 - prevalence)}$$

- The negative predictive value (`Neg Pred Value`) is the probability of an observation being classified as a non-event and it truly isn't an event. The formula for this is as follows:

$$NPV = \frac{specificity * (1 - prevalence)}{((1 - sensitivity) * (prevalence)) + (specificity) * (1 - prevalence)}$$

- `Prevalence` is the estimated population prevalence of events, calculated here as the total of the second column (the `1` column) divided by the total observations.
- `Detection Rate` is the rate of the true positives that have been identified.

- `Detection Prevalence` is the predicted prevalence rate or, in our case, the bottom row divided by the total observations.
- `Balanced Accuracy` is the average accuracy obtained from either class. This measure accounts for a potential bias in the classifier algorithm, thus potentially over predicting the most frequent class. This is simply:
  Sensitivity + Specificity divided by 2.

You can discern some model weakness in `Sensitivity` and positive predictive value. Feel free to try on your own changing different distance weighting options and see if you can improve performance. Otherwise, let's proceed to SVM and compare the performance alongside what we just completed.

Support vector machine

If you recall from a previous section, the first thing we did was perform RFE to reduce our input features. We'll repeat that step in the following. We'll redo our control function:

```
> ctrl <- caret::rfeControl(
    functions = caret::lrFuncs,
    method = "cv",
    number = 10,
    verbose = TRUE
  )
```

I say we shoot for around 20 to 30 total features and set our random seed:

```
> subsets <- c(20:30)

> set.seed(54321)
```

Now, in selecting the features you can use the SVM linear or the kernel functions. Let's proceed with linear, which means our specification for the following method will be `svmLinear`. If, for instance, you wanted to change to a polynomial kernel, then you would specify `svmPoly` instead or `svmRadial` for the radial basis function:

```
> svmProfile <- caret::rfe(
    train_df,
    train_y,
    sizes = subsets,
    rfeControl = ctrl,
    method = "svmLinear",
    metric = "Kappa"
  )
```

```
> svmProfile
Recursive feature selection

Outer resampling method: Cross-Validated (10 fold)

Resampling performance over subset size:

 Variables Accuracy Kappa  AccuracySD KappaSD Selected
        20   0.8357 0.5206   0.008253 0.02915
        21   0.8350 0.5178   0.008624 0.03091
        22   0.8359 0.5204   0.008277 0.02948
        23   0.8361 0.5220   0.009435 0.02979
        24   0.8383 0.5292   0.008560 0.02572  *
        25   0.8375 0.5261   0.008067 0.02323
        26   0.8379 0.5290   0.010193 0.02905
        27   0.8375 0.5276   0.009205 0.02667
        28   0.8372 0.5259   0.008770 0.02437
        29   0.8361 0.5231   0.008074 0.02319
        30   0.8368 0.5252   0.008069 0.02401
        39   0.8377 0.5290   0.009290 0.02711

The top 5 variables (out of 24):
   V74, V35, V22, V78, V20
```

The optimal Kappa and accuracy are with 24 features. Notice that the top five features are the same as when we ran this with KNN. Here's how to plot the Kappa score per number of features:

```
> svm_results <- svmProfile$results

> ggplot2::ggplot(svm_results, aes(Variables, Kappa)) +
    ggplot2::geom_line(color = 'steelblue', size = 2) +
    ggthemes::theme_fivethirtyeight()
```

The output of the preceding code is as follows:

Let's select a dataframe with only the optimal features:

```
> svm_vars <- svmProfile$optVariables

> x_selected <-
    train_df[, (colnames(train_df) %in% svm_vars)]
```

With our features selected, we can train a model with cross-validation, and in the process tune the hyperparameter, C. If you recall from previously, this is the regularization parameter. We'll go forward with caret's train() function:

```
> grid <- expand.grid(.C = c(1, 2, 3))

> svm_control <- caret::trainControl(method = 'cv', number = 10)

> set.seed(1918)

> svm <- caret::train(x_selected,
    train_y,
    method = "svmLinear",
    trControl = svm_control,
    tuneGrid = grid,
    metric = "Kappa")

> svm
Support Vector Machines with Linear Kernel

4491 samples
  24 predictor
   2 classes: '0', '1'

No pre-processing
Resampling: Cross-Validated (10 fold)
Summary of sample sizes: 4041, 4042, 4042, 4041, 4042, 4043, ...
Resampling results across tuning parameters:

  C Accuracy Kappa
  1 0.8372287 0.5223355
  2 0.8367833 0.5210972
  3 0.8374514 0.5229846

Kappa was used to select the optimal model using the
 largest value.
The final value used for the model was C = 3.
```

Excellent! We have optimal `C = 3`, so let's build that model. By the way, be sure to specify we want a probability model with `prob.model = TRUE`. The linear kernel is specified with `vanilladot`:

```
> svm_fit <-
    kernlab::ksvm(
    as.matrix(x_selected),
    train_y,
    kernel = "vanilladot",
    prob.model = TRUE,
    kpar = "automatic",
    C = 3
  )
```

Do we want a dataframe of predicted probabilities on the train data? I'm glad you asked:

```
> svm_pred_train <-
    kernlab::predict(svm_fit, x_selected, type = "probabilities")

> svm_pred_train <- data.frame(svm_pred_train)
```

Our density plot in the following looks about as good as what we saw with KNN:

```
> classifierplots::density_plot(train_y, svm_pred_train$X1)
```

The output of the preceding code is as follows:

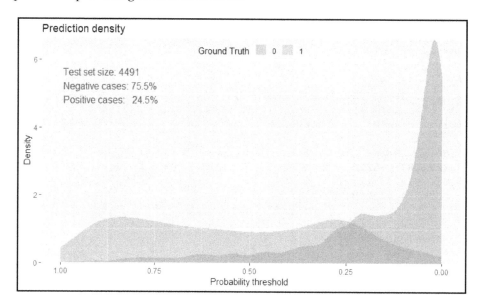

Two things before moving on to the test data, and that is AUC and the optimal score cutoff:

```
> Metrics::auc(train_y, svm_pred_train$X1)
[1] 0.8940114

> InformationValue::optimalCutoff(train_y, svm_pred_train$X1)
[1] 0.3879227
```

OK, the AUC is inferior to KNN on the training data, but the proof must be in our test data:

```
> test_svm <- test[, (colnames(test) %in% svm_vars)]

> svm_pred_test <-
    kernlab::predict(svm_fit, test_svm, type = "probabilities")

> svm_pred_test <- as.data.frame(svm_pred_test)
```

I insist we take a look at the density plot:

```
> classifierplots::density_plot(test_y, svm_pred_test$`1`)
```

The output of the preceding code is as follows:

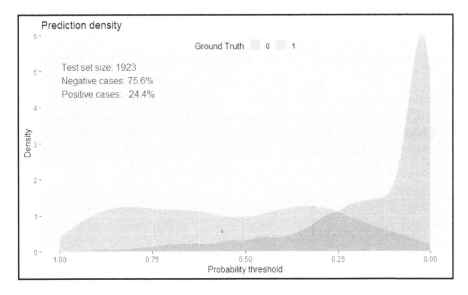

I would put forward that we have a good overall fit here:

```
> Metrics::auc(test_y, svm_pred_test$`1`)
[1] 0.8951011
```

That's more like it: excellent bias/variance tradeoff. We can start the overall comparison with KNN by moving forward with the confusion matrix and relevant stats:

```
> svm_pred_class <- as.factor(ifelse(svm_pred_test$`1` >= 0.275, "1", "0"))

> caret::confusionMatrix(data = svm_pred_class, reference = test_y,
positive = "1")
Confusion Matrix and Statistics
          Reference
Prediction    0    1
         0 1206  104
         1  247  366
              Accuracy : 0.8175
                95% CI : (0.7995, 0.8345)
   No Information Rate : 0.7556
   P-Value [Acc > NIR] : 0.00000000004314737
                 Kappa : 0.5519
Mcnemar's Test P-Value : 0.00000000000003472
           Sensitivity : 0.7787
           Specificity : 0.8300
        Pos Pred Value : 0.5971
        Neg Pred Value : 0.9206
            Prevalence : 0.2444
        Detection Rate : 0.1903
  Detection Prevalence : 0.3188
     Balanced Accuracy : 0.8044
      'Positive' Class : 1
```

When you compare the results across methods, we see better values for the SVM almost across the board, especially a better Kappa as well as better balanced accuracy. In the past couple of chapters, we've produced ROC plots where the various models were overlaid on the same plot. We can recreate that same plot here as well, as follows:

```
> pred.knn <- ROCR::prediction(knn_pred_test$X1, test_y)

> perf.knn <- ROCR::performance(pred.knn, "tpr", "fpr")

> ROCR::plot(perf.knn, main = "ROC", col = 1)

> pred.svm <- ROCR::prediction(svm_pred_test$`1`, test_y)

> perf.svm <- ROCR::performance(pred.svm, "tpr", "fpr")

> ROCR::plot(perf.svm, col = 2, add = TRUE)

> legend(0.6, 0.6, c("KNN", "SVM"), 1:2)
```

The output of the preceding code is as follows:

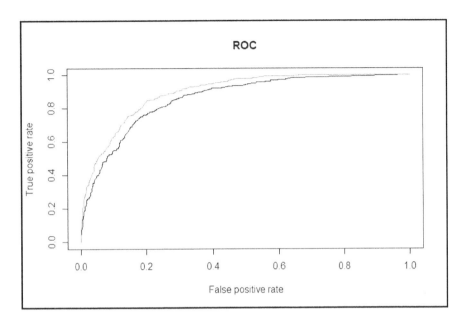

The plot shows a clear separation in the curves between the two models. Therefore, given what we've done here, the SVM algorithm performed better than KNN. Indeed, we could try a number of different methods to improve either algorithm, which could include a different feature selection and a different weighting for KNN (or kernels for SVM).

Summary

In this chapter, we reviewed two classification techniques: KNN and SVM. The goal was to discover how these techniques work and ascertain the differences between them, by building and comparing models on a common dataset. KNN involved both unweighted and weighted nearest neighbor algorithms, and for SVM, only a linear model was developed, which outperformed all other models.

We examined how to use Recursive Feature Elimination to find an optimal set of features for both methods. We used the extremely versatile `caret` package to train the models. We expanded our exploration of model performance using a confusion matrix, and the relevant statistics that one can derive from the matrix. We'll now use tree-based classifiers, which are very powerful and very popular.

Tree-Based Classification

6

"The classifiers most likely to be the best are the random forest (RF) versions, the best of which (implemented in R and accessed via caret), achieves 94.1 percent of the maximum accuracy, overcoming 90 percent in 84.3 percent of the data sets."

- Fernández-Delgado et al. (2014)

This quote from Fernández-Delgado et al. in the *Journal of Machine Learning Research* is meant to demonstrate that the techniques in this chapter are quite powerful, particularly when used for classification problems.

In previous chapters, we examined techniques used to predict label classification on three different datasets. Here, we'll apply tree-based methods with an eye to see whether we can improve our predictive power on the Santander data used in `Chapter 3`, *Logistic Regression*, and the data used in `Chapter 4`, *Advanced Feature Selection in Linear Models*.

The first item of discussion is the basic decision tree, which is simple to both build and to understand. However, the single decision tree method isn't likely to perform as well as the other methods that you've already learned, for example, **Support Vector Machines (SVMs)**, or the ones that we've yet to learn, such as neural networks. Therefore, we'll discuss the creation of multiple, sometimes hundreds, of different trees with their individual results combined, leading to a single overall prediction.

These methods, as the paper referenced at the beginning of this chapter states, perform as well as, or better than, any technique in this book. These methods are known as **random forests** and **gradient boosted trees**. Additionally, we'll work on how to use the random forest method to assist in feature elimination/selection.

Following are the topics that we'll be covering in this chapter:

- An overview of the techniques
- Datasets and modeling

An overview of the techniques

We'll now get to an overview of the techniques, covering classification trees, random forests, and gradient boosting. This will set the stage for their practical use.

Understanding a regression tree

To establish an understanding of tree-based methods, it's probably easier to start with a quantitative outcome and then move on to how it works in a classification problem. The essence of a tree is that the features are partitioned, starting with the first split that improves the RSS the most. These binary splits continue until the termination of the tree. Each subsequent split/partition isn't done on the entire dataset, but only on the portion of the prior split that it falls under. This top-down process is referred to as **recursive partitioning**. It's also a process that's **greedy**, a term you may stumble upon in reading about **machine learning** (**ML**) methods. Greedy means that during each split in the process, the algorithm looks for the greatest reduction in the RSS without any regard to how well it will perform on the later partitions. The result is that you may end up with a full tree of unnecessary branches leading to a low bias but a high variance. To control this effect, you need to appropriately prune the tree to an optimal size after building a full tree.

This diagram provides a visualization of this technique in action:

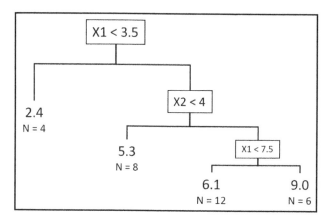

Regression tree with three splits and four terminal nodes, and the corresponding node average and number of observations

The data is hypothetical with 30 observations, a response ranging from 1 to 10, and two predictor features, both ranging in value from 0 to 10 named **X1** and **X2**. The tree has three splits leading to four terminal nodes. Each split is basically an `if...then` statement or uses the R syntax `ifelse()`. The first split is: if **X1** is less than **3.5**, then the response is split into four observations with an average value of **2.4** and the remaining 26 observations. The left branch of four observations is a terminal node as any further splits would not substantially improve the RSS. The predicted value for these four observations is that the partition of the tree becomes the average. The next split is at **X2 < 4**, and finally **X1 < 7.5**.

An advantage of this method is that it can handle highly nonlinear relationships; however, can you see a couple of potential problems? The first issue is that an observation is given the average of the terminal node under which it falls. This can hurt the overall predictive performance (high bias). Conversely, if you keep partitioning the data further and further to achieve a low bias, a high variance can become an issue. As with the other methods, you can use cross-validation to select the appropriate tree depth size.

Classification trees

Classification trees operate under the same principle as regression trees, except that the splits aren't determined by the RSS but by an error rate. The error rate used isn't what you would expect where the calculation is simply the misclassified observations divided by the total observations. As it turns out, when it comes to tree-splitting, a misclassification rate, by itself, may lead to a situation where you can gain information with a further split but not improve the misclassification rate. Let's look at an example.

Suppose we have a node, let's call it `N0`, where you have seven observations labeled `No` and three observations labeled `Yes`. We can say that the misclassified rate is 30%. With this in mind, let's calculate a common alternative error measure called the **Gini index**. The formula for a single node Gini index is as follows:

$$Gini = 1 - (probability\ of\ Class\ 1)^2 - (probability\ of\ Class\ 2)^2$$

Then, for `N0`, the Gini is $1 - (.7)^2 - (.3)^2$, which is equal to *0.42*, versus the misclassification rate of 30%.

Taking this example further, we'll now create node *N1* with three observations from `Class 1` and none from `Class 2`, along with *N2*, which has four observations from `Class 1` and three from `Class 2`. Now, the overall misclassification rate for this branch of the tree is still 30%, but look at how the overall Gini index has improved:

- *Gini(N1) = 1 - (3/3)^2 - (0/3)^2 = 0*
- *Gini(N2) = 1 - (4/7)^2 - (3/7)^2 = 0.49*
- *New Gini index = (proportion of N1 x Gini(N1)) + (proportion of N2 x Gini(N2)),* which is equal to *(0.3 x 0) + (0.7 x 0.49)* or *0.343*

By doing a split on a surrogate error rate, we actually improved our model impurity, reducing it from *0.42* to *0.343*, whereas the misclassification rate didn't change. This is the methodology that's used by the `rpart()` package, which we'll be using in this chapter.

Random forest

To greatly improve our model's predictive ability, we can produce numerous trees and combine the results. The random forest technique does this by applying two different tricks in model development. The first is the use of **bootstrap aggregation**, or **bagging**, as it's called.

In bagging, an individual tree is built on a random sample of the dataset, roughly two-thirds of the total observations (note that the remaining one-third is referred to as **out-of-bag (oob)**). This is repeated dozens or hundreds of times and the results are averaged. Each of these trees is grown and not pruned based on any error measure, and this means that the variance of each of these individual trees is high. However, by averaging the results, you can reduce the variance without increasing the bias.

The next thing that random forest brings to the table is that concurrently with the random sample of the data—that is, bagging—it also takes a random sampling of the input features at each split. In the `randomForest` package, we'll use the default random number of the predictors that're sampled, which, for classification problems, is the square root of the total predictors, and for regression, is the total number of the predictors divided by three. The number of predictors the algorithm randomly chooses at each split can be changed via the model tuning process.

By doing this random sample of the features at each split and incorporating it into the methodology, you can mitigate the effect of a highly correlated predictor becoming the main driver in all of your bootstrapped trees, preventing you from reducing the variance that you hoped to achieve with bagging. The subsequent averaging of the trees that're less correlated to each other is more generalizable and robust to outliers than if you only performed bagging.

Gradient boosting

Boosting methods can become extremely complicated to learn and understand, but you should keep in mind what's fundamentally happening behind the curtain. The main idea is to build an initial model of some kind (linear, spline, tree, and so on) called the base learner, examine the residuals, and fit a model based on these residuals around the so-called **loss function**. A loss function is merely the function that measures the discrepancy between the model and desired prediction, for example, a squared error for regression or the logistic function for classification. The process continues until it reaches some specified stopping criterion. This is sort of like the student who takes a practice exam and gets 30 out of 100 questions wrong and, as a result, studies only these 30 questions that were missed. In the next practice exam, they get 10 out of those 30 wrong and so only focus on those 10 questions, and so on. If you would like to explore the theory behind this further, a great resource for you is available in *Frontiers in Neurorobotics, Gradient boosting machines, a tutorial*, Natekin A., Knoll A. (2013), at
`http://www.ncbi.nlm.nih.gov/pmc/articles/PMC3885826/`.

As just mentioned, boosting can be applied to many different base learners, but here, we'll only focus on the specifics of **tree-based learning**. Each tree iteration is small and we'll determine how small with one of the tuning parameters referred to as interaction depth. In fact, it may be as small as one split, which is referred to as a stump.

Trees are sequentially fitted to the residuals, according to the loss function, up to the number of trees that we specified (our stopping criterion).

There're a number of parameters that require tuning in the model-building process using the Xgboost package, which stands for **eXtreme Gradient Boosting**. This package has become quite popular for online data contests because of its winning performance. There's excellent background material on boosting trees and on Xgboost at the following website:

`http://xgboost.readthedocs.io/en/latest/model.html`.

In the practical examples, we'll learn how to begin to optimize the hyperparameters and produce meaningful output and predictions. These parameters can interact with each other and, if you just tinker with one without considering the other, your model may worsen the performance. The `caret` package will help us in the tuning endeavor.

Datasets and modeling

We're going to be using two of the prior datasets, the simulated data from Chapter 4, *Advanced Feature Selection in Linear Models*, and the customer satisfaction data from Chapter 3, *Logistic Regression*. We'll start by building a classification tree on the simulated data. This will help us to understand the basic principles of tree-based methods. Then, we'll move on to random forest and boosted trees applied to the customer satisfaction data. This exercise will provide an excellent comparison to the generalized linear models from before. Finally, I want to show you an interesting feature selection method using random forest, using the simulated data. By interesting, I mean it's a valuable technique to add to your feature selection arsenal, but I'll point out a couple of caveats for you to consider in practical application.

Classification tree

This exercise will be an excellent introduction to tree-based methods. I recommend applying this method to any supervised learning method because, at a minimum, you'll get a better understanding of the data and establish a good baseline of predictive performance. It may also be the only thing you need to do to solve a problem for your business partners. An example I can share was where the marketing team tasked me to try and reverse-engineer a customer segmentation done by an external vendor nearly two years in the past. We had the original survey data and the customer segment labels, but no understanding of how the data drove the segmentation.

Well, I just used the methods described in this section, and we could predict a segment with almost 100% accuracy. Plus, as you'll see, it was easy to explain why:

1. Let's get the packages installed if needed:

```
library(magrittr)
install.packages("Boruta")
install.packages("caret")
install.packages("classifierplots")
install.packages("InformationValue")
install.packages("MLmetrics")
install.packages("randomForest")
```

```
install.packages("ROCR")
install.packages("rpart")
install.packages("rpart.plot")
install.packages("tidyverse")
install.packages("xgboost")
options(scipen=999)
```

2. As for the simulated data, I discuss how I created it in `Chapter 4`, *Advanced Feature Selection in Linear Models*. You can find it on GitHub at this link: `https://github.com/datameister66/MMLR3rd/blob/master/sim_df.csv`.

3. We now load it into R:

```
> sim_df <- read.csv("~/sim_df.csv", stringsAsFactors = FALSE)
```

4. The response we'll try and predict is called `y`. It's a numeric value of either 0 or 1 with 1 being the outcome of interest. It's slightly unbalanced, with about 30% of the responses labeled a 1. Let's confirm that and turn it into a factor, which will tell our tree function we're interested in classification:

```
> table(sim_df$y)

   0    1
7072 2928

> sim_df$y <- as.factor(sim_df$y)
```

5. Create the train/test split using the same random seed as in `Chapter 4`, *Advanced Feature Selection in Linear Models*:

```
> set.seed(1066)

> index <- caret::createDataPartition(sim_df$y, p = 0.7, list = F)

> train <- sim_df[index, ]

> test <- sim_df[-index, ]
```

6. To create our classification tree, we'll be using the `rpart()` function, using the common formula syntax:

```
> tree_fit <- rpart::rpart(y ~ ., data = train)
```

7. The next thing I like to do is look at the `cptable` from our model object:

```
> tree_fit$cptable
          CP nsplit rel error    xerror       xstd
1 0.20878049      0 1.0000000 1.0000000 0.01857332
```

```
2 0.19609756        1 0.7912195 0.7595122 0.01697342
3 0.01585366        2 0.5951220 0.6029268 0.01556234
4 0.01219512        6 0.5297561 0.5775610 0.01530000
5 0.01000000        8 0.5053659 0.5395122 0.01488626
```

This is an interesting table to analyze. The first column labeled CP is the cost complexity parameter. The second column, `nsplit`, is the number of splits in the tree. The `rel error` column stands for relative error. Both `xerror` and `xstd` are based on ten-fold cross-validation, with `xerror` being the average error and `xstd` the standard deviation of the cross-validation process. We can see that eight splits produced the lowest error on the `full` dataset and on cross-validation.

8. You can examine this using `plotcp()`:

```
> rpart::plotcp(tree_fit)
```

The output of the preceding actions is as follows:

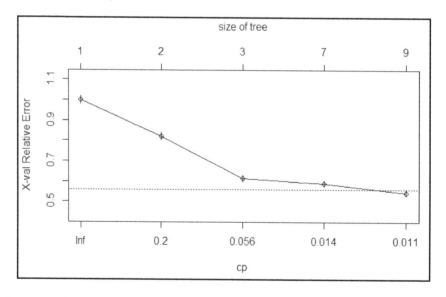

The plot shows us the cross-validated relative error by tree size with the corresponding error bars. The horizontal line on the plot is the upper limit of the lowest standard error. Selecting a different tree size, say seven, you would create an object of your desired **cp** and prune the tree simply by specifying that object in the `prune()` function, or you can just give the function the cp number. It would look as follows:

```
> cp = tree_fit$cptable[4, 1]
```

```
> cp
[1] 0.01219512

> cp <- min(tree_fit$cptable[, 3])
# not run
# rpart::prune(tree_fit, cp = cp)
# Or
# rpart::prune(tree_fit, cp = 0.01219512)
```

You can plot and explore the tree in a number of different ways. I prefer the version from the `rpart.plot` package. There's an excellent vignette on how to use it at the following website:

`http://www.milbo.org/rpart-plot/prp.pdf.`

Here's the first one, `type = 3` with `extra = 2` (see the vignette for more options):

```
> rpart.plot::rpart.plot(
    tree_fit,
    type = 3,
    extra = 2,
    branch = .75,
    under = TRUE
  )
```

The output of the preceding command is as follows:

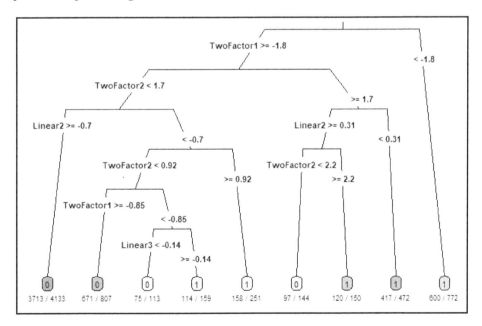

The preceding plot shows the feature at each split and the value related to that split. The first split in the tree is the feature **TwoFactor1**. If the value is less than **-1.8** then those observations end up in a terminal node. In this version of the tree, **772** observations are in that node (because the feature value is less than **-1.8**, and **600** of those observations are labeled **1**. So, you can say that the node probability is 78% (**600/772**) that an observation is a **1**. Now, if the value is equal to or greater than **-1.8**, then it goes to the next feature to split, which is **TwoFactor2**, and so forth until all observations are in a terminal node.

If you want to see all of those terminal node probabilities, a simple change to the syntax will suffice:

```
> rpart.plot::rpart.plot(
  tree_fit,
  type = 1,
  extra = 6,
  branch = .75,
  under = TRUE
  )
```

The output of the preceding command is as follows:

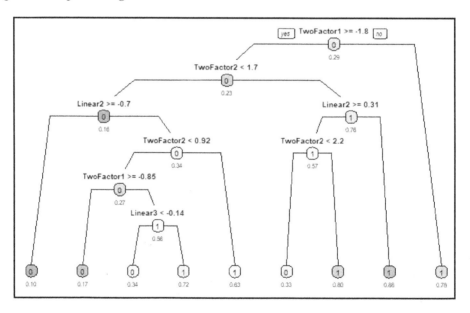

This different look shows the percentage of **1** in each terminal node and complements the preceding plot. If you want to see all of the rules leading for the nodes, you can run this:

```
> rpart.plot::rpart.rules(tree_fit)
    y
```

```
 0.10 when TwoFactor1 >= -1.75 & TwoFactor2 < 1.69 & Linear2 >= -0.70
 0.17 when TwoFactor1 >= -0.85 & TwoFactor2 < 0.92 & Linear2 < -0.70
 0.33 when TwoFactor1 >= -1.75 & TwoFactor2 is 1.69 to 2.20 & Linear2 >=
0.31
 0.34 when TwoFactor1 is -1.75 to -0.85 & TwoFactor2 < 0.92 & Linear2 <
-0.70 &
         Linear3 < -0.14
 0.63 when TwoFactor1 >= -1.75 & TwoFactor2 is 0.92 to 1.69 & Linear2 <
-0.70
 0.72 when TwoFactor1 is -1.75 to -0.85 & TwoFactor2 < 0.92 & Linear2 <
-0.70 &
         Linear3 >= -0.14
 0.78 when TwoFactor1 < -1.75
 0.80 when TwoFactor1 >= -1.75 & TwoFactor2 >= 2.20 & Linear2 >= 0.31
 0.88 when TwoFactor1 >= -1.75 & TwoFactor2 >= 1.69 & Linear2 < 0.31
```

We shall now see how this simple model performs on the test set. You may recall that with elastic net, we had an **area under the curve (AUC)** of over 0.87 and a log-loss of 0.37:

```
> rparty.test <- predict(tree_fit, newdata = test)

> rparty.test <- rparty.test[, 2]

> classifierplots::density_plot(test$y, rparty.test)
```

The output of the preceding code is as follows:

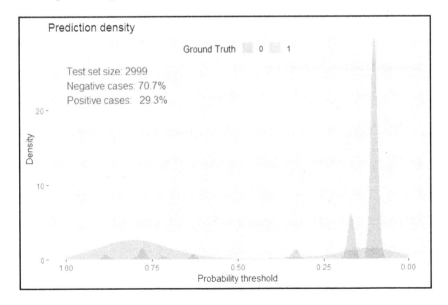

Notice the spikes in the density. The plot is capturing the probabilities from those terminal nodes. The real test will be our two favorite metrics, AUC and log-loss:

```
> ynum <- as.numeric(ifelse(test$y == "1", 1, 0))

> MLmetrics::AUC(rparty.test, ynum)
[1] 0.8201691

> MLmetrics::LogLoss(rparty.test, ynum)
[1] 0.4140015
```

OK, the performance isn't as good as using elastic net and so on, but overall I don't believe that's too bad for such a simple model that even someone in marketing can understand. We'll see if complicating things with a random forest can surpass elastic net when we look at using it for feature selection. Our next task is to use random forest and boosted trees in a classification problem.

Random forest

The customer satisfaction data was covered in Chapter 3, *Logistic Regression*. The GitHub links to the CSV and an RData file are as follows:

- https://github.com/datameister66/MMLR3rd/blob/master/santander_prepd.RData
- https://github.com/datameister66/MMLR3rd/blob/master/santander_prepd.csv

I'll show you how to load the RData file:

```
> santander <- readRDS("santander_prepd.RData")
```

The data has an unbalanced response:

```
> table(santander$y)

    0     1
73012  3008
```

We'll split the train and test sets using the same random seed as in Chapter 3, *Logistic Regression*:

```
> set.seed(1966)

> trainIndex <- caret::createDataPartition(santander$y, p = 0.8, list =
FALSE)
```

```
> train <- santander[trainIndex, ]

> test <- santander[-trainIndex, ]
```

With this split, we end up with one zero variance features, which we'll find and remove:

```
> train_zero <- caret::nearZeroVar(train, saveMetrics = TRUE)

> table(train_zero$zeroVar)

FALSE  TRUE
  142     1

> train <- train[, train_zero$zeroVar == 'FALSE']
```

I like to put the predictors in a matrix, and we'll need the response as a factor:

```
> x <- as.matrix(train[, -142])

> y <- as.factor(train$y)
```

We're now ready to start training a model. Recall that we have a highly unbalanced response. One of the things I highly recommend in such an instance is to structure your sample size. In fact, this can actually become a key parameter to tune. In the training data, there are only 2,405 ones alongside 58,411 zeros. I'll show an example of forcing the sample at each bagged sample in the algorithm. Again, this will take some trial and error on your part to identify the right ratio of *downsampling* the majority class to minority class. In the following example, I'm sampling 1,200 of the minority class and 3,600 of the majority class. This was some simple trial and error on my part, so see if you can do better. What this does to your predicted probabilities is skew them towards the minority class—in other words, you have a relative probability. This might not be what the business desires, so you can apply a correction to produce the corrected probability:

$$CorrectedProbability = 1/(1 + ((1/population proportion) - 1)/((1/sample proportion) - 1) * ((1/predicted probability) - 1))$$

The population proportion is the actual, or the estimated proportion of the minority class, and the sample proportion is from your oversample. Predicted probability equates to the model's probability for a given observation.

The other thing I specify here is the number of trees, and 200 for starters is sufficient. In some instances, you may need a thousand or more:

```
> set.seed(1999)

> forest_fit <- randomForest::randomForest(x = x, y = y,
      ntree = 200,
      sampsize = c(3600, 1200))
```

Calling the fitted object gives us the following results:

```
> forest_fit

Call:
 randomForest(x = x, y = y, ntree = 200, sampsize = c(3600, 1200))
               Type of random forest: classification
                     Number of trees: 200
No. of variables tried at each split: 11

        OOB estimate of  error rate: 9.51%
Confusion matrix:
      0    1 class.error
0 53946 4465  0.07644108
1  1321 1084  0.54927235
```

You can notice that the out-of-bag error rate is under 10%, and it gives us a confusion matrix. My advice is to not pay that much attention to this and just make a note of it. We'll use our relative probabilities to find the best split. Besides, as we've talked about in other chapters, error/accuracy isn't the best metric to judge a model. One thing that's good to look at is the number of trees that minimized the error. That way, you can limit the number of trees in an attempt to avoid overfitting:

```
> which.min(forest_fit$err.rate[, 1])
[1] 105

> forest_fit$err.rate[105]
[1] 0.0934458
```

There you have it: only 105 trees are needed to minimize the error versus all 200. In this model, we used all 142 features. That's just computationally inefficient and prone to cause overfitting.

I'll show you what has worked quite well for me on a number of projects to reduce features. Before we go there, here's the standard feature importance plot:

```
> randomForest::varImpPlot(forest_fit)
```

The output of the preceding code is as follows:

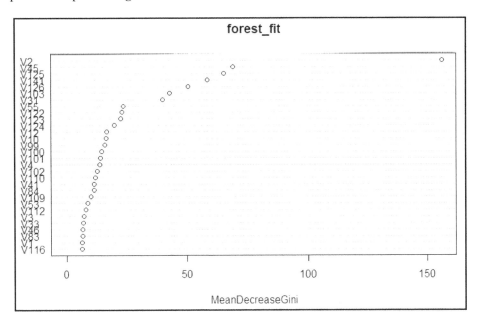

The feature importance is based on the average decrease in Gini. We can see that there're roughly a dozen or so features driving predictions, and the **V2** feature is quite suspicious. I talk about the notorious **V2** feature in Chapter 3, *Logistic Regression* so I won't belabor the point here.

What I'm about to present you may find controversial or unscientific. Well, I have to agree. However, it works. What I do is find the descriptive statistics for feature importance and decide, based on some experimental value or business expertise, where to filter the features. It's best to demonstrate how in our example:

```
> ff <- data.frame(unlist(forest_fit$importance))

> ff$var <- row.names(ff)

> summary(ff)
 MeanDecreaseGini              var
 Min.    :   0.00000    Length:141
 1st Qu. :   0.02172    Class :character
 Median  :   0.36412     Mode :character
 Mean    :   6.12824
 3rd Qu. :   4.02137
 Max.    : 155.86878
```

In the lack of subject matter expertise or otherwise, we can cut the features based on mean Gini decrease above the third quantile:

```
> my_forest_vars <- dplyr::filter(ff, MeanDecreaseGini > 4.02)

> my_forest_vars <- my_forest_vars$var

> x_reduced <- x[, my_forest_vars]

> dim(x_reduced)
[1] 60816 36
```

That gave us just 36 input features. We could reduce it even further, but I'll let you experiment with different results. Now, build the new model with reduced features:

```
> set.seed(567)

> forest_fit2 <- randomForest::randomForest(x = x_reduced, y = y,
    ntree = 110,
    sampsize = c(3600, 1200))

> which.min(forest_fit2$err.rate[, 1])
[1] 98
```

Examine how it does on the training data first:

```
> rf_prob <- predict(forest_fit, type = "prob")

> y_prob <- rf_prob[, 2]

> classifierplots::density_plot(y, y_prob)
```

The output of the preceding code is as follows:

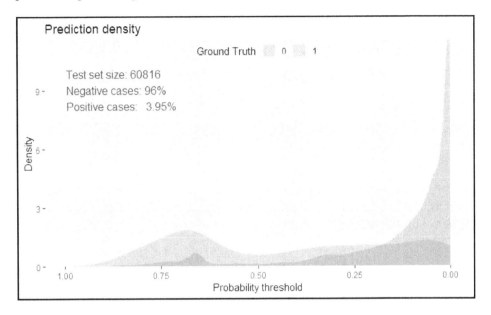

Now, pursue identifying the metrics:

```
> ynum <- as.numeric(ifelse(y == "1", 1, 0))

> MLmetrics::AUC(y_prob, ynum)
[1] 0.8154905

> MLmetrics::LogLoss(y_prob, ynum)
[1] 0.2652151
```

The AUC seems about what came about what we would expect, but the log-loss is quite a bit worse. Why? Ah, yes, our problem is the relative probabilities. We need to adjust the predicted probabilities, then recalculate log-loss. I'll make it straightforward to do this by taking the formula I discussed previously and putting it into a function:

```
> corrected_prob <- function(result, population_fraction, sample_fraction){
    value <- 1/(1+(1/population_fraction-1) /
(1/sample_fraction-1)*(1/result-1))
    return(value)
}
```

Then, we apply the function to the predicted results:

```
> yprob_corrected <- corrected_prob(result = y_prob,
    population_fraction = 0.04,
    sample_fraction = .33
```

We can see that the AUC hasn't changed, but the log-loss has improved:

```
> MLmetrics::AUC(yprob_corrected, ynum)
[1] 0.8154905

> MLmetrics::LogLoss(yprob_corrected, ynum)
[1] 0.188308
```

In fact, it's more in line now with what we saw in `Chapter 3`, *Logistic Regression*. It's worth exploring whether it can be close to the 0.14 log-loss and 0.81 AUC values we achieved with the MARS model on the test set:

```
> rf_test <- predict(forest_fit, type = "prob", newdata = test)

> rf_test <- rf_test[, 2]

> ytest <- as.numeric(ifelse(test$y == "1", 1, 0))

> MLmetrics::AUC(rf_test, ytest)
[1] 0.8149009
```

Nicely done on the AUC! Correct those probabilities and get the log-loss:

```
> rftest_corrected <- corrected_probability(result = rf_test,
    population_fraction = 0.04,
    sample_fraction = 0.33)

> MLmetrics::LogLoss(rftest_corrected, ytest)
[1] 0.1787402
```

We actually improved the log-loss versus the training data, but didn't win the battle versus MARS. What to do? Well, we're going to give **XGboost** a try next. We could go back and and tune the number of trees, oversampling fraction, or the number of features sampled per tree or even just say that, on this dataset, MARS did its job. It's been my experience that, on unbalanced labels, random forest will outperform MARS.

However, this case does demonstrate the power of MARS as your go-to baseline model. Let's do one further drill-down and plot the AUC curves of random forest versus MARS. Please note that this last step requires you to have executed the code in Chapter 3, *Logistic Regression*. If you haven't saved the results, go back and run the MARS example before proceeding with the following:

```
pred.rf <- ROCR::prediction(rftest_corrected, test$y)

perf.rf <- ROCR::performance(pred.rf, "tpr", "fpr")

ROCR::plot(perf.rf, main = "ROC", col = 1)

pred.earth <- ROCR::prediction(test_pred, test$y)

perf.earth <- ROCR::performance(pred.earth, "tpr", "fpr")

ROCR::plot(perf.earth, col = 2, add = TRUE)
legend(0.6, 0.6, c("RF", "MARS"), 1:2)
```

The output of the preceding code is as follows:

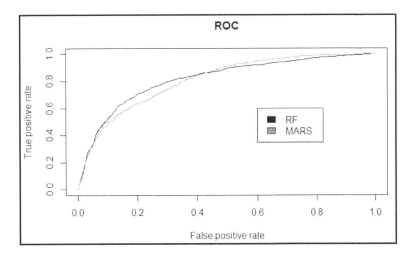

This is quite revealing. Here, we to very distinct curves where the AUC values are almost identical. Indeed, from a true positive rate of 0.4 to 0.8, random forest outperforms MARS. The key learning here is that a model performance value in and of itself isn't enough to guide model selection.

While random forest once again proved itself a capable tool for classification, let's see how gradient boosting trees can perform.

Extreme gradient boosting – classification

As mentioned previously, we'll be using the `xgboost` package in this section. Given the method's well-earned reputation, let's try it on the `santander` data.

As stated in the boosting overview, you can tune a number of parameters:

- `nrounds`: This is the maximum number of iterations (number of trees in the final model).
- `colsample_bytree`: This is the number of features, expressed as a ratio, to sample when building a tree. The default is 1 (100% of the features).
- `min_child_weight`: This is the minimum weight in the trees being boosted. The default is 1.
- `eta`: This is the learning rate, which is the contribution of each tree to the solution. The default is 0.3.
- `gamma`: This is the minimum loss reduction required to make another leaf partition in a tree.
- `subsample`: This is the ratio of data observations. The default is 1 (100%).
- `max_depth`: This is the maximum depth of the individual trees.

 Using the `expand.grid()` function, we'll build our experimental grid to run through the training process of the `caret` package. If you don't specify values for all of the preceding parameters, even if it's just a default, you'll receive an error message when you execute the function. The following values are based on a number of training iterations I've done previously. I encourage you to try your own tuning values.

Tuning this can be a daunting task computationally speaking. For our example, we'll just focus on tuning `eta` and `gamma`. Let's build the grid as follows:

```
> grid = expand.grid(
    nrounds = 100,
    colsample_bytree = 1,
    min_child_weight = 1,
    eta = c(0.1, 0.3, 0.5), #0.3 is default,
    gamma = c(0.25, 0.5),
    subsample = 1,
    max_depth = c(3)
  )
```

This creates a grid of six different models that the `caret` package will run to determine the best tuning parameters. A note of caution is in order. On a dataset of the size that we'll be working with, this process takes only a few minutes. However, in large datasets or tuning more parameters with more values per parameter, this can take hours. As such, you must apply your judgment and possibly experiment with smaller samples of the data in order to identify the tuning parameters, in case time is of the essence or you're constrained by the size of your hard drive.

Before using the `train()` function from the `caret` package, I would like to specify the `trainControl` argument by creating an object called `control`. This object will store the method that we want so as to train the tuning parameters. We'll use 5 fold cross-validation, as follows:

```
> cntrl = caret::trainControl(
+ method = "cv",
+ number = 5,
+ verboseIter = TRUE,
+ returnData = FALSE,
+ returnResamp = "final"
+ )
```

To utilize the `train.xgb()` function, just specify the formula as we did with the other models: the `train` dataset input values, labels, method, train control, metric, and experimental grid. Remember to set the random seed:

```
> set.seed(123)

> train.xgb = caret::train(
    x = x_reduced,
    y = y,
    trControl = cntrl,
    tuneGrid = grid,
    method = "xgbTree",
    metric = "Kappa"
  )
```

Since in `trControl` I set `verboseIter` to `TRUE`, you should have seen each training iteration within each k-fold.

Calling the object gives us the optimal parameters and the results of each of the parameter settings, as follows (this is abbreviated for simplicity):

```
> train.xgb
eXtreme Gradient Boosting
No pre-processing
Resampling: Cross-Validated (5 fold)
```

```
Summary of sample sizes: 48653, 48653, 48653, 48652, 48653
Resampling results across tuning parameters:

  eta gamma  Accuracy       Kappa
  0.1  0.25 0.9604545 0.001525813
  0.1  0.50 0.9604709 0.002323003
  0.3  0.25 0.9604216 0.014214973
  0.3  0.50 0.9604052 0.014215605
  0.5  0.25 0.9600434 0.015513354
  0.5  0.50 0.9599776 0.013964451

Tuning parameter 'nrounds' was held constant at a value of 100
 1
Tuning parameter 'min_child_weight' was held constant at a value of
 1
Tuning parameter 'subsample' was held constant at a value of 1
Kappa was used to select the optimal model using the largest value.
The final values used for the model were nrounds = 100, max_depth = 3, eta
 = 0.5, gamma = 0.25, colsample_bytree = 1, min_child_weight = 1
 and subsample = 1.
```

The best results are with $eta = 0.5$, and $gamma = 0.25$. Now it gets a little tricky, but this is what I've seen as best practice. First, create a list of parameters that will be used by the xgboost training function, xgb.train(). Then, turn the dataframe into a matrix of input features and a list of labeled numeric outcomes (0s and 1s). Then, turn the features and labels into the input required, as xgb.Dmatrix. Try this:

```
> param <- list( objective = "binary:logistic",
    booster = "gbtree",
    eval_metric = "error",
    eta = 0.5,
    max_depth = 3,
    subsample = 1,
    colsample_bytree = 1,
    gamma = 0.25
 )
> train.mat <- xgboost::xgb.DMatrix(data = x_reduced, label = ynum)
```

With all of that prepared, just create the model:

```
> set.seed(1232)

> xgb.fit <- xgboost::xgb.train(params = param, data = train.mat, nrounds =
    100)
```

Before seeing how it does on the test set, let's check the variable importance and plot it. You can examine three items: **gain**, **cover**, and **frequency**. **Gain** is the improvement in accuracy that feature brings to the branches it's on. **Cover** is the relative number of total observations related to this feature. **Frequency** is the percentage of times that feature occurs in all of the trees. The following code produces the desired output:

```
> impMatrix <- xgboost::xgb.importance(feature_names = dimnames(x)[[2]],
    model = xgb.fit)

> xgboost::xgb.plot.importance(impMatrix, main = "Gain by Feature")
```

The output of the preceding command is as follows:

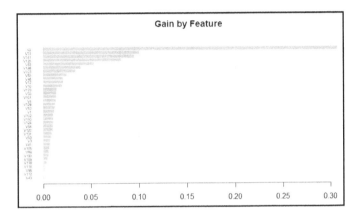

How does the feature importance compare to random forest? Feature **V2** remains the most important, and roughly the top ten are the same. Note that it does very well on the training data:

```
> pred <- predict(xgb.fit, x_reduced)

> MLmetrics::AUC(pred, y) #.88
[1] 0.8839242

> MLmetrics::LogLoss(pred, ynum) #.12
[1] 0.1209341
```

Impressed? Well, here is how we see it performed on the test set, which, like the training data, must be in a matrix:

```
> test_xgb <- as.matrix(test)

> test_xgb <- test_xgb[, my_forest_vars]
```

```
> xgb_test_matrix <- xgboost::xgb.DMatrix(data = test_xgb, label = ytest)

> xgb_pred <- predict(xgb.fit, xgb_test_matrix)

> Metrics::auc(ytest, xgb_pred) #.83
[1] 0.8282241

> MLmetrics::LogLoss(xgb_pred, ytest) #.138
[1] 0.1380904
```

What happened here is that the model had the lowest bias on the training data, but the performance falls off on the test data. Even so, it still has the highest AUC and lowest log-loss. Like we did with random forest, let's compare the ROC plot with `xgboost` added:

```
> ROCR::plot(perf.rf, main = "ROC", col = "black")

> ROCR::plot(perf.earth, col = "red", add = TRUE)

> pred.xgb <- ROCR::prediction(xgb_pred, test$y)

> perf.xgb <- ROCR::performance(pred.xgb, "tpr", "fpr")

> ROCR::plot(perf.xgb, col = "green", add = TRUE)

> legend(x = .75, y = .5,
    legend = c("RF", "MARS", "XGB"),
    fil = c("black", "red", "green"),
    col = c(1,2,3))
```

The output of the proceeding code is as follows:

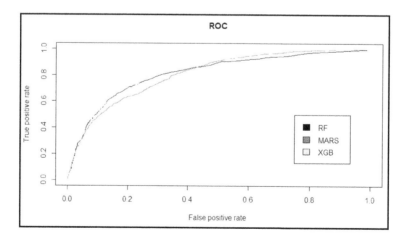

The `xgboost` model sort of combines the best of random forest and MARS in performance. All that will minimal tuning of hyperparameters. This clearly shows the power of the method and why it has become so popular.

Before we bring this chapter to a close, I want to introduce the powerful method of feature elimination using random forest techniques.

Feature selection with random forests

So far, we've looked at several feature selection techniques, such as regularization, stepwise, and recursive feature elimination. I now want to introduce an effective feature selection method for classification problems with random forests using the `Boruta` package. A paper is available that provides details on how it works in providing all the relevant features: *Kursa M., Rudnicki W. (2010), Feature Selection with the Boruta Package, Journal of Statistical Software, 36(11), 1 - 13.*

What I'll do here is provide an overview of the algorithm and then apply it to the simulated dataset. I've found it to be highly effective at eliminating unimportant features, but be advised it can be computationally intensive. However, it's usually time well spent.

At a high level, the algorithm creates **shadow attributes** by copying all of the input values and shuffling the order of their observations to decorrelate them. Then, a random forest model is built on all of the input values and a Z-score of the mean accuracy loss for each feature, including the shadow ones. Features with significantly higher Z-scores or significantly lower Z-scores than the shadow attributes are deemed **important** and **unimportant** respectively. The shadow attributes and those features with known importance are removed and the process repeats itself until all features are assigned an importance value. You can also specify the maximum number of random forest iterations. After completion of the algorithm, each of the original features will be labeled as **confirmed**, **tentative**, or **rejected**. You must decide on whether or not to include the tentative features for further modeling. Depending on your situation, you have some options:

- Change the random seed and rerun the methodology multiple (*k*) times and select only those features that are confirmed in all of the *k* runs
- Divide your data (training data) into *k* folds, run separate iterations on each fold, and select those features which are confirmed for all of the *k* folds

Note that all of this can be done with just a few lines of code. To get started, load the simulated data, `sim_df`, again. We'll create train and test sets as before:

```
> sim_df$y <- as.factor(sim_df$y)

> set.seed(1066)

> index <- caret::createDataPartition(sim_df$y, p = 0.7, list = F)

> train <- sim_df[index, ]

> test <- sim_df[-index, ]
```

To run the algorithm, you just need to call the `Boruta` package and create a formula in the `boruta()` function. Keep in mind that the labels must be a factor or the algorithm won't work. If you want to track the progress of the algorithm, specify `doTrace = 1`. But, I shall forgot that option in the following. Also, don't forget to set the random seed:

```
> set.seed(5150)

> rf_fs <- Boruta::Boruta(y ~ ., data = train)
```

As mentioned, this can be computationally intensive. Here's how long it took on my old-fashioned laptop:

```
> rf_fs$timeTaken #2.84 minutes workstation, 28.22
Time difference of 22.15982 mins
```

I ran this same thing on a high-powered workstation and it ran in two minutes.

A simple table will provide the count of the final importance decision. We see that the algorithm rejects five features and selects 11:

```
> table(rf_fs$finalDecision)

 Tentative Confirmed Rejected
         0        11        5
```

Using these results, it's simple to create a new dataframe with our selected features. We start out using the `getSelectedAttributes()` function to capture the feature names. In this example, let's only select those that are confirmed. If we wanted to include confirmed and tentative, we just specify `withTentative - TRUE` in the function:

```
> fnames <- Boruta::getSelectedAttributes(rf_fs) #withTentative = TRUE

> fnames
 [1] "TwoFactor1" "TwoFactor2" "Linear2"    "Linear3"    "Linear4"
"Linear5"
 [7] "Linear6"    "Nonlinear1" "Nonlinear2" "Nonlinear3" "random1"
```

Using the feature names, we create our subset of the data:

```
> boruta_train <- train[, colnames(train) %in% fnames]

> boruta_train$y <- train$y
```

We'll go ahead now and build a random forest algorithm with the selected features and see how it performs:

```
> boruta_fit <- randomForest::randomForest(y ~ ., data = train)

> boruta_pred <- predict(boruta_fit, type = "prob", newdata = test)

> boruta_pred <- boruta_pred[, 2]

> ytest <- as.numeric(ifelse(test$y == "1", 1, 0))

> MLmetrics::AUC(boruta_pred, ytest)
[1] 0.9604841

> MLmetrics::LogLoss(boruta_pred, ytest)
[1] 0.2704204
```

This is quite an impressive performance when you compare to the results from Chapter 4, *Advanced Feature Selection in Linear Models*. I think this example serves as a good validation of the technique. Go get some computing horsepower and start using it!

Summary

In this chapter, you learned both the power of tree-based learning methods for classification problems. Single trees, while easy to build and interpret, may not have the necessary predictive power for many of the problems that we're trying to solve. To improve on the predictive ability, we have the tools of random forest and gradient-boosted trees at our disposal. With random forest, hundreds or even thousands of trees are built and the results aggregated for an overall prediction. Each tree of the random forest is built using a sample of the data called bootstrapping as well as a sample of the predictive variables. As for gradient boosting, an initial, and a relatively small, tree is produced. After this initial tree is built, subsequent trees are produced based on the residuals/misclassifications. The intended result of such a technique is to build a series of trees that can improve on the weakness of the prior tree in the process, resulting in decreased bias and variance. We also saw that, in R, we can utilize random forests as an effective feature selection/reduction method.

While these methods are extremely powerful, they aren't some sort of nostrum in the world of machine learning. Different datasets require judgment on the part of the analyst as to which techniques are applicable. The techniques to be applied to the analysis, and the selection of the tuning parameters is equally important. This fine tuning can make all of the difference between a good predictive model and a great predictive model.

In the next chapter, we'll turn our attention to using R to build neural networks and deep learning models.

Neural Networks and Deep Learning

7

"Forget artificial intelligence – in the brave new world of big data, it's artificial idiocy we should be looking out for."

– Tom Chatfield

I recall that at some meeting circa mid-2012, I was part of a group discussing the results of some analysis or other, when one of the people around the table sounded off with a hint of exasperation mixed with a tinge of fright: *this isn't one of those neural networks, is it?* I knew of his past run-ins with, and deep-seated anxiety regarding, neural networks, so I assuaged his fears, making some sarcastic comment that neural networks have basically gone the way of the dinosaur. No one disagreed! Several months later, I was gobsmacked when I attended a local meeting where the discussion focused on, of all things, neural networks and this mysterious deep learning. Machine learning pioneers, such as Ng, Hinton, Salakhutdinov, and Bengio have revived neural networks and improved their performance.

Much media hype revolves around these methods, with high-tech companies such as Facebook, Google, and Netflix investing tens, if not hundreds, of millions of dollars. These methods have yielded promising results in voice recognition, image recognition, automation, and any practical data science project. If self-driving cars ever stop running off the road and into each other, it will certainly be due to the methods we've discussed here.

In this chapter, we will discuss how the methods work, their benefits, and their inherent drawbacks so that you can become conversationally competent about them. We will start slowly by working through a simple application of a neural network, which will give you a feel for what is happening. Then, we will pursue the deep learning methodology that has burst on the scene the past couple of years, TensorFlow, using Keras as the frontend.

The following topics will be covered in this chapter:

- Introduction to neural networks
- Deep learning, a not-so-deep overview
- Creating a simple neural network
- An example of deep learning

Introduction to neural networks

Neural network is a fairly broad term that covers a number of related methods but, in our case, we will focus on a **feedforward** network that trains with **backpropagation**. I'm not going to waste our time discussing how the machine learning methodology is similar or dissimilar to how a biological brain works. We only need to start with a working definition of what a neural network is.

 To know more about artificial neural networks, I think the Wikipedia entry is a good start: https://en.wikipedia.org/wiki/Artificial_neural_network.

To summarize, in machine learning and cognitive science, **artificial neural networks (ANNs)** are a family of statistical learning models inspired by biological neural networks (the central nervous systems of animals, the brain) and are used to estimate or approximate functions that can depend on a large number of inputs and are generally unknown.

The motivation or benefit of ANNs is that they allow the modeling of highly complex relationships between inputs/features and response variable(s), especially if the relationships are highly nonlinear. No underlying assumptions are required to create and evaluate the model, and it can be used with qualitative and quantitative responses. If this is the yin, then the yang is the common criticism that the results are a black box, which means that there is no equation with the coefficients to examine and share with the business partners. In fact, the results are *almost* uninterpretable. The other criticisms revolve around how results can differ by just changing the initial random inputs and that training ANNs is computationally expensive and time-consuming.

The mathematics behind ANNs is not trivial by any measure. However, it is crucial to at least get a working understanding of what is happening. A good way to intuitively develop this understanding is to start with a diagram of a simplistic neural network.

In this simple network, the inputs or covariates consist of two nodes or neurons. The neuron labeled as **1** represents a constant or, more appropriately, the intercept. **X1** represents a quantitative variable. **W** represents the weights that are multiplied by the input node values. These values become **input nodes** to the **hidden node**. You can have multiple hidden nodes, but the principle of what happens in just this one is the same. In the hidden node, **H1**, the *weight * value* computations are summed. As the intercept is notated as **1**, then that input value is simply the weight, **W1**. Now the magic happens. The summed value is then transformed with the **activation** function, turning the input signal to an output signal. In this example, as it is the only the **hidden node**, it is multiplied by **W3** and becomes the estimate of **Y**, our response. This is the feedforward portion of the algorithm:

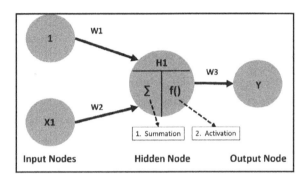

But wait, there's more! To complete the cycle or epoch, as it is known, backpropagation happens and trains the model based on what was learned. To initiate backpropagation, an error is determined based on a loss function such as **sum of squared error** or **cross-entropy**, among others. As the weights, **W1** and **W2**, were set to some initial random values between *[-1, 1]*, the initial error may be high. Working backward, the weights are changed to minimize the error in the loss function. The following diagram portrays the backpropagation portion:

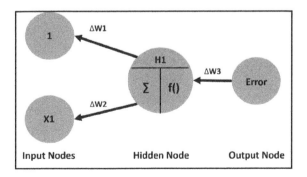

This completes one epoch. This process continues, using gradient descent (discussed in Chapter 5, *K-Nearest Neighbors and Support Vector Machines*) until the algorithm converges to the minimum error or a pre-specified number of epochs. If we assume that our activation function is simply linear, in this example, we would end up with the following:

$$Y = W3(W1(1) + W2(X1))$$

The networks can get complicated if you add numerous input neurons, multiple neurons in a hidden node, and even multiple hidden nodes. It is important to note that the output from a neuron is connected to all the subsequent neurons and has weights assigned to all these connections. This greatly increases the model's complexity. Adding hidden nodes and increasing the number of neurons in the hidden nodes has not improved the performance of ANNs as we had hoped. Thus, the development of deep learning occurs, which in part relaxes the requirement of all these neuron connections.

There are a number of activation functions that you can use/try, including a simple linear function, or for a classification problem, the sigmoid function, which is a special case of the logistic function (Chapter 3, *Logistic Regression*). Other common activation functions are Rectifier, Maxout, and tanh (hyperbolic tangent).

We can plot a sigmoid function in R, first creating an R function to calculate the sigmoid function values:

```
> sigmoid = function(x) {
 1 / ( 1 + exp(-x) )
 }
```

Then, it is a simple matter of plotting the function over a range of values, say −5 to 5:

```
> x <- seq(-5, 5, .1)
> plot(sigmoid(x))
```

The output of the preceding command is as follows:

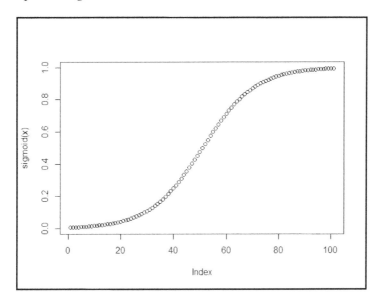

The `tanh` function (hyperbolic tangent) is a rescaling of the logistic `sigmoid` with the output between **-1** and **1**. The `tanh` function relates to `sigmoid` as follows, where x is the `sigmoid` function:

$$tanh(x) = 2 * sigmoid(2x) - 1$$

Let's plot the `tanh` and `sigmoid` functions for comparison purposes. Let's also use `ggplot`:

```
> install.packages("ggplot2")

> s <- sigmoid(x)

> t <- tanh(x)

> z <- data.frame(cbind(x, s, t))

> ggplot2::ggplot(z, ggplot2::aes(x)) +
    ggplot2::geom_line(ggplot2::aes(y = s, color = "sigmoid")) +
    ggplot2::geom_line(ggplot2::aes(y = t, color = "tanh"))
```

The output of the preceding command is as follows:

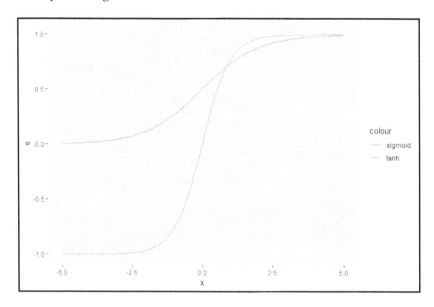

So, why use the `tanh` function versus `sigmoid`? It seems there are many opinions on the subject. In short, assuming you have scaled data with mean 0 and variance 1, the `tanh` function permits weights that are on average, close to zero (zero-centered). This helps in avoiding bias and improves convergence. Think about the implications of always having positive weights from an output neuron to an input neuron like in a `sigmoid` function activation. During backpropagation, the weights will become either all positive or all negative between layers. This may cause performance issues. Also, since the gradient at the tails of a `sigmoid` (0 and 1) are almost zero, during backpropagation, it can happen that almost no signal will flow between neurons of different layers. A full discussion of the issue is available from LeCun (1998). Keep in mind it is not a foregone conclusion that `tanh` is always better.

This all sounds fascinating, but the ANN almost went the way of disco as it just did not perform as well as advertised, especially when trying to use deep networks with many hidden layers and neurons. It seems that a slow, yet gradual revival came about with the seminal paper by Hinton and Salakhutdinov (2006) in the reformulated and, dare I say, rebranded neural network, deep learning.

Deep learning – a not-so-deep overview

So, what is this deep learning that is grabbing our attention and headlines? Let's turn to Wikipedia again to form a working definition: *Deep learning is a branch of machine learning based on a set of algorithms that attempt to model high-level abstractions in data by using model architectures, with complex structures or otherwise, composed of multiple nonlinear transformations.* That sounds as if a lawyer wrote it. The characteristics of deep learning are that it is based on ANNs where the machine learning techniques, primarily unsupervised learning, are used to create new features from the input variables. We will dig into some unsupervised learning techniques in the next couple of chapters, but you can think of it as finding structure in data where no response variable is available.

A simple way to think of it is the **periodic table of elements**, which is a classic case of finding a structure where no response is specified. Pull up this table online and you will see that it is organized based on atomic structure, with metals on one side and non-metals on the other. It was created based on latent classification/structure. This identification of latent structure/hierarchy is what separates deep learning from your run-of-the-mill ANN. Deep learning sort of addresses the question of whether there is an algorithm that better represents the outcome than just the raw inputs. In other words, can our model learn to classify pictures other than with just the raw pixels as the only input? This can be of great help in a situation where you have a small set of labeled responses but a vast amount of unlabeled input data. You could train your deep learning model using unsupervised learning and then apply this in a supervised fashion to the labeled data, iterating back and forth.

Identification of these latent structures is not trivial mathematically, but one example is the concept of regularization that we looked at in `Chapter 4`, *Advanced Feature Selection in Linear Models*. In deep learning, you can penalize weights with **regularization** methods such as *L1* (penalize non-zero weights), *L2* (penalize large weights), and **dropout** (randomly ignore certain inputs and zero their weight out). In standard ANNs, none of these regularization methods take place.

Another way is to reduce the dimensionality of the data. One such method is the `autoencoder`. This is a neural network where the inputs are transformed into a set of reduced dimension weights. In the following diagram, notice that **Feature A** is not connected to one of the hidden nodes:

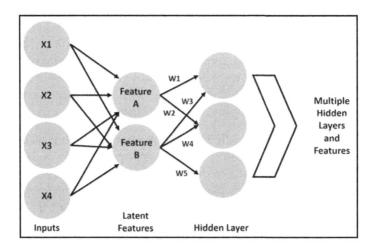

This can be applied recursively and learning can take place over many hidden layers. What you have seen happening, in this case, is that the network is developing features of features as they are stacked on each other. Deep learning will learn the weights between two layers in sequence first and then use backpropagation to fine-tune these weights. Other feature selection methods include **restricted Boltzmann machine** and **sparse coding model**.

The details of restricted Boltzmann machine and sparse coding model are beyond our scope, and many resources are available to learn about the specifics. Here are a couple of starting points:
`http://www.cs.toronto.edu/~hinton/`
and `http://deeplearning.net/`.

Deep learning has performed well on many classification problems, including winning a Kaggle contest or two. It still suffers from the problems of ANNs, especially the black box problem. Try explaining to the uninformed what is happening inside a neural network, regardless of the use of various in vogue methods. However, it is appropriate for problems where an explanation of *how* is not a problem and the important question is *what*. After all, do we really care why an autonomous car avoided running into a pedestrian, or do we care about the fact that it did not? Additionally, the Python community has a bit of a head start on the R community in deep learning usage and packages. As we will see in the practical exercise, the gap is closing.

While deep learning is an exciting undertaking, be aware that to achieve the full benefit of its capabilities, you will need a high degree of computational power along with taking the time to train the best model by fine-tuning the hyperparameters. Here is a list of some things that you will need to consider:

- An activation function
- Size and number of the hidden layers
- Dimensionality reduction, that is, restricted Boltzmann versus autoencoder
- The number of epochs
- The gradient descent learning rate
- The loss function
- Regularization

Deep learning resources and advanced methods

One of the more interesting visual tools you can use for both learning and explaining is the interactive widget provided by TensorFlow: `http://playground.tensorflow.org/`. This tool allows you to explore, or *tinker*, as the site calls it, the various parameters and how they impact on the response, be it a classification problem or a regression problem. I could spend – well, I have spent – hours tinkering with it.

Here is an interesting task: create your own experimental design and see how the various parameters affect your prediction.

At this point, the fastest-growing deep learning open source tool is TensorFlow. You can access TensorFlow with R, but it requires you to install Python first. What we will go through in the practical exercise is Keras, which is an API that can run on top of TensorFlow, or other backend neural networks such as Theano. The creators of Keras designed it to simplify the development and testing of deep neural networks. We will discuss TensorFlow and Keras a little more in-depth, prior to our implementation of a problem.

I also really like using MXNet, which does not require the installation of Python and is relatively easy to install and make operational. It also offers a number of trained models that allow you to start making predictions quickly. Several R tutorials are available at `http://mxnet.io/`.

I now want to take the time to enumerate some of the variations of deep neural networks along with the learning tasks where they have performed well.

Convolutional neural networks (CNNs) make the assumption that the inputs are images and create features from slices or small portions of the data, which are combined to create a feature map. Think of these small slices as filters or, probably more appropriately, kernels that the network learns during training. The activation function for a CNN is a rectified linear unit (ReLU). It is simply $f(x) = \max(0, x)$, where x is the input to the neuron. CNNs perform well on image classification, and object detection.

Recurrent neural networks (RNNs) are created to make use of sequential information. In traditional neural networks, the inputs and outputs are independent of each other. With RNNs, the output is dependent on the computations of previous layers, permitting information to persist across layers. So, take an output from a neuron (y); it is calculated not only on its input (t) but on all previous layers (t-1, t-n...). It is effective at handwriting and speech detection.

Long short-term memory (LSTM) is a special case of an RNN. The problem with an RNN is that it does not perform well on data with long signals. Thus, LSTMs were created to capture complex patterns in data. RNNs combine information during training from previous steps in the same way, regardless of the fact that information in one step is more or less valuable than other steps. LSTMs seek to overcome this limitation by deciding what to remember at each step during training. This multiplication of a weight matrix by the data vector is referred to as a gate, which acts as an information filter. A neuron in an LSTM will have two inputs and two outputs. The input from prior outputs and the memory vector passed from the previous gate. Then, it produces the output values and output memory as inputs to the next layer. LSTMs have the limitation of requiring a healthy dose of training data and are computationally intensive. LSTMs have performed well on speech recognition problems and in complicated time series analysis.

With that, let's move on to some practical applications.

Creating a simple neural network

For this task, we will develop a neural network to answer the question of when the now-defunct Space Shuttle should use its autolanding system. The default decision is to let the crew land the craft. However, the autoland capability may be required for situations of crew incapacitation or adverse effects of gravity upon re-entry after extended orbital operations. This data is based on computer simulations, not actual flights. In reality, the autoland system went through some trials and tribulations and, for the most part, the shuttle astronauts were in charge during the landing process. Here are a couple of links for further background information:

- http://www.spaceref.com/news/viewsr.html?pid=10518
- https://waynehale.wordpress.com/2011/03/11/breaking-through/

Data understanding and preparation

To start, we will load the necessary packages and put the required ones in the environment. The data is in the MASS package:

```
> library(magrittr)

> install.packages(caret)

> install.packages(MASS)

> library(MASS)

> install.packages("neuralnet")

> install.packages("vtreat")
```

The neuralnet package will be used for building the model and caret for data preparation. Let's load the data and examine its structure:

```
> data(shuttle)

> str(shuttle)
```

The data consists of 256 observations and 7 features. Notice that all of the features are categorical and the response is `use` with two levels, `auto` and `noauto`, as follows:

- `stability`: This is stable positioning or not (`stab`/`xstab`)
- `error`: This is the size of the error (`MM` / `SS` / `LX`)
- `sign`: This is the sign of the error, positive or negative (`pp`/`nn`)
- `wind`: This is the `wind` sign (`head` / `tail`)
- `magn`: This is the `wind` strength (`Light` / `Medium` / `Strong` / `Out of Range`)
- `vis`: This is the visibility (`yes` / `no`)

Here, we will look at a table of the response/outcome:

```
> table(shuttle$use)
 auto noauto
 145      111
```

Almost 57% of the time, the decision is to use the autolander. We'll now get our training and testing data set up for modeling:

```
> set.seed(1942)

> trainIndex <-
    caret::createDataPartition(shuttle$use, p = .6, list = FALSE)

> shuttleTrain <- shuttle[trainIndex, -7]

> shuttleTest <- shuttle[-trainIndex, -7]
```

We are going to treat the data to create numeric features, and also drop the `cat_P` features that the function creates. We covered the idea of treating a dataframe in Chapter 1, *Preparing and Understanding Data*:

```
> treatShuttle <- vtreat::designTreatmentsZ(shuttleTrain,
colnames(shuttleTrain))

> train_treated <- vtreat::prepare(treatShuttle, shuttleTrain)

> train_treated <- train_treated[, c(-1,-2)]

> test_treated <- vtreat::prepare(treatShuttle, shuttleTest)

> test_treated <- test_treated[, c(-1, -2)]
```

The next couple portions of code I find awkward. Because `neuralnet()` requires a formula and the data in a dataframe, we have to turn the response into a numeric list and then add it to our treated train and test data:

```
> shuttle_trainY <- shuttle[trainIndex, 7]

> train_treated$y <- ifelse(shuttle_trainY == "auto", 1, 0)

> shuttle_testY <- shuttle[-trainIndex, 7]

> test_treated$y <- ifelse(shuttle_testY == "auto", 1, 0)
```

The function in `neuralnet` will call for the use of a formula as we used elsewhere, such as *y~x1+x2+x3+x4, data = df*. In the past, we used *y~* to specify all the other variables in the data as inputs. However, `neuralnet` does not accommodate this at the time of writing. The way around this limitation is to use the `as.formula()` function. After first creating an object of the variable names, we will use this as an input to paste the variables properly on the right-hand side of the equation:

```
> n <- names(train_treated)

> form <- as.formula(paste("y ~", paste(n[!n %in% "y"], collapse = " + ")))
```

The object `form` give us what we need to build our model.

Modeling and evaluation

In the `neuralnet` package, the function that we will use is appropriately named `neuralnet()`. Other than the formula, there are four other critical arguments that we will need to examine:

- `hidden`: This is the number of hidden neurons in each layer, which can be up to three layers; the default is 1
- `act.fct`: This is the activation function with the default logistic and `tanh` available
- `err.fct`: This is the function used to calculate the error with the default `sse`; as we are dealing with binary outcomes, we will use `ce` for cross-entropy
- `linear.output`: This is a logical argument on whether or not to ignore `act.fct` with the default `TRUE`, so for our data, this will need to be `FALSE`

You can also specify the algorithm. The default is resilient with backpropagation and we will use it along with the default of one hidden neuron for simplicity:

```
> nnfit <- neuralnet::neuralnet(form, data = train_treated, err.fct = "ce",
linear.output = FALSE)
```

Here is an abbreviated output of weights for the overall result:

```
> head(nnfit$result.matrix)
                                              1
error                              0.024293436369
reached.threshold                  0.009929147409
steps                            181.000000000000
Intercept.to.1layhid1              0.573783967352
stability_lev_x_stab.to.1layhid1  -2.072585716776
stability_lev_x_xstab.to.1layhid1  6.859369770672
```

We can see that the error is extremely low at `0.024`. The number of steps required for the algorithm to reach the threshold, which is when the absolute partial derivatives of the error function, become smaller than this error (default = 0.1).

You can also look at what is known as generalized weights. According to the authors of the `neuralnet` package, the generalized weight is defined as the contribution of the *i*th covariate to the log-odds:

The generalized weight expresses the effect of each covariate x_i and thus has an analogous interpretation as the ith regression parameter in regression models. However, the generalized weight depends on all other covariates (Gunther and Fritsch, 2010).

 The weights can be called and examined. I've abbreviated the output to the first four variables and six observations only. Note that if you sum each row, you will get the same number, which means that the weights are equal for each covariate combination. Please note that your results might be slightly different because of random weight initialization.

The results are as follows:

```
> head(fit$generalized.weights[[1]])
             [,1]             [,2]             [,3]             [,4]
1 0.0004057906237 -0.001342992917 -0.0010654093452 -0.00010947079069
2 0.0003792401307 -0.001255122173 -0.0009957006291 -0.00010230822138
3 0.0003929874040 -0.001300619751 -0.0010317943007 -0.00010601684547
4 0.0003672745975 -0.001215521390 -0.0009642849428 -0.00009908026019
5 0.0273129186450 -0.090394045943 -0.0717104759663 -0.00736825009054
6 0.0255281981170 -0.084487386479 -0.0670246655557 -0.00688678315678
```

To visualize the neural network, simply use the `plot()` function:

```
> plot(fit)
```

The following is the output of the preceding command:

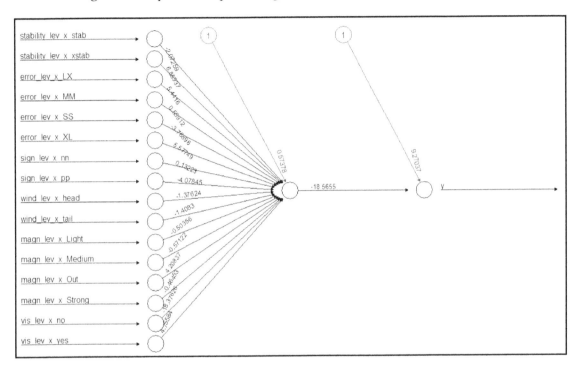

This plot shows the weights of the features and intercepts.

We now want to see how well the model performs. This is done with the `compute()` function and specifying the fit model and covariates:

```
> test_pred <- neuralnet::compute(nnfit, test_treated[, 1:16])

> test_prob <- test_pred$net.result
```

These results are in probabilities, so let's turn them into 0 or 1 and follow this up with a confusion matrix and log-loss:

```
> pred <- ifelse(test_prob >= 0.5, 1, 0)

> table(pred, test_treated$y)
pred  0  1
   0 41  0
```

```
     1   3 58
 > MLmetrics::LogLoss(test_prob, test_treated$y)
 [1] 0.2002453861
```

The model achieved near-perfect accuracy on the test set but had three false negatives. I'll leave it to you to see if you can build a neural network that achieves 100% accuracy!

An example of deep learning

Shifting gears away from the Space Shuttle, let's work through how to set up, train, and evaluate a deep learning model. You see these used quite a bit for image classification, NLP, and so on. However, let's look at using it for regression. You don't find too many examples of that in my opinion. As such, let's go with our Ames housing price data we used back in `Chapter 2`, *Linear Regression*. Before that, let's briefly discuss what Tensor, TensorFlow, and Keras are.

Keras and TensorFlow background

I mentioned earlier that Keras is an API, a frontend if you will, for several deep learning backends. It was originally available only for Python but has been available in R since, mid-2017. It is important to spend some time reviewing its capabilities at its documentation source: `https://keras.io/why-use-keras/`.

I must confess my colleagues brought me into Keras and using TensorFlow kicking and screaming. If *I* can get this to work, I would say that you certainly can. I must thank them, as it is very powerful, even though I have a slight bias toward MXNet. As the old saying goes, it is tough to teach old dogs new tricks!

The backend of choice, of course, is TensorFlow. We must now take a few sentences to put in plain English what a tensor is, and what TensorFlow is. A tensor is an *n*-dimensional array. Thus, a vector is a one-dimensional tensor, a matrix is a two-dimensional tensor and so forth. Let's say you have a multivariate time series, which would consist of a three-dimensional tensor: one dimension is the observations or length of your data, another dimension is the features, and another the timesteps or, more concretely, the lagged values. TensorFlow as a backend is an open source platform, created by Google, that uses tensors, of course, for high-performance and scalable computation. The base frontend for TensorFlow is Python. Therefore, to use Keras and R as the frontend, you must install Python, in particular the Python platform Anaconda: `https://www.anaconda.com/`.

So, if installing Anaconda becomes an issue, then the following exercise will require you to use a different backend, which is outside the scope of this discussion. Let's look at how to get this up and running. Keep in mind that I'm using a Windows-based computer:

 As a caveat, it is important to inform you that I in no way guarantee that the following code will work for you as I exactly lay it out. I've installed this on several computers, and each time I encountered different problems that required me to search the internet for a specific solution. The one common factor is that you have installed Anaconda on your computer and that it is fully functional.

```
# Install reticulate package as it allows R to call python
> install.packages("reticulate")

> install.packages("keras")

> keras::install_keras() # loads the necessary python packages and may take
some time to complete

> library(keras)

> library(reticulate)
```

That was the code that worked for me on this laptop. Again, your results may vary. Also, note that I've run into a number of issues that required me to run install_keras() again to get it working properly.

Assuming all is well, let's get our data loaded.

Loading the data

As for this data, it is the same that we used in Chapter 2, *Linear Regression*. What is different is that I've prepared the data exactly as before, but saved the features and response as an RData file. You can download that from GitHub: https://github.com/datameister66/MMLR3rd/blob/master/amesDL.RData.

Once you have that in your working directory, load it into the environment:

```
> load("amesDL.RData")
```

Notice that you now have four new objects:

- `trained`: The training data features
- `tested`: The testing data features
- `train_logy`: The log of home sales
- `test_logy`: The log of home sales

It is essential that the data is centered and scaled for a neural network (in the prior exercise, all features were either zero or one, which is acceptable). To perform this task, a function is available in the `caret` package. Let's use the training data to create the mean and standard deviation values that we will apply to both train and test data:

```
> prep <- caret::preProcess(trained, method = c("center", "scale"))

> trainT <- predict(prep, trained)
```

This gives us our transformed training data. However, Keras will not accept a dataframe as an input. It needs an array for both the features and the response. This is an easy fix with the `data.matrix()` function:

```
> train_logy <- data.matrix(train_logy)

> trainT <- data.matrix(trainT)
```

Now, you can just repeat these steps with the test data features:

```
> testT <- predict(prep, tested)

> testT <- data.matrix(testT)
```

It's about to get interesting.

Creating the model function

OK, we are going to create a model function, but not the model. The key function is `keras_model_sequential()`. There is a ton of stuff you can specify. What I'm going to show are two hidden layers with 64 neurons each. In both layers, the activation function is `relu`, which I covered earlier, and they work well for a regression problem. After the first layer, I demonstrate how to incorporate a dropout layer of 30%. Then, after the second hidden layer, I incorporate L1 regularization or LASSO, which we discussed in `Chapter 4`, *Advanced Feature Selection in Linear Models*. I thought it was important to show how to use both regularization methods, so you can use and adjust them as you deem fit.

The next function within the function is `compile()`, where I specify the loss as **mean-squared-error (MSE)** and the validation data metric as mean-absolute-error:

```
> model <- keras_model_sequential() %>%
    layer_dense(units = 64, activation = "relu",
                input_shape = dim(trainT)[2]
    ) %>%
    layer_dropout(0.3) %>%
    layer_dense(units = 64, activation = "relu",
                kernel_regularizer = regularizer_l1(l = 0.001)) %>%
    #layer_dropout(0.5) %>%
    layer_dense(units = 1)
  model %>% compile(
    loss = "mse",
    optimizer = optimizer_rmsprop(),
    metrics = list("mean_absolute_error")
  )
  model
}
```

Now, you can build the model and examine it. One thing of note, and something I don't see in very many vignettes out there, is to specify the seed, otherwise your results *will* vary wildly:

```
> use_session_with_seed(1800)

> model <- build_model()

> model %>% summary()
```

The output of the preceding code is as follows:

Layer (type)	Output Shape	Param #
dense_1 (Dense)	(None, 64)	7360
dropout_1 (Dropout)	(None, 64)	0
dense_2 (Dense)	(None, 64)	4160
dense_3 (Dense)	(None, 1)	65

Total params: 11,585

```
Trainable params: 11,585
Non-trainable params: 0
```

The output should be self-explanatory, which means we can finally train the model.

Model training

Training the model is quite interesting, I believe. We will pass the model to the `fit()` function, having specified the features, response, number of epochs, and validation percentage at each epoch. Here, I have gone with 100 epochs, and 20% of the training data for validation:

```
> epochs <- 100

> # Fit the model and store training stats

> history <- model %>% fit(
    trainT,
    train_logy,
    epochs = epochs,
    validation_split = 0.2,
    verbose = 0
)
```

You can examine the history object on your own, but what is very powerful is to plot the training and validation error for each epoch:

```
> plot(history, metrics = "mean_absolute_error", smooth = FALSE)
```

The output of the preceding code is as follows:

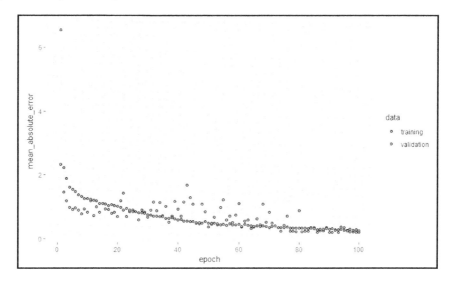

Notice how much the error differs between training and validation until we get above 80 epochs. This leads me to believe we should do well on the test data. Let's get our training baseline!

```
> min(history$metrics$mean_absolute_error)
[1] 0.248
```

To get the predicted values on the test data, just pipe the model to the `predict()` function:

```
> test_predictions <- model %>% predict(testT)
```

We now call up our metrics as we've done in other chapters. We should look at MAE obviously, but also the % error, and the R-squared:

```
> MLmetrics::MAE(test_predictions, test_logy)
[1] 0.162

> MLmetrics::MAPE(test_predictions, test_logy)
[1] 0.0133

> MLmetrics::R2_Score(test_predictions, test_logy)
[1] 0.6765795
```

Well done, I must say. To conclude evaluation, let's examine a base R plot of the predicted values versus the actuals (the log values):

```
> plot(test_predictions, test_logy)
```

The output of the preceding code is as follows:

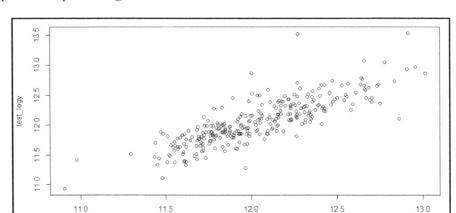

This compares similarly to what we did in Chapter 2, *Linear Regression*, with a number of outliers and some erratic performance on the lower- and higher-priced houses – all that with hardly any effort to adjust parameters such as the number of hidden neurons, layers, regularization, and maybe adding a linear activation unit somewhere.

In summary, using Keras with TensorFlow can challenge your sanity to code it properly to produce the results you desire, but what we've done here is establish a pipeline to make it possible for regression, and with a couple of changes, it will work for classification. All that, with very little effort around optimizing parameters, which I think is indicative of the power of the technique. Go and do likewise.

Summary

In this chapter, the goal was to get you up and running in the exciting world of neural networks and deep learning. We examined how the methods work, their benefits, and their inherent drawbacks, with applications to two different datasets. These techniques work well where complex, nonlinear relationships exist in the data. The first example was of a simple neural network on a simple dataset. The second example showed the power of using Keras with TensorFlow backend on a challenging dataset, and the performance was exemplary. I hope you will apply these methods by themselves or supplement other methods in an ensemble modeling fashion. Good luck and good hunting!

In the next chapter, we will learn about, ensembles, understand the data, and dive in deeper in modeling and evaluation.

8
Creating Ensembles and Multiclass Methods

"This is how you win ML competitions: you take other people's work and ensemble them together."

- Vitaly Kuznetsov, NIPS2014

You may have already realized that we've discussed ensemble learning. It's defined on www.scholarpedia.org as *the process by which multiple models, such as classifiers or experts, are strategically generated and combined to solve a particular computational intelligence problem*. In random forest and gradient boosting, we combined the *votes* of hundreds or thousands of trees to make a prediction. Hence, by definition, those models are ensembles. This methodology can be extended to any learner to create ensembles, which some refer to as meta-ensembles or meta-learners. We'll look at one of these methods referred to as **stacking**. In this methodology, we'll produce a number of classifiers and use their predicted class probabilities as input features to another classifier. This method *can* result in improved predictive accuracy. In the previous chapters, we focused on classification problems focused on binary outcomes. We'll now look at methods to predict those situations where the data consists of more than two outcomes (multiclass), a very common situation in real-world datasets.

The following are the topics that will be covered in this chapter:

- Ensembles
- Data understanding
- Modeling and evaluation

Ensembles

The quote at the beginning of this chapter mentions using ensembles to win machine learning competitions. However, they do have practical applications. I've provided a definition of what ensemble modeling is, but why does it work? To demonstrate this, I've co-opted an example from the following blog, which goes into depth at a number of ensemble methods: http://mlwave.com/kaggle-ensembling-guide/.

As I write this chapter, we're only a day away from the 2018 College Football Championship—the Clemson Tigers versus the Alabama Crimson Tide. Let's say we want to review our probability of winning a friendly wager where we want to take the Tide minus the points (5.5 points at the time of writing).

Assume that we've been following three expert prognosticators who said, *All have the same probability of predicting that the Patriots will cover the spread (60%)*. Now, if we favor any one of the so-called experts, it's clear that we have a 60% chance of winning. However, let's see what creating an ensemble of their predictions can do to increase our chances of profiting and humiliating friends and family.

Start by calculating the probability of each possible outcome for the experts picking Alabama, and let's assume that the probability is the same at 60%. If all three pick Alabama, we have *0.6 x 0.6 x 0.6* or a *21.6%* chance that all three are correct.

If any two of the three pick Alabama, then we have *(0.6 x 0.6 x 0.3) x 3* for a total of *43.2%*.

By using majority voting, if at least two of the three pick Alabama, then our probability of winning becomes almost *65% (21.6 + 43.2)*, which is an absolute improvement of *5%*.

This is a rather simplistic example but representative nonetheless. In machine learning, it can manifest itself by incorporating the predictions from several OK or even weak learners to improve overall accuracy. The diagram that follows shows how this can be accomplished:

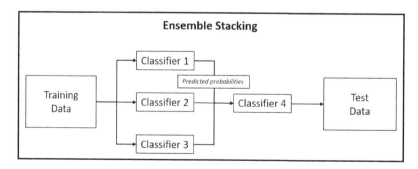

In this graphic, we build three different classifiers and use their predicted probabilities as input values to a fourth and different classifier in order to make predictions on the test data. Let's see how to apply this with R.

Data understanding

The dataset for analysis here is DNA pulled from mlbench. You don't have to install the package as I've put it in a CSV file and placed it on GitHub: `https://github.com/datameister66/MMLR3rd/blob/master/dna.csv`.

Install the packages as needed and load the data:

```
> library(magrittr)

> install.packages("earth")

> install.packages("glmnet")

> install.packages("mlr")

> install.packages("randomForest")

> install.packages("tidyverse")

dna <- read.csv("dna.csv")
```

The data consists of 3,181 observations, 180 input features coded as binary indicators, and the Class response. The response is a factor with three labels indicating a DNA type either ei, ie, or neither—coded as n. The following is a table of the target labels:

```
> table(dna$Class)

  ei  ie    n
 767 765 1654
```

This data should be ready for analysis, but let's run some quick checks to verify, starting with missing values:

```
> na_count <-
    sapply(dna, function(y)
    sum(length(which(is.na(
    y
))))))

> table(na_count)
```

```
na_count
    0
  181
```

With no missing values, we check for zero variance features:

```
> feature_variance <- caret::nearZeroVar(dna[, -181], saveMetrics = TRUE)

> table(feature_variance$zeroVar)

FALSE
  180
```

One of the things the authors of `mlbench` did with this data is transform the nucleotide factor features (A, C, G, T) into indicator features. They also de-identified the features naming them V1 through V180.

As such, let's check feature correlation:

```
> high_corr <- caret::findCorrelation(dna[, -181], cutoff = 0.9)

> length(high_corr)
[1] 173
```

It's a highly correlated dataset. We could run our feature selection methods as we've done in previous chapters, but let's press on with all features and see what happens.

Before doing so, let's get the train and test sets created:

```
> set.seed(555)

> index <- caret::createDataPartition(y = dna$Class, p = 0.8, list = FALSE)

> train <- dna[index, ]

> test <- dna[-index, ]
```

This created an 80/20 split for us and we can move on to building an algorithm.

Modeling and evaluation

We're going to explore the use of the `mlr` package, which stand for machine learning in R. The package supports multiple classes and ensemble methods. If you're familiar with `sci-kit learn` for Python, we could say that `mlr` endeavors to provide the same functionality for R. I intend to demonstrate how to use the package on a multiclass problem, then conclude by showing how to do an ensemble on the same data, so we can compare performances.

For the multiclass problem, we'll look at how to tune a random forest and then examine how to build an ensemble using random forest in conjunction with MARS, stacking those models by calling the generalized linear model function from the `glmnet` package.

Random forest model

There are a number of approaches to learning in multiclass problems. Techniques such as random forest and discriminant analysis will deal with multiclass while some techniques and/or packages won't—for example, generalized linear models, `glm()`, in base R. The functionality built into `mlr` allows you to run a number of techniques for supervised and unsupervised learning. However, leveraging its power the first couple of times you use it can be a little confusing. If you follow the process outlined in the following, you'll be well on your way to developing powerful learning pipelines. We'll be using random forest in this demonstration. You can see the full list of models available here, plus you can utilize your own: `https://mlr-org.github.io/mlr-tutorial/release/html/integrated_learners/index.html`.

We've created the training and testing sets, which you can do in `mlr`, but I still prefer the technique we've been doing using the `caret` package. One of the unique things about the `mlr` package is that you have to put your training data into a task structure, specifically, in this problem, a classification task. Optionally, you can place your test set in a task as well. You specify the dataset and the target containing the labels:

```
> dna_task <- mlr::makeClassifTask(data = train, target = "Class")
```

There are many ways to use `mlr` in your analysis, but I recommend creating a resample object.

In the following code block, we create a resampling object to help us in tuning the number of trees for our random forest, consisting of five subsamples. Keep in mind that you have similar flexibility in the resampling method just like the `caret` package with techniques such as cross-validation and repeated cross-validation:

```
> rdesc <- mlr::makeResampleDesc("Subsample", iters = 5)
```

The next object establishes the grid of trees for tuning with the minimum number of trees, set to 50, and the maximum set to 200. You can also establish multiple parameters as we did with the `caret` package. Your options can be explored by calling help for the function with `makeParamSet`:

```
> param <-
+ ParamHelpers::makeParamSet(ParamHelpers::makeDiscreteParam("ntree",
values = c(50, 75, 100, 150, 175, 200)))
```

Next, create a control object, establishing a numeric grid:

```
> ctrl <- makeTuneControlGrid()
```

With the preliminary objects created, we can now go ahead and tune the hyperparameter for the optimal number of trees in the random forest, as per our grid. Notice that we're specifying `classif.randomForest`. The previous link on the available models of `mlr` gives us all of the proper syntax you use for your desired method. One thing we should do is bring the `mlr` library into the environment, so we can use that syntax. We also use the objects we just created:

```
> library(mlr)

> tuning <-
    mlr::tuneParams(
      "classif.randomForest",
      task = dna_task,
      resampling = rdesc,
      par.set = param,
      control = ctrl)
```

Once the algorithm completes its iterations, you can call up both the optimal number of trees and the associated out-of-sample error:

```
> tuning$x
$`ntree`
[1] 175

> tuning$y
mmce.test.mean
    0.04635294
```

The optimal number of trees as per our experiment grid is 175 with a mean misclassification error of 0.046 percent. It's now a simple matter of setting this parameter for training as a wrapper around the makeLearner() function. Notice that I set the predicted type to "prob" as the default is the predicted class and not the probability:

```
> rf <-
    mlr::setHyperPars(mlr::makeLearner("classif.randomForest", predict.type
= "prob"),
    par.vals = tuning$x)
```

Now we train the model again with just 175 trees:

```
> fit_rf <- mlr::train(rf, dna_task)
```

You can see the confusion matrix on the train data:

```
> fit_rf$learner.model

        OOB estimate of error rate: 5.14%
Confusion matrix:
     ei  ie    n class.error
ei 563  26   25 0.08306189
ie  16 575   21 0.06045752
n   10  33 1281 0.03247734
```

That's better than I expected with an out-of-bag error of just over 5%. Also, there is no error for a class that's way out of balance. Additionally, it performs pretty well on the test data:

```
> mlr::calculateConfusionMatrix(pred)
        predicted
true     ei  ie    n -err.-
  ei    139   4   10     14
  ie      3 147    3      6
  n       2   3  325      5
  -err.-  5   7   13     25
```

The package has a full set of metrics available. Here, I pull up the test accuracy and log-loss:

```
> mlr::performance(pred, measures = list(acc, logloss))
      acc    logloss
0.9606918 0.2863458
```

It has an impressive 96% accuracy on the test set and a baseline log-loss of `0.286`. This leads us to the next step, where we see whether creating an ensemble by just combining the predictions of random forest and MARS can improve performance.

Creating an ensemble

Using the functionality of `mlr` again, we first need to create an object with our base learners. This is once again `classif.randomForest` and, for a MARS model, we call the `earth` package with `classif.earth`:

```
> base <- c("classif.randomForest", "classif.earth")
```

You now make a learner with those base learners, and then specify that you want the output of those learners as the predicted probability:

```
> learns <- lapply(base, makeLearner)

> learns <- lapply(learns, setPredictType, "prob")
```

The process of building the base learning object is complete. I stated earlier that the ensembling learning algorithm will be GLM from `glmnet`. For just two base learners, a CART might be more appropriate, but let's demonstrate what's possible. There are a number of methods for stacking. In the following code block, I stack with cross-validation:

```
> sl <-
    mlr::makeStackedLearner(
    base.learners = learns,
    super.learner = "classif.glmnet",
    predict.type = "prob",
    method = "stack.cv"
  )
```

Now, it gets exciting as we train our stacked model:

```
stacked_fit <- mlr::train(sl, dna_task)
```

And we establish the predicted probabilities for the test data:

```
> prod_stacked <- predict(stacked_fit, newdata = test)
```

Just for a sanity check, let's look at the confusion matrix:

```
> mlr::calculateConfusionMatrix(pred_stacked)
        predicted
true     ei  ie   n -err.-
   ei   144   4   5      9
   ie     5 146   2      7
    n     2   1 327      3
 -err.-   7   5   7     19
```

The stacked model produced six fewer classification errors. The proof is in the metrics:

```
> mlr::performance(pred_stacked, measures = list(acc, logloss))
      acc    logloss
0.9701258 0.1101400
```

Of course, accuracy is better, but even better the log-loss improved substantially.

What have we learned? Using primarily one package, `mlr`, we built a good model with random forest, but by stacking random forest and MARS, we improved performance. Although all of that was with just a few lines of code, it's important to understand how to create and implement the pipeline.

Summary

In this chapter, we looked at very important machine learning methods for creating an ensemble model by stacking in the framework. In stacking, we used base models (learners) to create predicted probabilities that were used on input features to another model (a super learner) to make our final predictions. Indeed, the stacked method showed an improvement over the individual base model. We performed all of this using `mlr` (machine learn), which is a powerful tool for any R machine learning practitioner.

Up next, we're going to delve into the world of unsupervised learning, where we're not trying to predict a label or quantitative outcome, but rather to understand patterns in the observations or features.

9
Cluster Analysis

"Quickly bring me a beaker of wine, so that I may wet my mind and say something clever."

- Aristophanes, Athenian Playwright

In the earlier chapters, we focused on trying to learn the best algorithm in order to solve an outcome or response, for example, customer satisfaction or home prices. In all these cases, we had y, and that y is a function of x, or $y = f(x)$. In our data, we had the actual y values and we could train x accordingly. This is referred to as **supervised learning**. However, there are many situations where we try to learn something from our data, and either we do not have the y, or we actually choose to ignore it. If so, we enter the world of **unsupervised learning**. In this world, we build and select our algorithm based on how well it addresses our business needs versus how accurate it is.

Why would we try and learn without supervision? First of all, unsupervised learning can help you understand and identify patterns in your data, which may be valuable. Second, you can use it to transform your data in order to improve your supervised learning techniques.

This chapter will focus on the former and the next chapter on the latter.

So, let's begin by tackling a popular and powerful technique known as **cluster analysis**. With cluster analysis, the goal is to group the observations into a number of groups (k-groups), where the members in a group are as similar as possible while the members between groups are as different as possible. There are many examples of how this can help an organization; here are just a few:

- The creation of customer types or segments
- The detection of high-crime areas in a geography
- Image and facial recognition
- Genetic sequencing and transcription
- Petroleum and geological exploration

There are many uses of cluster analysis, but there are also many techniques. We will focus on the two most common: **hierarchical** and **k-means**. They are both effective clustering methods, but may not always be appropriate for the large and varied datasets that you may be called upon to analyze. Therefore, we will also examine **partitioning around medoids (PAM)** using a **Gower-based** metric dissimilarity matrix as the input. Finally, we will examine a new methodology I recently learned and applied using **random forest** to transform your data. The transformed data can then be used as an input to unsupervised learning.

A final comment before moving on: you may be asked whether these techniques are more art than science, as the learning is unsupervised. I think the clear answer is, *it depends*. In early 2016, I presented the methods here at a meeting of the Indianapolis, Indiana R-User Group. To a person, we all agreed that it is the judgment of the analysts and the business users that makes unsupervised learning meaningful and determines whether you have, say, three versus four clusters in your final algorithm. This quote sums it up nicely:

> *"The major obstacle is the difficulty in evaluating a clustering algorithm without taking into account the context: why does the user cluster his data in the first place, and what does he want to do with the clustering afterwards? We argue that clustering should not be treated as an application-independent mathematical problem, but should always be studied in the context of its end-use."*

- Luxburg et al. (2012)

The following are the topics that we will be covering in this chapter:

- Hierarchical clustering
- K-means clustering
- Gower and PAM
- Random forests
- Dataset background
- Data understanding and preparation
- Modeling

Hierarchical clustering

The hierarchical clustering algorithm is based on a dissimilarity measure between observations. A common measure, and what we will use, is **Euclidean distance**. Other distance measures are also available.

Hierarchical clustering is an agglomerative or bottom-up technique. By this, we mean that all observations are their own cluster. From there, the algorithm proceeds iteratively by searching all the pairwise points and finding the two clusters that are the most similar. So, after the first iteration, there are *n-1* clusters, and after the second iteration, there are *n-2* clusters, and so forth.

As the iterations continue, it is important to understand that in addition to the distance measure, we need to specify the linkage between the groups of observations. Different types of data will demand that you use different cluster linkages. As you experiment with the linkages, you may find that some create highly unbalanced numbers of observations in one or more clusters. For example, if you have 30 observations, one technique may create a cluster of just one observation, regardless of how many total clusters that you specify. In this situation, your judgment will likely be needed to select the most appropriate linkage as it relates to the data and business case.

The following table lists the types of common linkages, but note that there are others:

Linkage	Description
Ward	This minimizes the total within-cluster variance as measured by the sum of squared errors from the cluster points to its centroid.
Complete	The distance between two clusters is the maximum distance between an observation in one cluster and an observation in the other cluster.

Single	The distance between two clusters is the minimum distance between an observation in one cluster and an observation in the other cluster.
Average	The distance between two clusters is the mean distance between an observation in one cluster and an observation in the other cluster.
Centroid	The distance between two clusters is the distance between the cluster centroids.

The output of hierarchical clustering will be a **dendrogram**, which is a tree-like diagram that shows the arrangement of the various clusters.

As we will see, it can often be difficult to identify a clear-cut breakpoint in the selection of the number of clusters. Once again, your decision should be iterative in nature and focused on the context of the business decision.

Distance calculations

As mentioned previously, Euclidean distance is commonly used to build the input for hierarchical clustering. Let's look at a simple example of how to calculate it with two observations and two variables/features.

Let's say that observation *A* costs $5.00 and weighs 3 pounds. Further, observation *B* costs $3.00 and weighs 5 pounds. We can place these values in the distance formula: *distance between A and B is equal to the square root of the sum of the squared differences*, which in our example would be as follows:

$$d(A, B) = square\ root((5 - 3)^2 + (3 - 5)^2), \text{ which is equal to } 2.83$$

The value of *2.83* is not a meaningful value in and of itself, but is important in the context of the other pairwise distances. This calculation is the default in R for the `dist()` function. You can specify other distance calculations (maximum, manhattan, canberra, binary, and minkowski) in the function. We will avoid going in to detail on why or where you would choose these over Euclidean distance. This can get rather domain-specific; for example, a situation where Euclidean distance may be inadequate is where your data suffers from high-dimensionality, such as in a genomic study. It will take domain knowledge and/or trial and error on your part to determine the proper distance measure.

 One final note is to scale your data with a mean of zero and standard deviation of one, so that the distance calculations are comparable. If not, any variable with a larger scale will have a larger effect on distances.

K-means clustering

With k-means, we will need to specify the exact number of clusters that we want. The algorithm will then iterate until each observation belongs to just one of the k-clusters. The algorithm's goal is to minimize the within-cluster variation as defined by the squared Euclidean distances. So, the kth-cluster variation is the sum of the squared Euclidean distances for all the pairwise observations divided by the number of observations in the cluster.

Due to the iteration process that is involved, one k-means result can differ greatly from another result even if you specify the same number of clusters. Let's see how this algorithm plays out:

1. **Specify** the exact number of clusters you desire (k)
2. **Initialize:** k observations are randomly selected as the initial *means*
3. **Iterate**:
    - K clusters are created by assigning each observation to its closest cluster center (minimizing within-cluster sum of squares)
    - The centroid of each cluster becomes the new *mean*
    - This is repeated until convergence, that is, the cluster centroids do not change

As you can see, the final result will vary because of the initial assignment in step 1. Therefore, it is important to run multiple initial starts and let the software identify the best solution. In R, this can be a simple process, as we will see.

Gower and PAM

As you conduct clustering analysis in real life, one of the things that can quickly become apparent is the fact that neither hierarchical nor k-means is specifically designed to handle mixed datasets. By mixed data, I mean both quantitative and qualitative or, more specifically, nominal, ordinal, and interval/ratio data.

The reality of most datasets that you will use is that they will probably contain mixed data. There are a number of ways to handle this, such as doing **principal components analysis (PCA)** first in order to create latent variables, then using them as input in clustering or using different dissimilarity calculations. We will discuss PCA in the next chapter.

With the power and simplicity of R, you can use the **Gower dissimilarity coefficient** to turn mixed data to the proper feature space. In this method, you can even include factors as input variables. Additionally, instead of k-means, I recommend using the **PAM clustering algorithm**.

PAM is very similar to k-means but offers a couple of advantages. They are listed as follows:

1. First, PAM accepts a dissimilarity matrix, which allows the inclusion of mixed data
2. Second, it is more robust to outliers and skewed data because it minimizes a sum of dissimilarities, instead of a sum of squared Euclidean distances (Reynolds, 1992)

This is not to say that you must use Gower and PAM together. If you choose, you can use the Gower coefficients with hierarchical, and I've seen arguments for and against using it in the context of k-means. Additionally, PAM can accept other linkages. However, when paired, they make an effective method to handle mixed data. Let's take a quick look at both of these concepts before moving on.

Gower

The Gower coefficient compares cases pairwise and calculates a dissimilarity between them, which is essentially the weighted mean of the contributions of each variable. It is defined for two cases called i and j as follows:

$$S_{ij} = \text{sum}(W_{ijk} * S_{ijk}) / \text{sum}(W_{ijk})$$

Here, S_{ijk} is the contribution provided by the k_{th} variable, and W_{ijk} is 1 if the k_{th} variable is valid, or else 0.

For ordinal and continuous variables, $S_{ijk} = 1 - (absolute\ value\ of\ x_{ij} - x_{ik}) / r_k$, where r_k is the range of values for the k_{th} variable.

For nominal variables, $S_{ijk} = 1$ if $x_{ij} = x_{jk}$, or else 0.

For binary variables, S_{ijk} is calculated based on whether an attribute is present (+) or not present (-), as shown in the following table:

Variables	Value of attribute k			
Case i	+	+	-	-
Case j	+	-	+	-
Sijk	1	0	0	0
Wijk	1	1	1	0

PAM

For **PAM**, let's first define a **medoid**.

 A medoid is an observation of a cluster that minimizes the dissimilarity (in our case, calculated using the Gower metric) between the other observations in that cluster. So, similar to k-means, if you specify five clusters, you will have five partitions of the data.

With the objective of minimizing the dissimilarity of all the observations to the nearest medoid, the PAM algorithm iterates over the following steps:

1. Randomly select k observations as the initial medoid
2. Assign each observation to the closest medoid
3. Swap each medoid and non-medoid observation, computing the dissimilarity cost
4. Select the configuration that minimizes the total dissimilarity
5. Repeat steps 2 through 4 until there is no change in the medoids

Both Gower and PAM can be called using the `cluster` package in R. For Gower, we will use the `daisy()` function in order to calculate the dissimilarity matrix and the `pam()` function for the actual partitioning. With this, let's get started with putting these methods to the test.

Random forest

Like our motivation with the use of the Gower metric in handling mixed, in fact, *messy* data, we can apply random forest in an unsupervised fashion. Selecting this method has a number of advantages:

- Robust against outliers and highly skewed variables
- No need to transform or scale the data
- Handles mixed data (numeric and factors)
- Can accommodate missing data
- Can be used on data with a large number of variables; in fact, it can be used to eliminate useless features by examining variable importance
- The dissimilarity matrix produced serves as an input to the other techniques discussed earlier (hierarchical, k-means, and PAM)

A couple of words of caution. It may take some trial and error to properly tune the random forest with respect to the number of variables sampled at each tree split (`mtry = ?` in the function) and the number of trees grown. Studies done show that the more trees grown, up to a point, provide better results, and a good starting point is to grow 2,000 trees (Shi, T. & Horvath, S., 2006).

This is how the algorithm works, given a dataset with no labels:

- The current observed data is labeled as class 1
- A second (synthetic) set of observations is created of the same size as the observed data; this is created by randomly sampling from each of the features from the observed data, so if you have 20 observed features, you will have 20 synthetic features
- The synthetic portion of the data is labeled as class 2, which facilitates using random forest as an artificial classification problem
- Create a random forest model to distinguish between the two classes
- Turn the model's proximity measures of just the observed data (the synthetic data is now discarded) into a dissimilarity matrix
- Utilize the dissimilarity matrix as the clustering input features

So what exactly are these proximity measures?

 A proximity measure is a pairwise measure between all the observations. If two observations end up in the same terminal node of a tree, their proximity score is equal to one, otherwise zero.

At the termination of the random forest run, the proximity scores for the observed data are normalized by dividing by the total number of trees. The resulting NxN matrix contains scores between zero and one, naturally with the diagonal values all being one. That's all there is to it. An effective technique that I believe is underutilized and one that I wish I had learned years ago.

Dataset background

Until a year ago, I was unaware that there were less than 300 certified Master Sommeliers in the entire world. The exam, administered by the Court of Master Sommeliers, is notorious for its demands and high failure rate.

The trials, tribulations, and rewards of several individuals pursuing the certification are detailed in the critically acclaimed documentary, *Somm*. So, for this exercise, we will try and help a hypothetical individual struggling to become a Master Sommelier find a latent structure in Italian wines.

Data understanding and preparation

Let's start with installing the R packages needed for this chapter, if you have not done so already:

```
> library(magrittr)

> install.packages("cluster")

> install.packages("dendextend")

> install.packages("ggthemes")

> install.packages("HDclassif")

> install.packages("NbClust")

> install.packages("tidyverse")

> options(scipen=999)
```

The dataset is in the `HDclassif` package. Load the data and examine the structure with the `str()` function:

```
> library(HDclassif)

> data(wine)

> str(wine)
'data.frame': 178 obs. of 14 variables:
 $ class: int 1 1 1 1 1 1 1 1 1 1 ...
 $ V1 : num 14.2 13.2 13.2 14.4 13.2 ...
 $ V2 : num 1.71 1.78 2.36 1.95 2.59 1.76 1.87 2.15 1.64 1.35 ...
 $ V3 : num 2.43 2.14 2.67 2.5 2.87 2.45 2.45 2.61 2.17 2.27 ...
 $ V4 : num 15.6 11.2 18.6 16.8 21 15.2 14.6 17.6 14 16 ...
 $ V5 : int 127 100 101 113 118 112 96 121 97 98 ...
 $ V6 : num 2.8 2.65 2.8 3.85 2.8 3.27 2.5 2.6 2.8 2.98 ...
 $ V7 : num 3.06 2.76 3.24 3.49 2.69 3.39 2.52 2.51 2.98 3.15 ...
 $ V8 : num 0.28 0.26 0.3 0.24 0.39 0.34 0.3 0.31 0.29 0.22 ...
 $ V9 : num 2.29 1.28 2.81 2.18 1.82 1.97 1.98 1.25 1.98 1.85 ...
 $ V10 : num 5.64 4.38 5.68 7.8 4.32 6.75 5.25 5.05 5.2 7.22 ...
 $ V11 : num 1.04 1.05 1.03 0.86 1.04 1.05 1.02 1.06 1.08 1.01 ...
 $ V12 : num 3.92 3.4 3.17 3.45 2.93 2.85 3.58 3.58 2.85 3.55 ...
 $ V13 : int 1065 1050 1185 1480 735 1450 1290 1295 1045 1045 ...
```

The data consists of 178 wines with 13 variables of the chemical composition and one variable, `Class`, the label for the cultivar or plant variety. We won't use this in the clustering, but as a test of model performance. The variables, `V1` through `V13`, are the measures of the chemical composition, as follows:

- `V1`: alcohol
- `V2`: malic acid
- `V3`: ash
- `V4`: alkalinity of ash
- `V5`: magnesium
- `V6`: total phenols
- `V7`: flavonoids
- `V8`: non-flavonoid phenols
- `V9`: proanthocyanidins
- `V10`: color intensity
- `V11`: hue
- `V12`: OD280/OD315
- `V13`: proline

The variables are all quantitative. We should rename them to something meaningful for our analysis. This is easily done with the `colnames()` function:

```
> colnames(winc) <- c(
    "Class",
    "Alcohol",
    "MalicAcid",
    "Ash",
    "Alk_ash",
    "magnesium",
    "T_phenols",
    "Flavanoids",
    "Non_flav",
    "Proantho",
    "C_Intensity",
    "Hue",
    "OD280_315",
    "Proline"
  )
```

As the variables are not scaled, we will need to do this using the `scale()` function. This will first center the data where the column mean is subtracted from each individual in the column. Then the centered values will be divided by the corresponding column's standard deviation. We can also use this transformation to make sure that we only include columns 2 through 14, dropping class and putting it in a data frame. This can all be done with one line of code:

```
> wine_df <- as.data.frame(scale(wine[, -1]))
```

Before moving on, and out of curiosity, let's do a quick table to see the distribution of the cultivars or `Class`:

```
> table(wine$Class)

 1  2  3
59 71 48
```

We can now move on to the unsupervised learning models.

Modeling

Having created our data frame, `df`, we can begin to develop the clustering algorithms. We will start with hierarchical and then try our hand at k-means. After this, we will need to manipulate our data a little bit to demonstrate how to incorporate mixed data with Gower and random forest.

Hierarchical clustering

To build a hierarchical cluster model in R, you can utilize the `hclust()` function in the base `stats` package. The two primary inputs needed for the function are a distance matrix and the clustering method. The distance matrix is easily done with the `dist()` function. For the distance, we will use Euclidean distance. A number of clustering methods are available, and the default for `hclust()` is complete linkage.

We will try this, but I also recommend Ward's linkage method. Ward's method tends to produce clusters with a similar number of observations.

The complete linkage method results in the distance between any two clusters, that is, the maximum distance between any one observation in a cluster and any one observation in the other cluster. Ward's linkage method seeks to cluster the observations in order to minimize the within-cluster sum of squares.

It is noteworthy that the R method `ward.D2` uses the squared Euclidean distance, which is indeed Ward's linkage method. In R, `ward.D` is available but requires your distance matrix to be squared values. As we will be building a distance matrix of non-squared values, we will require `ward.D2`.

Now, the big question is how many clusters should we create? As stated in the introduction, the short, and probably not very satisfying, answer is that it depends. Even though there are cluster validity measures to help with this dilemma – which we will look at – it really requires an intimate knowledge of the business context, underlying data, and, quite frankly, trial and error. As our sommelier partner is fictional, we will have to rely on the validity measures. However, that is no panacea to selecting the numbers of clusters as there are several dozen validity measures.

As exploring the positives and negatives of the vast array of cluster validity measures is way outside the scope of this chapter, we can turn to a couple of papers and even R itself to simplify this problem for us. A paper by Miligan and Cooper, 1985, explored the performance of 30 different measures/indices on simulated data. The top five performers were CH index, Duda Index, Cindex, Gamma, and Beale Index. Another well-known method to determine the number of clusters is the **gap statistic** (Tibshirani, Walther, and Hastie, 2001). These are two good papers for you to explore if your cluster validity curiosity gets the better of you.

With R, we can use the NbClust() function in the NbClust package to pull results on 23 indices, including the top five from Miligan and Cooper and the gap statistic. You can see a list of all the available indices in the help file for the package. There are two ways to approach this process: one is to pick your favorite index or indices and call them with R; the other is to include all of them in the analysis and go with the majority rules method, which the function summarizes for you nicely. The function will also produce a couple of plots as well.

With the stage set, let's walk through the example of using the complete linkage method. When using the function, you will need to specify the minimum and maximum number of clusters, distance measures, and indices in addition to the linkage. As you can see in the following code, we will create an object called numComplete. The function specifications are for Euclidean distance, minimum number of clusters two, maximum number of clusters six, complete linkage, and all indices. When you run the command, the function will automatically produce an output similar to what you can see here—a discussion on both the graphical methods and majority rules conclusion:

```
> numComplete <- NbClust::NbClust(
    wine_df,
    distance = "euclidean",
    min.nc = 2,
    max.nc = 6,
    method = "complete",
    index = "all"
 )
*** : The Hubert index is a graphical method of determining the number of
clusters.
  In the plot of Hubert index, we seek a significant knee that corresponds
to a
  significant increase of the value of the measure that is, the significant
peak in Hubert
  index second differences plot.

*** : The D index is a graphical method of determining the number of
clusters.
  In the plot of D index, we seek a significant knee (the significant peak
```

```
in Dindex
 second differences plot) that corresponds to a significant increase of the
value of
 the measure.
********************************************************************
* Among all indices:
* 1 proposed 2 as the best number of clusters
* 11 proposed 3 as the best number of clusters
* 6 proposed 5 as the best number of clusters
* 5 proposed 6 as the best number of clusters

 ***** Conclusion *****
* According to the majority rule, the best number of clusters is 3
********************************************************************
```

Going with the majority rules method, we would select three clusters as the optimal solution, at least for hierarchical clustering. The two plots that are produced contain two graphs each. As the preceding output states, you are looking for a significant knee in the plot (the graph on the left-hand side) and the peak of the graph on the right-hand side. This is the **Hubert Index** plot:

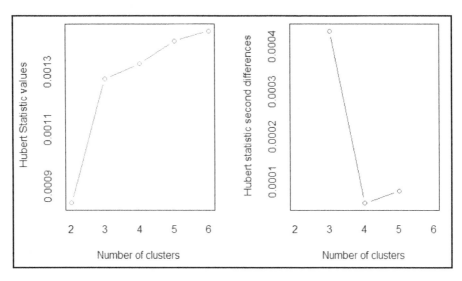

You can see that the bend or knee is at three clusters in the graph on the left-hand side. Additionally, the graph on the right-hand side has its peak at three clusters. The following **Dindex** plot provides the same information:

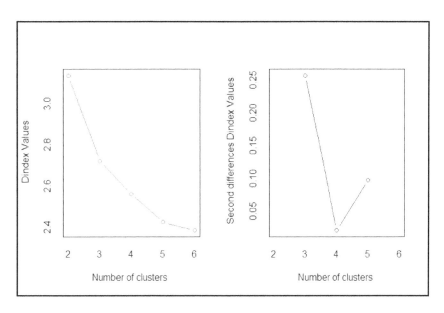

There are a number of values that you can call with the function and there is one that I would like to show. This output is the best number of clusters for each index and the index value for that corresponding number of clusters. This is done with $Best.nc. I've abbreviated the output to the first few indices:

```
> numComplete$Best.nc
                       KL        CH Hartigan    CCC     Scott
Number_clusters   5.0000    3.0000   3.0000  5.000    3.0000
Value_Index      14.2227   48.9898  27.8971  1.148  340.9634
```

You can see that the first index, KL, has the optimal number of clusters as five and the next index, CH, has it as three.

With three clusters as the recommended selection, we will now compute the distance matrix and build our hierarchical cluster object. This builds the distance matrix:

```
> euc_dist <- dist(wine_df, method = "euclidean")
```

Then, we will use this matrix as the input for the actual clustering with `hclust()`:

```
> hc_complete <- hclust(euc_dist, method = "complete")
```

The common way to visualize hierarchical clustering is to plot a **dendrogram**. We will do this with the functionality provided by the `dendextend` package:

```
> dend1 <- dendextend::color_branches(dend_complete, k = 3)
```

```
> plot(dend1, main = "Complete-Linkage")
```

The output of the preceding code is as follows:

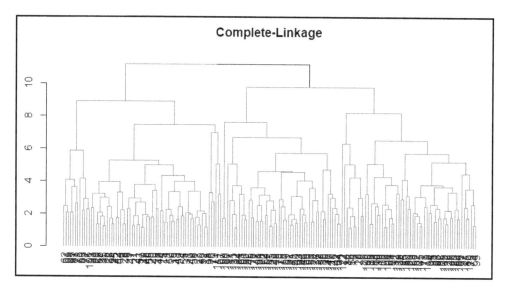

The dendrogram is a tree diagram that shows you how the individual observations are clustered together. The arrangement of the connections (branches, if you will) tells us which observations are similar. The height of the branches indicates how much the observations are similar or dissimilar to each other from the distance matrix.

Here is the table of cluster counts:

```
> complete_clusters <- cutree(hc_complete, 3)

> table(complete_clusters)
complete_clusters
 1  2  3
69 58 51
```

Out of curiosity, let's compare how this clustering algorithm compares to the **cultivar** labels:

```
> table(complete_clusters, wine$Class)
complete_clusters  1   2   3
                1 51  18   0
                2  8  50   0
                3  0   3  48
```

In this table, the rows are the clusters and columns are the cultivars. This method matched the cultivar labels at an 84 percent rate. Note that we are not trying to use the clusters to predict a cultivar, and in this example, we have no a priori reason to match clusters to the cultivars, but it is revealing nonetheless.

We will now try Ward's linkage. This is the same code as before; it first starts with trying to identify the number of clusters, which means that we will need to change the method to `Ward.D2`:

```
> numWard <- NbClust::NbClust(
    wine_df,
    distance = "euclidean",
    min.nc = 2,
    max.nc = 6,
    method = "ward.D2",
    index = "all"
)
# Output abbreviated to just show the algorithm's conclusion.
                  ***** Conclusion *****
    * According to the majority rule, the best number of clusters is 3
```

Once again, the majority rules were for a three-cluster solution. I'll let you peruse the plots on your own.

Let's move on to the actual clustering and production of the dendrogram for Ward's linkage:

```
> hc_ward <- hclust(euc_dist, method = "ward.D2")

> dend_ward <- as.dendrogram(hc_ward)

> dend2 <- dendextend::color_branches(dend_ward, k = 3)

> plot(dend2, main = "Ward Method")
```

This is the output:

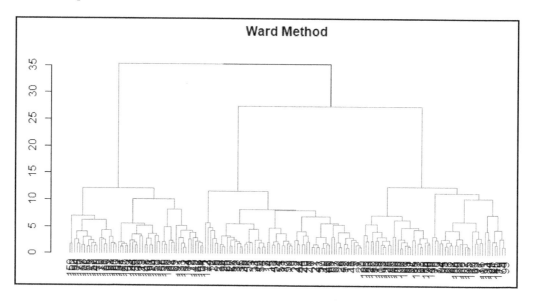

The plot shows three pretty distinct clusters that are roughly equal in size. Let's get a count of the cluster size and show it in relation to the cultivar labels:

```
> ward_clusters <- cutree(hc_ward, 3)

> table(ward_clusters, wine$Class)
ward_clusters  1   2   3
            1 59   5   0
            2  0  58   0
            3  0   8  48
```

So, cluster one has 64 observations, cluster two has 58, and cluster three has 56. This method matches the cultivar categories closer than using complete linkage.

With another table, we can compare how the two methods match observations:

```
> table(complete_clusters, ward_clusters)
                   ward_clusters
complete_clusters  1   2   3
               1  53  11   5
               2  11  47   0
               3   0   0  51
```

While cluster three for each method is exact, the other two are not. The question now is how do we identify what the differences are for the interpretation? In many examples, the datasets are very small and you can look at the labels for each cluster. In the real world, this is often impossible. I like to aggregate results by cluster and compare accordingly.

Putting aggregated results by cluster into an interactive spreadsheet or business intelligence tool facilitates understanding by you and your business partners, helping to select the appropriate clustering method and number of clusters.

I'm going to demonstrate this by looking at the mean of the features grouped by the clusters from Ward's method. First, create a separate data frame with the scaled data (or original data, if you prefer) and the results:

```
> ward_df <- wine_df %>%
    dplyr::mutate(cluster = ward_clusters)
```

Now, do the aggregation:

```
> ward_df %>%
    dplyr::group_by(cluster) %>%
    dplyr::summarise_all(dplyr::funs(mean)) -> ward_results
```

You now can view that data frame in RStudio, or export it to your favorite BI tool. Maybe you are interested in a plot? If so, give this a try:

```
> ggplot2::ggplot(ward_results, ggplot2::aes(cluster, Alcohol)) +
    ggplot2::geom_bar(stat = "identity") +
    ggthemes::theme_stata()
```

This is the output:

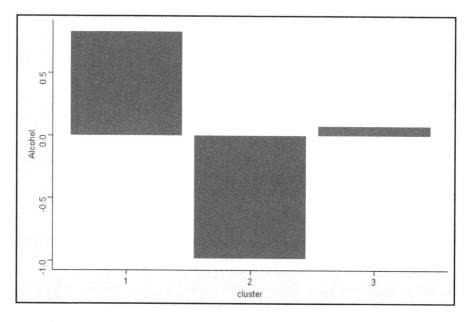

A clear separation exists between the clusters in alcohol content. With that said, let's move on to k-means.

K-means clustering

As we did with hierarchical clustering, we can also use NbClust() to determine the optimum number of clusters for k-means. All you need to do is specify kmeans as the method in the function. Let's also loosen up the maximum number of clusters to 15. I've abbreviated the following output to just the conclusion:

```
> numKMeans <- NbClust::NbClust(wine_df,
    min.nc = 2,
    max.nc = 15,
    method = "kmeans")
***** Conclusion *****

* According to the majority rule, the best number of clusters is 3
```

Once again, three clusters appears to be the optimum solution.

In R, we can use the kmeans() function to do this analysis. In addition to the input data, we have to specify the number of clusters we are solving for and a value for random assignments, the nstart argument. We will also need to specify a random seed:

```
> set.seed(1234)
> km <- kmeans(df, 3, nstart = 25)
```

Creating a table of the clusters gives us a sense of the distribution of the observations between them:

```
> table(km$cluster)
 1   2   3
62  65  51
```

The number of observations per cluster is well balanced. I have seen on a number of occasions with larger datasets and many more features that no number of k-means yields a promising and compelling result. Another way to analyze the clustering is to look at a matrix of the cluster centers for each variable in each cluster:

```
> km$centers
     Alcohol   MalicAcid        Ash    Alk_ash   magnesium    T_phenols
1  0.8328826 -0.3029551  0.3636801 -0.6084749  0.57596208   0.88274724
2 -0.9234669 -0.3929331 -0.4931257  0.1701220 -0.49032869  -0.07576891
3  0.1644436  0.8690954  0.1863726  0.5228924 -0.07526047  -0.97657548
    Flavanoids    Non_flav    Proantho C_Intensity        Hue   OD280_315
1   0.97506900 -0.56050853  0.57865427   0.1705823  0.4726504   0.7770551
2   0.02075402 -0.03343924  0.05810161  -0.8993770  0.4605046   0.2700025
3  -1.21182921  0.72402116 -0.77751312   0.9388902 -1.1615122  -1.2887761
       Proline
1   1.1220202
2  -0.7517257
3  -0.4059428
```

Note that cluster one has, on average, a higher alcohol content. Let's produce a box plot to look at the distribution of alcohol content and compare it to Ward's:

```
> par(mfrow = c(1, 2))

> boxplot(wine$Alcohol ~ km$cluster, data = wine,
    main = "Alcohol Content, K-Means")

> boxplot(wine$Alcohol ~ ward_clusters, data = wine,
    main = "Alcohol Content, Ward's")
```

This is the output:

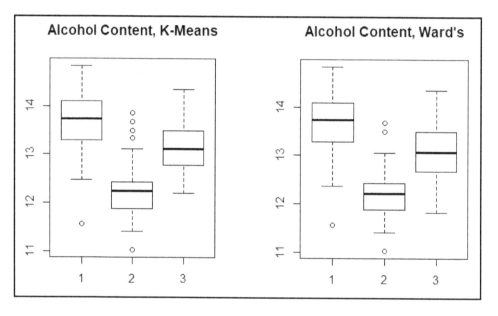

The alcohol content for each cluster is almost exactly the same. On the surface, this tells me that three clusters is the proper latent structure for the wines and there is little difference between using k-means or hierarchical clustering. Finally, let's do a comparison of the k-means clusters versus the cultivars:

```
> table(km$cluster, wine$Class)
      1   2   3
  1  59   3   0
  2   0  65   0
  3   0   3  48
```

This is very similar to the distribution produced by Ward's method, and either one would probably be acceptable to our hypothetical sommelier.

However, to demonstrate how you can cluster on data with both numeric and non-numeric values, let's work through some more examples.

Gower and PAM

To begin this step, we will need to wrangle our data a little bit. As this method can take variables that are factors, we will convert alcohol to either high or low content. It also takes only one line of code utilizing the `ifelse()` function to change the variable to a factor. What this will accomplish is if alcohol is greater than zero, it will be `High`, otherwise, it will be `Low`:

```
> wine_df$Alcohol <- as.factor(ifelse(df$Alcohol > 0, "High", "Low"))
```

We are now ready to create the dissimilarity matrix using the `daisy()` function from the `cluster` package and specifying the method as `gower`:

```
> gower_dist <- cluster::daisy(wine[, -1], metric = "gower")
```

The creation of the cluster object is done with the `pam()` function, which is a part of the `cluster` package. We will create three clusters in this example and create a table of the cluster size:

```
> set.seed(123)

> pam_cluster <- cluster::pam(gower_dist, k = 3)

> table(pam_cluster$clustering)

 1  2  3
62 71 45
```

Now, let's see how it does compared to the cultivar labels:

```
> table(pam_cluster$clustering, wine$Class)
     1   2   3
  1 57   5   0
  2  2  64   5
  3  0   2  43
```

You can run a similar aggregation and exploration exercise with this method as described previously. Let's see how the distribution of alcohol is across the three clusters:

```
> table(pam_cluster$clustering, wine$Alcohol)
   High Low
1    62   0
2     1  70
3    29  16
```

This table shows the proportion of the factor levels by the cluster. The Gower metric is very powerful for data with labels, factors, characters, missing values, and so on. I highly recommend it. One of the drawbacks with any distance matrix is that it can become a computational problem with large datasets. An effective solution is to run k-samples and compare results. Done well, you can then build a classifier to predict the cluster for your population.

Finally, we'll create a dissimilarity matrix with random forest and create three clusters with PAM.

Random forest and PAM

To perform this method in R, you can use the `randomForest()` function. After setting the random seed, simply create the model object. In the following code, I specify the number of trees as 2000 and set proximity measure to TRUE. You don't have to run this on scaled data:

```
> set.seed(1918)

> rf <- randomForest::randomForest(x = wine[, -1], ntree = 2000, proximity
= T)

> rf

Call:
 randomForest(x = wine[, -1], ntree = 2000, proximity = T)
               Type of random forest: unsupervised
                     Number of trees: 2000
No. of variables tried at each split: 3
```

As you can see, placing a call to rf did not provide any meaningful output other than the variables sampled at each split (mtry). Let's examine the first five rows and first five columns of the *N x N* matrix:

```
> dim(rf$proximity)
[1] 178 178

> rf$proximity[1:5, 1:5]
           1          2         3          4          5
1 1.0000000 0.27868852 0.4049296 0.36200717 0.12969283
2 0.2786885 1.00000000 0.2142857 0.12648221 0.04453441
3 0.4049296 0.21428571 1.0000000 0.26865672 0.14942529
4 0.3620072 0.12648221 0.2686567 1.00000000 0.07692308
5 0.1296928 0.04453441 0.1494253 0.07692308 1.00000000
```

One way to think of the values is that they are the percentage of times those two observations show up in the same terminal nodes! Looking at variable importance, we see that the transformed Alcohol input could possibly be dropped. We will keep it for simplicity:

```
> randomForest::importance(rf)
            MeanDecreaseGini
Alcohol             3.692748
MalicAcid          12.650096
Ash                10.842885
Alk_ash            11.636227
magnesium          10.672465
T_phenols          17.733783
Flavanoids         21.410838
Non_flav           11.527873
Proantho           14.494229
C_Intensity        14.795900
Hue                14.296274
OD280_315          17.815508
Proline            15.922621
```

It is now just a matter of creating the dissimilarity matrix, which transforms the proximity values (*square root(1 - proximity)*) as follows:

```
> rf_dist <- sqrt(1 - rf$proximity)

> rf_dist[1:2, 1:2]
          1         2
1 0.0000000 0.8493006
2 0.8493006 0.0000000
```

We now have our input features, so let's run a PAM clustering as we did earlier:

```
> set.seed(1776)

> pam_rf <- cluster::pam(rf_dist, k = 3)

> table(pam_rf$clustering)

 1  2  3
52 82 44

> table(pam_rf$clustering, wine$Class)
     1  2  3
  1 52  0  0
  2  7 70  5
  3  0  1 43
```

These results are comparable to the other techniques applied. Lesson learned here? If you have messy data for a clustering problem, consider using random forest to create a distance matrix, and even eliminate features from your clustering algorithm.

Summary

In this chapter, we started exploring unsupervised learning techniques. We focused on cluster analysis to both provide data reduction and data understanding of the observations.

Four methods were introduced: the traditional hierarchical and k-means clustering algorithms, along with PAM, incorporating two different inputs (Gower and random forest). We applied these four methods to find a structure in Italian wines coming from three different cultivars and examined the results.

In the next chapter, we will continue exploring unsupervised learning, but instead of finding structure among the observations, we will focus on finding structure among the variables in order to create new features that can be used in a supervised learning problem.

10
Principal Component Analysis

"The only easy day was yesterday."

- A Special Forces motivational saying

This chapter is the second one where we will focus on unsupervised learning techniques. In the previous chapter, we covered cluster analysis, which provides us with the groupings of similar observations. In this chapter, we will see how to reduce the dimensionality and improve the understanding of our data by grouping the correlated variables with **principal components analysis (PCA)**. Then, we will use the principal components in supervised learning.

In many datasets, particularly in the social sciences, you will see many variables highly correlated with each other. They may additionally suffer from high-dimensionality or, as it is better known, the **curse of dimensionality**. This is a problem because the number of samples needed to estimate a function grows exponentially with the number of input features. In such datasets, it may be the case that some variables are redundant as they end up measuring the same constructs, for example, income and poverty or depression and anxiety. The goal then is to use PCA in order to create a smaller set of variables that capture most of the information from the original set of variables, thus simplifying the dataset and often leading to hidden insights. These new variables (principal components) are highly uncorrelated with each other. In addition to supervised learning, it is also very common to use these components to perform data visualization.

From over a decade of either doing or supporting analytics using PCA, it has been my experience that it is widely used but poorly understood, especially among people who don't do the analysis but consume the results. It is intuitive to understand that you are creating a new variable from the other correlated variables. However, the technique itself is shrouded in potentially misunderstood terminology and mathematical concepts that often bewilder the layperson. The intention here is to provide a good foundation on what it is and how to use it by covering the following:

- Preparing a dataset for PCA
- Conducting PCA
- Selecting our principal components
- Building a predictive model using principal components
- Making out-of-sample predictions using the predictive model

An overview of the principal components

PCA is the process of finding the principal components. What exactly are these?

We can consider that a component is a normalized linear combination of the features (James, 2012). The first principal component in a dataset is the linear combination that captures the maximum variance in the data. A second component is created by selecting another linear combination that maximizes the variance with the constraint that its direction is perpendicular to the first component. The subsequent components (equal to the number of variables) would follow this same rule.

A couple of things here. This definition describes the **linear combination**, which is one of the key assumptions in PCA. If you ever try and apply PCA to a dataset of variables having a low correlation, you will likely end up with a meaningless analysis. Another key assumption is that the mean and variance for a variable are sufficient statistics. What this tells us is that the data should fit a normal distribution so that the covariance matrix fully describes our dataset, that is, **multivariate normality**. PCA is fairly robust to non-normally distributed data and is even used in conjunction with binary variables, so the results are still interpretable.

Now, what is this direction described here and how is the linear combination determined? The best way to grasp this subject is with visualization. Let's take a small dataset with two variables and plot it. PCA is sensitive to scale, so the data has been scaled with a mean of zero and standard deviation of one. You can see in the following diagram that this data happens to form the shape of an oval with the diamonds representing each observation:

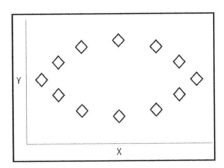

Looking at the plot, the data has the most variance along the x axis, so we can draw a dashed horizontal line to represent our **first principal component**, as shown in the following diagram. This component is the linear combination of our two variables or $PC1 = \alpha_{11}X_1 + \alpha_{12}X_2$, where the coefficient weights are the variable loading on the principal component. They form the basis of the direction along which the data varies the most. This equation is constrained by *1* in order to prevent the selection of arbitrarily high values. Another way to look at this is that the dashed line minimizes the distance between itself and the data points. This distance is shown for a couple of points as arrows, as follows:

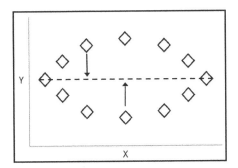

The **second principal component** is then calculated in the same way, but it is uncorrelated with the first, that is, its direction is at a right angle or orthogonal to the first principal component. The following plot shows the second principal component added as a dotted line:

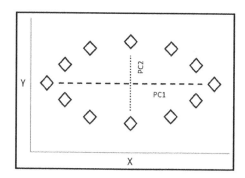

With the principal component loading calculated for each variable, the algorithm will then provide us with the principal component scores. The scores are calculated for each principal component for each observation. For **PC1** and the first observation, this would equate to the formula $Z_{11} = \alpha_{11} * (X_{11}$ - average of $X_1) + \alpha_{12} * (X_{12}$ - average of $X_2)$. For **PC2** and the first observation, the equation would be $Z_{12} = \alpha_{21} * (X_{11}$ - average of $X_2) + \alpha_{22} * (X_{12}$ - average of $X_2)$. These principal component scores are now the new feature space to be used in whatever analysis you will undertake.

Recall that the algorithm will create as many principal components as there are variables, accounting for 100 percent of the possible variance. So, how do we narrow down the components to achieve the original objective in the first place? There are some heuristics that one can use, and in the upcoming modeling process, we will look at the specifics; but a common method to select a principal component is if its **eigenvalue** is greater than one. While the algebra behind the estimation of eigenvalues and **eigenvectors** is outside the scope of this book, it is important to discuss what they are and how they are used in PCA.

The optimized linear weights are determined using linear algebra in order to create what is referred to as an eigenvector. They are optimal because no other possible combination of weights could explain variation better than they do. The eigenvalue for a principal component then is the total amount of variation that it explains in the entire dataset.

Recall that the equation for the first principal component is $PC1 = \alpha_{11}X_1 + \alpha_{12}X_2$.

As the first principal component accounts for the largest amount of variation, it will have the largest eigenvalue. The second component will have the second highest eigenvalue and so forth. So, an eigenvalue greater than one indicates that the principal component accounts for more variance than any of the original variables do by themselves. If you standardize the sum of all the eigenvalues to one, you will have the percentage of the total variance that each component explains. This will also aid you in determining a proper cut-off point.

The eigenvalue criterion is certainly not a hard-and-fast rule and must be balanced with your knowledge of the data and business problem at hand. Once you have selected the number of principal components, you can rotate them in order to simplify their interpretation.

Rotation

Should you rotate or not? As stated previously, rotation helps in the interpretation of the principal components by modifying the loading of each variable, but makes the results technically no longer a principal component. The overall variation explained by the rotated number of components will not change, but the contributions to the total variance explained by each component will change. What you will find by rotation is that the loading values will either move farther or closer to zero, theoretically aiding in identifying those variables that are important to each principal component. This is an attempt to associate a variable to only one principal component. Remember that this is unsupervised learning, so you are trying to understand your data, not test some hypothesis. In short, rotation aids you in this endeavor. I have seen both the non-rotated and rotated components used to calculate the loading. I like to use the rotated components.

The most common form of principal component rotation is known as **varimax**. There are other forms, such as **quartimax** and **equimax**, but we will focus on varimax rotation. In my experience, I've never seen the other methods provide better solutions. Trial and error on your part may be the best way to decide the issue.

 With varimax, we are maximizing the sum of the variances of the squared loading. The varimax procedure rotates the axis of the feature space and their coordinates without changing the locations of the data points.

Perhaps the best way to demonstrate this is via another simple illustration. Let's assume that we have a dataset of variables **A** through **G** and we have two principal components. Plotting this data, we will end up with the following diagram:

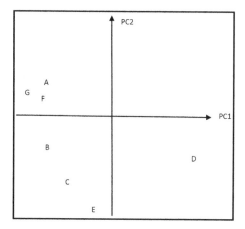

For the sake of argument, let's say that variable A's loading are -0.4 on **PC1** and 0.1 on **PC2**. Now, let's say that variable D's loading are 0.4 on **PC1** and -0.3 on **PC2**. For point E, the loading are -0.05 and -0.7, respectively. Note that the loading will follow the direction of the principal component. After running a varimax procedure, the rotated components will look as follows:

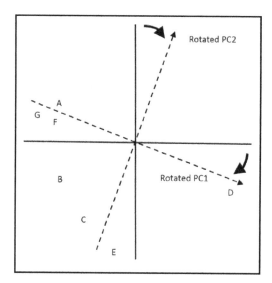

The following are the new loading on **PC1** and **PC2** after rotation:

- **Variable A**: -0.5 and 0.02
- **Variable D**: 0.5 and -0.3
- **Variable E**: 0.15 and -0.75

The loading have changed but the data points have not. With this simple illustration, we can't say that we have simplified the interpretation, but this should help you understand what is happening during the rotation of the principal components.

Data

We will be using what is referred to as the ANSUR dataset, which stands for US Army Anthropometric Survey. It consists of two separate files: one for female soldiers and one for male soldiers. I've combined the results into one dataset. You can download the data here: `https://github.com/datameister66/MMLR3rd/blob/master/army_ansur.RData`.

I found this data on a data repository site called `data.world`, which allows members to share any dataset they have of interest. For example, I have a version of the Gettysburg data we used in `Chapter 1`, *Preparing and Understanding Data*, on the site. This ANSUR data consists of research done by the **Natick Soldier Research, Development and Engineering Center** (**NSRDEC**) on over 6000 Active Duty, Reserve, and National Guard soldiers for the US Army. The features are of 93 different body measurements along with assorted demographic data. The US Army and contractors use this information to order the proper quantity and size of equipment, design new equipment, and so on. As you can imagine, many of these features are highly correlated, making this data perfect for PCA.

We'll put those body measurements through the PCA process, then use that to predict body weight in pounds, using a MARS model as we learned in prior chapters. Why soldier weight? Why not? We'll lump males and females together. We could use that data as an input feature, but I won't. Use age, race, gender, or the like in a model in the banking industry subject to review, and prepare to, at a minimum, answer some tough questions. OK, enough of the introduction, let's get cracking.

Data loading and review

To begin with, load the necessary packages:

```
> library(magrittr)

> install.packages("caret")

> install.packages("DataExplorer")

> install.packages("earth")

> install.packages("ggthemes")

> install.packages("psych")

> install.packages("tidyverse")

> options(scipen = 999)
```

Now, read the data into your environment:

```
> army_ansur <- readRDS("army_ansur.RData")
```

The feature names are fairly straightforward. Here, I just put in the last few features as output:

```
> colnames(army_ansur)
  [93] "wristcircumference"      "wristheight"
  [95] "Gender"                  "Date"
  [97] "Installation"            "Component"
  [99] "Branch"                  "PrimaryMOS"
 [101] "SubjectsBirthLocation"   "SubjectNumericRace"
 [103] "Ethnicity"               "DODRace"
 [105] "Age"                     "Heightin"
 [107] "Weightlbs"               "WritingPreference"
 [109] "SubjectId"
```

I'm interested in looking at the breakdown of the "Component" and "Gender" columns:

```
> table(army_ansur$Component)

Army National Guard    Army Reserve   Regular Army
               2708             220           3140
```

```
> table(army_ansur$Gender)

Female   Male
  1986   4082
```

If we look at missing values, we can see something of interest. Here is the abbreviated output:

```
> sapply(army_ansur, function(x) sum(is.na(x)))
        PrimaryMOS   SubjectsBirthLocation   SubjectNumericRace
                 0                       0                    0
          Ethnicity                 DODRace                  Age
              4647                       0                    0
          Heightin               Weightlbs     WritingPreference
                 0                       0                    0
         SubjectId
              4082
```

We have a bunch of missing subject IDs. Fine, let's take care of that right now:

```
> army_ansur$subjectid <- seq(1:6068)
```

Since weight is what we will predict after we build our unsupervised model, let's have a look at it:

```
> sjmisc::descr(army_ansur$Weightlbs)

## Basic descriptive statistics
 var    type label    n NA.prc  mean    sd   se  md trimmed       range
skew
  dd integer    dd 6068      0 174.8 33.69 0.43 173   173.4 321 (0-321)
0.39
```

Look at the range! We have someone who weighs zero. A plot of this data is in order, I believe:

```
> ggplot2::ggplot(army_ansur, ggplot2::aes(x = Weightlbs)) +
    ggplot2::geom_density() +
    ggthemes::theme_wsj()
```

The output of the preceding code is as follows:

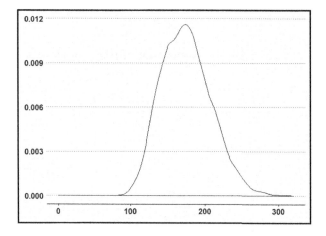

So, I would estimate we only have one or two observations of implausible weight values. Indeed, this code will confirm that assumption:

```
> dplyr::select(army_ansur, Weightlbs) %>%
    dplyr::arrange(Weightlbs)
# A tibble: 6,068 x 1
   Weightlbs
       <int>
 1         0
 2        86
 3        88
 4        90
 5        95
 6        95
 7        95
 8        96
 9        98
10       100
# ... with 6,058 more rows
```

Removing that observation is important:

```
> armyClean <- dplyr::filter(army_ansur, Weightlbs > 0)
```

We can now transition to bundling our features for PCA and creating training and testing dataframes.

Training and testing datasets

Here, we are going to put the numeric features into a dataframe along with the quantitative response. Then, we'll carve this up into train and test sets with an 80/20 split. As a closing effort, we'll scale the data, which is required for PCA.

Here, I grab those input features, including height in inches, while dropping weight in kilograms. I also include the `subjectid`:

```
> army_subset <- armyClean[, c(1:91, 93, 94, 106, 107)]
```

We've used the `dplyr` and `caret` packages to create train and test sets, and here I demonstrate the `dplyr` method:

```
> set.seed(1812)

> army_subset %>%
    dplyr::sample_frac(.8) -> train

> army_subset %>%
    dplyr::anti_join(train, by = "subjectid") -> test
```

I mentioned previously that this data had a number of high correlations. Even if you take just the first five features, that becomes clear:

```
> DataExplorer::plot_correlation(train[, 2:6])
```

The output of the preceding code is as follows:

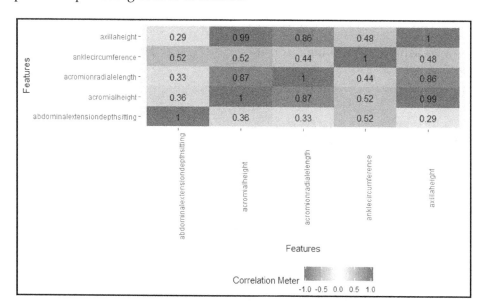

Axilla height and acromial height are 99 percent correlated. These refer to the armpit and point of the shoulder respectively.

We need to preserve the y-values for the training data. Additionally, we have to scale the data, that is, just the input features, so drop the `subjectid` and y-values:

```
> trainY <- train$Weightlbs

> train_scale <- data.frame(scale(train[, c(-1, -95)]))
```

With that complete, we can move on to creating principal components and using them in a supervised learning example.

PCA modeling

For the modeling process, we will use the following steps:

1. Extract the components and determine the number to retain
2. Rotate the retained components
3. Interpret the rotated solution
4. Create scores from the non-rotated components
5. Use the scores as input variables for regression analysis with MARS and evaluate the performance on the test data

There are many different ways and packages used to conduct PCA in R, including what seems to be the most commonly used `prcomp()` and `princomp()` functions in base R. However, for my money, it seems that the `psych` package is the most flexible with the best options.

Component extraction

To extract the components with the `psych` package, you will use the `principal()` function. The syntax will include the data and whether or not we want to rotate the components at this time:

```
> pca <- principal(train_scale, rotate = "none")
```

You can examine the components by calling the `pca` object that we created. However, my primary intent is to determine what should be the number of components to retain. For that, a scree plot will suffice. A scree plot can aid you in assessing the components that explain the most variance in the data. It shows the `Component` number on the *x* axis and their associated `Eigenvalues` on the *y* axis. For simplicity of interpretation, I include only the first 10 components:

```
> plot(pca$values[1:10], type = "b", ylab = "Eigenvalues", xlab =
"Component")
```

The following is the output of the preceding command:

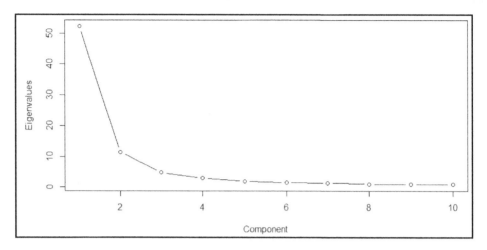

What you are looking for is a point in the scree plot where the rate of change decreases. This will be what is commonly called an elbow or bend in the plot. That elbow point in the plot captures the fact that additional variance explained by a component does not differ greatly from one component to the next. In other words, it is the breakpoint where the plot flattens out. In the plot, maybe four, five, or six components looks compelling. I think more information is needed. Here, we can see the eigenvalues of those 10 components. A rule of thumb recommends selecting all components with an eigenvalue greater than 1:

```
> head(pca$values, 10)
 [1] 52.2361 11.3294 4.7375 3.0193 1.9830 1.5153 1.2896 1.0655 1.0275
[10]  0.9185
```

Another rule I've learned over the years is that you should capture about 70 percent of the total variance, which means that the cumulative variance explained by each of the selected components accounts for 70 percent of the variance explained by all the components. That is pretty simple to do. I'm inclined to go with five components:

```
> sum(pca$values)
[1] 93

> sum(pca$values[1:5])
[1] 73.31
```

We are capturing 79 percent of the total variance with just 5 components. Let's put that together:

```
> pca_5 <- psych::principal(train_scale, nfactors = 5, rotate = "none")
```

Calling the object gives a number of results. Here are the abbreviated results for the top portion of the output:

```
> pca_5
Principal Components Analysis
Call: psych::principal(r = train_scale, nfactors = 5, rotate = "none")
Standardized loading (pattern matrix) based upon correlation matrix
                                PC1    PC2  PC3   PC4    PC5   h2    u2  com
abdominalextensiondepthsitting 0.58  0.66 0.09 -0.08 -0.26 0.85 0.146 2.4
acromialheight                 0.92 -0.27 0.13  0.19 -0.03 0.98 0.025 1.3
acromionradialelength          0.84 -0.29 0.16 -0.04 -0.11 0.83 0.167 1.4
anklecircumference             0.67  0.34 0.00  0.02  0.34 0.69 0.314 2.0
```

Here, we see the feature loading on each of the five components. For example, `acromialheight` has the highest positive loading of the features on component 1. Here, I paste the part of the output that shows the sum of squares:

```
                      PC1    PC2   PC3  PC4  PC5
SS loading          52.24 11.33 4.74 3.02 1.98
Proportion Var       0.56  0.12 0.05 0.03 0.02
Cumulative Var       0.56  0.68 0.73 0.77 0.79
Proportion Explained 0.71  0.15 0.06 0.04 0.03
Cumulative Proportion 0.71 0.87 0.93 0.97 1.00
```

Here, the numbers are the eigenvalues for each component. When they are normalized, you will end up with the `Proportion Explained` row, which, as you may have guessed, stands for the proportion of the variance explained by each component. You can see that principal component 1 explains 56 percent of all the variance explained by the five components. Remember we previously examined the heuristic rule that your selected components should account for a minimum of 70 percent of the total variation. The `Cumulative Var` row shows the cumulative variance is 79 percent, as demonstrated previously.

Orthogonal rotation and interpretation

As we discussed previously, the point behind rotation is to maximize the loading of the variables on a specific component, which helps in simplifying the interpretation by reducing/eliminating the correlation among these components. The method to conduct orthogonal rotation is known as **varimax**. There are other non-orthogonal rotation methods that allow correlation across factors/components. The choice of the rotation methodology that you will use in your profession should be based on the pertinent literature, which exceeds the scope of this chapter. Feel free to experiment with this dataset. I think that when in doubt, the starting point for any PCA should be an orthogonal rotation.

For this process, we will simply turn back to the `principal()` function, slightly changing the syntax to account for five components and orthogonal rotation, as follows:

```
> pca_rotate <- psych::principal(train_scale, nfactors = 5, rotate =
"varimax")
```

Given the number of features, I just normally save this into a CSV file and examine it in a spreadsheet, in particular with a subject matter expert. Here, we save it and I'll come back with what are high-level summaries. When I worked in oncology market research, we always ended up with a component around the drug's efficacy, one around the drug's side effect profile, and then maybe one or two components regarding dosing, cost, or something of that ilk. The code here just removes the crazy `loading` class from the object so we can save it as a dataframe:

```
> pca_loading <- unclass(pca_rotate$loading)

> pca_loading <- data.frame(pca_loading)

> pca_loading$features <- row.names(pca_loading)

> readr::write_csv(pca_loading, "pca_loading.csv")
```

Welcome back! There is no correct answer, but my guess as to how to summarize these components would be something like this:

- **PC1**: A catchall component; 44 features have loading higher than 0.5
- **PC2**: Hips, thighs, and buttocks...with a dash of waist and chest
- **PC3**: Neck, shoulders, arms
- **PC4**: Some height measures
- **PC5**: Oddly enough, head and foot measures

This can be a fun exercise naming the components. I fondly recall the days of naming such components compassionate conservatives, pragmatic practitioners, and so on. Be that as it may, we need to create scores from these components so we can give supervised learning a go.

Creating scores from the components

We will now need to capture the component loading as the scores for each observation. These scores indicate how each observation (soldier) relates to a component. Let's do this and capture the scores in a dataframe as we will need to use it for our analysis:

```
> pca_scores <- data.frame(round(pca_5$scores, digits = 2))

> head(pca_scores)
    PC1   PC2   PC3   PC4   PC5
1 -1.37  0.29  1.06  0.09  0.29
2 -1.19 -0.45 -0.22 -1.61  0.22
3 -0.04 -1.19 -0.45 -0.69  0.05
4  1.44 -0.96  0.43 -1.87 -0.16
5  1.37  2.07  0.26  0.15  2.05
6 -0.09  0.29 -0.96 -0.07  0.17
```

We now have the scores for each component for each soldier. These are simply the features for each observation multiplied by the loading on each component and then summed. We now can bring in the response as a column in the data:

```
> pca_scores$weight <- trainY
```

With this done, I think we are compelled to examine the correlation of this data:

```
> DataExplorer::plot_correlation(pca_scores)
```

The output of the preceding code is as follows:

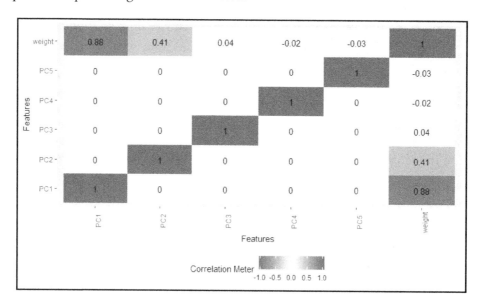

We see that components 1 and 2 are positively correlated to weight while the others seem meaningless. We must keep in mind this is univariate and our model may prove something different.

Regression with MARS

To do this part of the process, we will build a model with the `earth` package, review it on the training data, then see how it performs on the test data. We'll run a 10-fold cross-validation with the algorithm:

```
> set.seed(1492)

> earth_fit <-
    earth::earth(
    x = pca_scores[, 1:5],
    y = pca_scores[, 6],
    pmethod = 'cv',
    nfold = 10,
    degree = 1,
    minspan = -1
  )
```

Calling the summary of the model object gives us seven total terms with three of the features:

```
> summary(earth_fit)
Call: earth(x=pca_scores[,1:5], y=pca_scores[,6], pmethod="cv", degree=1,
nfold=10,
            minspan=-1)

            coefficients
(Intercept)      174.182
h(0.1-PC1)       -26.380
h(PC1-0.1)        33.806
h(0.01-PC2)      -13.181
h(PC2-0.01)       13.842
h(0.02-PC5)        1.333
h(PC5-0.02)       -0.869

Selected 7 of 7 terms, and 3 of 5 predictors using pmethod="cv"
Termination condition: RSq changed by less than 0.001 at 7 terms
Importance: PC1, PC2, PC5, PC3-unused, PC4-unused
Number of terms at each degree of interaction: 1 6 (additive model)
GRSq 0.9518 RSq 0.952 mean.oof.RSq 0.9512 (sd 0.0151)

pmethod="backward" would have selected the same model:
    7 terms 3 preds, GRSq 0.9518 RSq 0.952 mean.oof.RSq 0.9512
```

The model achieved a tremendous r-squared of 0.952 with components 1, 2, and 5. It can be a little easier to see the hinge functions at play with `plotmo`:

```
> plotmo::plotmo(earth_fit)
```

The output of the preceding code is as follows:

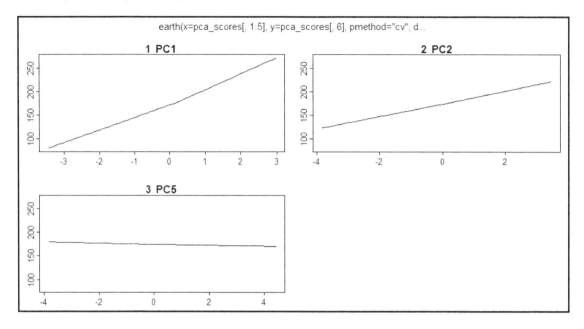

It's kind of a challenge to discern those subtle hinge functions from `plotmo`, with the exception of PC1. To see how this model really performs, save the predicted values and run some plots:

```
> ggplot2::ggplot(pca_scores, ggplot2::aes(x = earthpred, y = weight)) +
    ggplot2::geom_point() +
    ggplot2::stat_smooth(method = "lm", se = FALSE) +
    ggthemes::theme_pander()
```

The output of the preceding code is as follows:

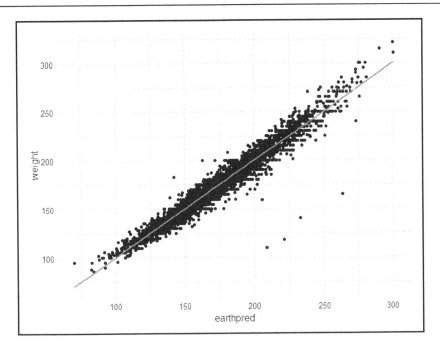

We see a nice linear relationship, but we have several outliers that make us scratch our heads. You mean our model predicts a weight of almost 225 pounds, but the soldier is less than 125 pounds? Something isn't right with those outlier predictions, perhaps measurement or data entry error; they are interesting observations nonetheless, worthy of further investigation, *time permitting*.

How about the residuals?

```
> ggplot2::ggplot(pca_scores, ggplot2::aes(x = earthpred, y = earthresid))
+
    ggplot2::geom_point() +
    ggplot2::stat_smooth(method = "loess", se = FALSE) +
    ggthemes::theme_few()
```

The output of the preceding code is as follows:

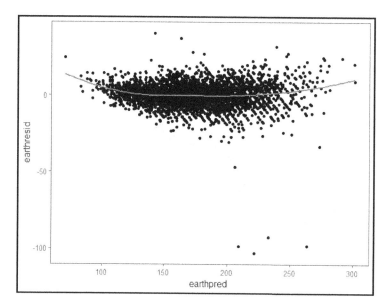

Just the slightest curvilinear relationship. We are seeing that the algorithm is underestimating, minimally, soldiers' weight at the extreme values. We already have r-squared, but RMSE and MAE are quickly callable:

```
> caret::postResample(pred = pca_scores$earthpred,
    obs = pca_scores$weight)
   RMSE Rsquared   MAE
  7.336    0.952 5.219
```

The mean absolute error is just 5 percent. Let's see if this holds on the test data.

Test data evaluation

One of the things you need to do on out-of-sample data is scale it according to the original (training) data. The predict function that comes with the `psych` package allows you to do this effortlessly. We put those scaled and scored values into a dataframe we can then use to make the out-of-sample predictions:

```
> test_reduced <- as.matrix(test[, c(-1, -95)])

> test_scores <- data.frame(predict(pca_5, test_reduced, old.data = train[,
  c(-1, -95)]))
```

Here, we just add the predicted and actual values:

```
> test_scores$testpred <- predict(earth_fit, test_scores)

> test_scores$weight <- test$Weightlbs
```

The results look good:

```
> caret::postResample(pred = test_scores$testpred,
    obs = test_scores$weight)
    RMSE Rsquared    MAE
  7.8735   0.9468 5.1937
```

The performance declined just a little bit. I think we can move forward with this model. Further exploration of the outliers is in order to see whether there is measurement error, drop them from the analysis, or truncate them. In closing, let's see the plot of actual versus predicted:

```
> ggplot2::ggplot(test_scores, ggplot2::aes(x = testpred, y = weight)) +
    ggplot2::geom_point() +
    ggplot2::stat_smooth(method = "lm", se = FALSE) +
    ggthemes::theme_excel_new()
```

The output of the preceding code is as follows:

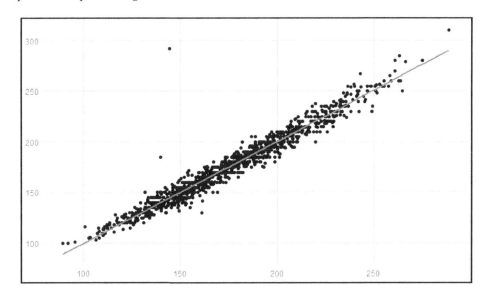

It looks similar to the training data plot. Once again, there is at least one anomaly. How can our model predict a soldier to be about 140 pounds but they are actually almost 300? We could amuse ourselves pursuing this further, but let's move on.

Summary

In this chapter, we took a second stab at unsupervised learning techniques by exploring PCA, examining what it is, and applying it in a practical fashion. We explored how it can be used to reduce the dimensionality and improve the understanding of the dataset when confronted with numerous highly correlated variables. Then, we applied it to real data of anthropometric measurements of US Army soldiers, using the resulting principal components in a regression analysis with MARS to predict a soldier's weight. Additionally, we explored ways to visualize the data and model results.

As an unsupervised learning technique, it requires some judgment along with trial and error to arrive at an optimal solution that is acceptable to business partners. Nevertheless, it is a powerful tool to extract latent insights and to support supervised learning.

In the next chapter, we will examine using unsupervised learning to look at association analysis.

11
Association Analysis

If we have data, let's look at data. If all we have are opinions, let's go with mine.

- Jim Barksdale, former Netscape CEO

You would have to live on the dark side of the Moon to not see the results of the techniques that we're about to discuss in this chapter every day. If you visit www.amazon.com, watch movies on www.netflix.com, or visit any retail website, you'll be exposed to terms such as *related products, because you watched..., customers who bought x also bought y,* and *recommended for you,* at every twist and turn. With large volumes of historical real-time or near real-time information, retailers utilize various algorithms in an attempt to increase both the quantity of buyers' purchases and the value of those purchases.

The techniques to do this can be broken down into two categories: association rules and recommendation engines. Association rule analysis is commonly referred to as market basket analysis, as it's concerned with understanding what items are purchased together. With recommendation engines, the goal is to provide a customer with other items that they'll enjoy based on how they've rated items they've viewed or purchased previously.

In this chapter, we'll focus on association analysis. It's applicable not only to making recommendations, product placement, and promotional pricing, but can be used in manufacturing, web usage, healthcare, and so on. If you're interested in how items occur together, apply what you're about to learn.

An overview of association analysis

Association analysis is a data mining technique that has the purpose of finding the optimal combination of products or services and allows marketers to exploit this knowledge to provide recommendations, optimize product placement, or develop marketing programs that take advantage of cross-selling. In short, the idea is to identify which items go well together, and profit from this.

You can think of the results of the analysis as an `if...then` statement. If a customer buys an airplane ticket, then there is a 46 % probability that they'll buy a hotel room, and if they go on to buy a hotel room, then there is a 33 % probability that they'll rent a car.

However, it isn't just for sales and marketing. It's also used in fraud detection and healthcare; for example, if a patient undergoes treatment A, then there's a 26 % probability that they'll exhibit symptom X. Before going into the details, we should have a look at some terminology, as follows:

- **Itemset**: This is a collection of one or more items in the dataset.
- **Support**: This is the proportion of the transactions in the data that contain an itemset of interest.
- **Confidence**: This is the conditional probability that, if a person purchases or does x, they'll purchase or do y; the act of doing x is referred to as the *antecedent* or **left-hand side (LHS)**, and y is the *consequence* or **right-hand side (RHS)**.
- **Lift**: This is the ratio of the support of x occurring together with y divided by the probability that x and y occur if they are independent. It's the **confidence** divided by the probability of x times the probability of y; for example, say that we have the probability of x and y occurring together as 10 %, and the probability of x is 20 %, and y is 30 %, then the lift would be 10 % (20 % times 30 %) or 16.67 %.

The package in R that you can use to perform a market basket analysis is **arules: Mining Association Rules and Frequent with Itemsets**. The package offers two different methods for finding rules **apriori** and **ECLAT**. There are other algorithms we can use to conduct a market basket analysis, but apriori is used most frequently, and so will be our focus.

With apriori, the principle is that, if an itemset is frequent, then all of its subsets must also be frequent. A minimum frequency (support) is determined by the analyst before executing the algorithm, and once established, the algorithm will run as follows:

- Let $k=1$ (the number of items)
- Generate itemsets of a length that is equal to or greater than the specified support
- Iterate $k + (1...n)$, pruning those that are infrequent (less than the support)
- Stop the iteration when no new frequent itemsets are identified

Once you have an ordered summary of the most frequent itemsets, you can continue the analysis process by examining the confidence and lift to offers the associations of interest.

Before we delve into the analysis, it's necessary to understand how to put your raw data into the appropriate structure, referred to as R class transactions. This can be a confusing task, so I'm going to spend some time on this before moving on to a full demonstration of association analysis.

Creating transactional data

In the world of the Internet of Things, you receive a ton of data. As you monitor devices for anomalies or failures, let's say you get some fault codes. How would you put the raw data into something meaningful for analysis in R? Well, here's a case study. We'll put together a random dataset and turn it into the proper form for use with R's `arules` package. Here's the dataframe:

```
> set.seed(270)

> faults <- data.frame(
    serialNumber = sample(1:20, 100, replace = T),
    faultCode = paste("fc", sample(1:12, 100, replace = T), sep = "")
)
```

This gives us 20 different serial numbers, which tells us which devices being monitored have had faults. Each device has a possibility of 12 different fault codes. The limitation of association analysis as we're doing it is the fact that the transaction order isn't included. Let's assume that isn't an issue in this example and proceed. First, given the random generation of this data, we will remove the duplicates:

```
> faults <- unique(faults)
```

The structure of the dataframe before turning it into transactions is critical. The identifier column needs to be as an integer. So, if you have a customer or equipment identifier such as `123abc`, you must turn it into an integer. Then, the item of interest must be a factor. Here, we confirm that we have the proper dataframe structure:

```
> str(faults)
'data.frame': 80 obs. of 2 variables:
 $ serialNumber: int 9 8 1 18 11 20 2 16 10 20 ...
 $ faultCode : Factor w/ 12 levels "fc1","fc10","fc11",..: 2 5 1 12 1 3 6
10 11 1 ...
```

Notice that this data is in the long format, which is usually how it's produced. As such, create a column where all values are TRUE and use tidyverse to reshape the data into the wide format:

```
> faults$indicator <- TRUE

> faults_wide <- tidyr::spread(faults, key = faultCode, value = indicator)
```

We now have a dataframe with the associated faults labeled as TRUE for each item of interest. Next, turn the data into a matrix while dropping the ID:

```
> faults_matrix <- as.matrix(faults_wide[,-1])
```

You must turn the missing `na` into something understood, so let's make them `FALSE`:

```
> faults_matrix[is.na(faults_matrix)] <- FALSE
```

Finally, we can turn this data into the `transactions` class:

```
> faults_transactions <- as(faults_matrix, "transactions")
```

To confirm it all worked, create a plot of the top 10 item frequency:

```
> arules::itemFrequencyPlot(faults_transactions, topN = 10)
```

The output of the preceding code is as follows:

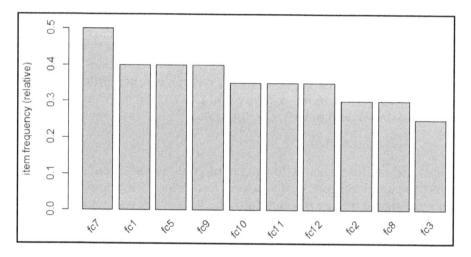

Success! Following the preceding process will get you from raw data to the appropriate structure. We'll transition to an example using data from the `arules` package itself, which you can apply to any analysis you want.

Data understanding

For our business case, we'll focus on identifying the association rules for a grocery store. The dataset will be from the `arules` package and is called `Groceries`. This dataset consists of actual transactions over 30 days from a real-world grocery store and consists of 9,835 different purchases. All of the items purchased are put into one of 169 categories, for example, bread, wine, meat, and so on.

Let's say that we want to develop an understanding of what potential customers will purchase along with beer to identify the right product placement within the store or support a cross-selling campaign.

Data preparation

For this analysis, we'll only need to load two packages, as well as the Groceries dataset:

```
> install.packages("arules")

> install.packages("arulesViz")

> library(arules)

> data(Groceries)

> str(Groceries)
    Formal class 'transactions' [package "arules"] with 3 slots
      ..@ data :Formal class 'ngCMatrix' [package "Matrix"] with 5
        slots
      .. .. ..@ i : int [1:43367] 13 60 69 78 14 29 98 24 15 29 ...
      .. .. ..@ p : int [1:9836] 0 4 7 8 12 16 21 22 27 28 ...
      .. .. ..@ Dim : int [1:2] 169 9835
      .. .. ..@ Dimnames:List of 2
      .. .. .. ..$ : NULL
      .. .. .. ..$ : NULL
      .. .. ..@ factors : list()
      ..@ itemInfo :'data.frame': 169 obs. of 3 variables:
      .. ..$ labels: chr [1:169] "frankfurter" "sausage" "liver loaf"
        "ham" ...
      .. ..$ level2: Factor w/ 55 levels "baby food","bags",..: 44 44
    44 44 44 44
    44 42 42 41 ...
      .. ..$ level1: Factor w/ 10 levels "canned food",..: 6 6 6 6 6 6
    6 6 6 6
      ...
      ..@ itemsetInfo:'data.frame': 0 obs. of 0 variables
```

This dataset is structured as a sparse matrix object, known as the `transaction` class, which we created previously.

So, once the structure is that of the class transaction, our standard exploration techniques won't work, but the `arules` package offers us other methods to explore the data. The best way to explore this data is with an item frequency plot using the `itemFrequencyPlot()` function in the `arules` package. You'll need to specify the transaction dataset, the number of items with the highest frequency to plot, and whether or not you want the relative or absolute frequency of the items. Let's first look at the absolute frequency and the top 10 items only:

```
> arules::itemFrequencyPlot(Groceries, topN = 10, type = "absolute")
```

The output of the preceding command is as follows:

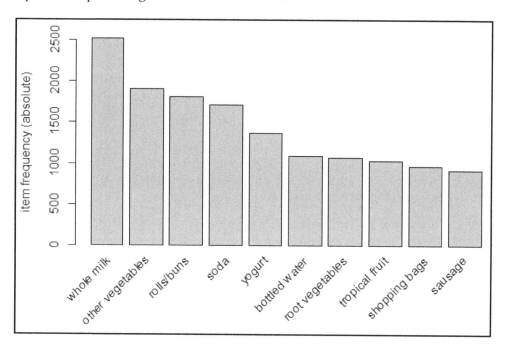

The top item purchased was **whole milk** with roughly **2,500** of the 9,836 transactions in the basket. For a relative distribution of the top 15 items, let's run the following code:

```
> arules::itemFrequencyPlot(Groceries, topN = 15)
```

The following is the output of the preceding command:

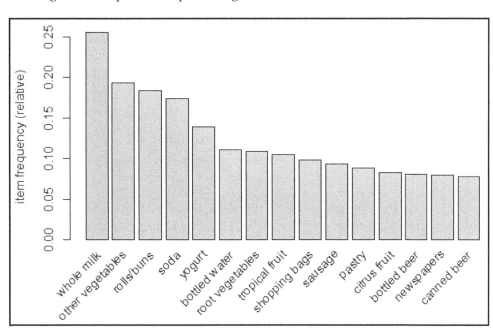

Alas, here we see that beer shows up as the 13th and 15th most purchased item at this store. Just under 10 % of the transactions related to **bottled beer** and/or **canned beer**.

For this exercise, this is all we need to do; therefore, we can move right on to the modeling and evaluation.

Modeling and evaluation

We'll start by mining the data for the overall association rules before moving on to our rules for beer specifically. Throughout the modeling process, we'll use the apriori algorithm, which is the appropriately named `apriori()` function in the `arules` package. The two main things that we'll need to specify in the function are the dataset and parameters. As for the parameters, you'll need to apply judgment when determining the minimum support, confidence, and the minimum and/or maximum length of basket items in an itemset. Using item frequency plots, along with trial and error, let's set the minimum support at 1 in 1,000 transactions and the minimum confidence at 90 %.

Additionally, let's establish the maximum number of items to be associated as 4. The following code creates the object that we'll call `rules`:

```
rules <-
  arules::apriori(Groceries, parameter = list(
    supp = 0.001,
    conf = 0.9,
    maxlen = 4
))
```

Calling the object shows how many rules the algorithm produced:

```
> rules
set of 67 rules
```

There are many ways to examine rules. The first thing that I recommend is setting the number of displayed digits to only two, with the `options()` function in base R. Then, sort and inspect the top five rules based on the lift that they provide, as follows:

```
> options(digits = 2)
> rules <- arules::sort(rules, by = "lift", decreasing = TRUE)
> arules::inspect(rules[1:5])
     lhs                       rhs                  support confidence lift
1 {liquor, red/blush wine}      => {bottled beer}        0.0019
   0.90 11.2
2 {root vegetables, butter, cream cheese }      => {yogurt}
   0.0010       0.91   6.5
3 {citrus fruit, root vegetables, soft cheese}=> {other vegetables}
   0.0010       1.00   5.2
4 {pip fruit, whipped/sour cream, brown bread}=> {other vegetables}
   0.0011       1.00   5.2
5 {butter,whipped/sour cream, soda}     => {other vegetables}
   0.0013       0.93   4.8
```

Lo and behold! The rule that offers the best overall lift is the purchase of `liquor` and `red wine` on the probability of purchasing `bottled beer`. I have to admit that this is pure chance and not intended on my part. As I always say, it's better to be lucky than good. Although, it's still not a very common transaction with support for only 1.9 per 1,000.

You can also sort by the support and confidence, so let's have a look at the first five rules by=`"confidence"` in descending order, as follows:

```
> rules <- arules::sort(rules, by = "confidence", decreasing = TRUE)

> arules::inspect(rules[1:5])
     lhs                  rhs                  support confidence lift
  1 {citrus fruit, root vegetables, soft cheese}=> {other vegetables}
```

```
     0.0010              1   5.2
  2 {pip fruit, whipped/sour cream, brown bread}=> {other vegetables}
     0.0011              1   5.2
  3 {rice, sugar}   => {whole milk}           0.0012         1   3.9
  4 {canned fish, hygienc articles} => {whole milk} 0.0011   1   3.9
  5 {root vegetables, butter, rice} => {whole milk} 0.0010   1   3.9
```

You can see in the table that `confidence` for these transactions is 100 %. Moving on to our specific study of beer, we can utilize a function in `arules` to develop cross - tabulations—the `crossTable()` function—and then examine whatever suits our needs. The first step is to create a table with our dataset:

```
> tab <- arules::crossTable(Groceries)
```

With `tab` created, we can now investigate joint occurrences between the items. Here, we'll look at just the first three rows and columns:

```
> tab[1:3, 1:3]
             frankfurter sausage liver loaf
  frankfurter         580      99          7
  sausage              99     924         10
  liver loaf            7      10         50
```

As you might imagine, shoppers only selected liver loaf 50 times out of the 9,835 transactions. Additionally, of the 924 times, people gravitated toward sausage, ten times they felt compelled to grab `liver loaf`. (Desperate times call for desperate measures!) If you want to look at a specific example, you can either specify the row and column number or spell that item out:

```
> tab["bottled beer","bottled beer"]
[1] 792
```

This tells us that there were 792 transactions of `bottled beer`. Let's see what the joint occurrence between `bottled beer` and `canned beer` is:

```
> tab["bottled beer","canned beer"]
[1] 26
```

I would expect this to be low as it supports my idea that people lean toward drinking beer from either a bottle or a can. I strongly prefer a bottle. It also makes a handy weapon to protect yourself from all these ruffian protesters such as *Occupy Wallstreet* and the like.

We can now move on and derive specific rules for `bottled beer`. We'll again use the `apriori()` function, but this time, we'll add a syntax around `appearance`. This means that we'll specify in the syntax that we want the left-hand side to be items that increase the probability of purchasing `bottled beer`, which will be on the right-hand side. In the following code, notice that I've adjusted the `support` and `confidence` numbers. Feel free to experiment with your settings:

```
> beer.rules <- arules::apriori(
    data = Groceries,
    parameter = list(support
    = 0.0015, confidence = 0.3),
    appearance = list(default = "lhs",
    rhs = "bottled beer"))

> beer.rules
set of 4 rules
```

We find ourselves with only 4 association rules. We've seen one of them already; now let's bring in the other three rules in descending order by lift:

```
> beer.rules <- arules::sort(beer.rules, decreasing = TRUE, by = "lift")
 > arules::inspect(beer.rules)
lhs rhs support confidence lift
1 {liquor, red/blush wine} => {bottled beer} 0.0019 0.90 11.2
2 {liquor} => {bottled beer} 0.0047 0.42 5.2
3 {soda, red/blush wine} => {bottled beer} 0.0016 0.36 4.4
4 {other vegetables, red/blush wine} => {bottled beer}0.0015 0.31
3.8
```

In all of the instances, the purchase of `bottled beer` is associated with booze, either `liquor` and/or red wine, which is no surprise to anyone. What's interesting is that white wine isn't in the mix here. Let's take a closer look at this and compare the joint occurrences of `bottled beer` and types of wine:

```
> tab["bottled beer", "red/blush wine"]
[1] 48
> tab["red/blush wine", "red/blush wine"]
[1] 189
> 48/189
[1] 0.25
> tab["white wine", "white wine"]
[1] 187
> tab["bottled beer", "white wine"]
[1] 22
> 22/187
[1] 0.12
```

It's interesting that 25 % of the time when someone purchased `red wine`, they also purchased `bottled beer`; but with `white wine`, a joint purchase only happened in 12 % of the instances. We certainly don't know why in this analysis, but this could potentially help us to determine how we should position our product in this grocery store. Another thing before we move on is to look at a plot of the rules. This is done with the `plot()` function in the `arulesViz` package.

There are many graphics options available. For this example, let's specify that we want `graph` showing `lift` and the rules provided and shaded by `confidence`. The following syntax will provide this accordingly:

```
> library(arulesViz)
Loading required package: grid

> plot(beer.rules,
+ method = "graph",
+ measure = "lift",
+ shading = "confidence")
```

The following is the output of the preceding command:

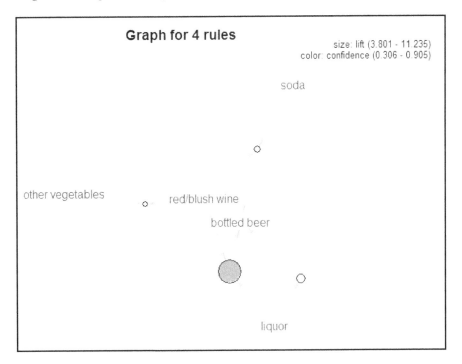

This graph shows that **liquor/red wine** provides the best **lift** and the highest level of **confidence** with both the **size** of the circle and its shading.

What we've just done in this simple exercise is show how easy it is with R to conduct a market basket analysis. It doesn't take much imagination to figure out the analytical possibilities that we can include with this technique, for example, in corporate customer segmentation, longitudinal purchase history, and so on, as well as how to use it in advert displays, co-promotions, and so on.

Summary

In this chapter, the goal was to provide an introduction to how to use R in order to build and test association rule mining (market basket analysis). Market basket analysis tries to understand what items are purchased together or what items occur together, so you can apply the analysis to healthcare, fraud-detection, and even exploring mechanical issues. As such, we learned how to transform raw data into a transactional structure for use in the `arules` package.

We're now going to shift gears back to supervised learning. In the next chapter, we're going to cover some poorly understood but essential methods in practical machine learning, that is, analyzing time series data and determining causality.

12
Time Series and Causality

"An economist is an expert who will know tomorrow why the things he predicted yesterday didn't happen today."

- Laurence J. Peter

A univariate time series is where the measurements are collected over a standard measure of time, which could be by the minute, hour, day, week, month, and so on. What makes the time series problematic over other data is that the order of the observations matters. This dependency of order can cause standard analysis methods to produce an unnecessarily high bias or variance.

It seems that there's a paucity of literature on machine learning and time series data or it's substandard. For example, I was at a data science conference in the spring of 2018, and a highly regarded machine learning expert mentioned that vector autoregression requires the data to be stationary. We'll discuss this later. When I heard this, I almost fell over. Fake data news! I informed my colleagues trained in econometrics to their horror and dismay. This is unfortunate as so much of real-world data involves a time component. Furthermore, time series analysis can be quite complicated and tricky. I would say that if you haven't seen a time series analysis done incorrectly, you haven't been looking close enough.

Another aspect involving time series that's often neglected is causality. Yes, we don't want to confuse correlation with causation but, in time series analysis, we can apply the technique of Granger causality in order to determine whether causality, statistically speaking, exists.

In this chapter, we'll apply time series/econometric techniques to identify univariate forecast models (including ensembles), vector autoregression models, and finally, Granger causality. After completing this chapter, you may not be a complete master of the time series analysis, but you'll know enough to perform an effective analysis and understand the fundamental issues to consider when building time series models and creating predictive models (forecasts).

Following are the topics that will be covered in this chapter:

- Univariate time series analysis
- Time series data
- Modeling and evaluation

Univariate time series analysis

We'll focus on two methods to analyze and forecast a single time series: **exponential smoothing** and **Autoregressive Integrated Moving Average** (**ARIMA**) models. We'll start by looking at exponential smoothing models.

Like moving average models, exponential smoothing models use weights for past observations. But unlike moving average models, the more recent the observation, the more weight it's given relative to the later ones. There are three possible smoothing parameters to estimate: the overall smoothing parameter, a trend parameter, and the seasonal smoothing parameter. If no trend or seasonality is present, then these parameters become null.

The smoothing parameter produces a forecast with the following equation:

$$Yt + 1 = \alpha(Yt) + (1\text{--}\alpha)Yt - 1 + (1 - \alpha)2Yt - 2 + \ldots, where\ 0 < \alpha \leq 1$$

In this equation, Y_t is the value at the time, T, and alpha (α) is the smoothing parameter. Algorithms optimize the alpha (and other parameters) by minimizing the errors, **Sum of Squared Error** (**SSE**) or maximum likelihood.

The forecast equation along with trend and seasonality equations, if applicable, will be as follows:

- The forecast, where A is the preceding smoothing equation and h is the number of forecast periods: $Yt + h = A + hBt + St$
- The trend equation: $Bt = \beta(At\text{--} At - 1) + (1\text{--}\beta)Bt - 1$

- The seasonality, where m is the number of seasonal periods:
$St = \Omega(Yt - At - 1 - Bt - 1) + (1 - \Omega)St - m$

This equation is referred to as the **Holt-Winters method**. The forecast equation is additive in nature with the trend as linear. The method also allows the inclusion of a dampened trend and multiplicative seasonality, where the seasonality proportionally increases or decreases over time. With these models, you don't have to worry about the assumption of stationarity as in an ARIMA model. Stationarity is where the time series has a constant mean, variance, and correlation between all of the time periods. Having said this, it's still important to understand the ARIMA models as there will be situations where they have the best performance.

Starting with the autoregressive model, the value of Y at time T is a linear function of the prior values of Y. The formula for an autoregressive lag-1 model *AR(1)* is $Yt = constant + \Phi Yt - 1 + Et$. The critical assumptions for the model are as follows:

- *Et* denotes the errors that are identically and independently distributed with a mean zero and constant variance
- The errors are independent of *Yt*
- *Yt, Yt-1, Yt-n...* is stationary, which means that the absolute value of Φ is less than one

With a stationary time series, you can examine the **autocorrelation function** (**ACF**). The ACF of a stationary series gives correlations between *Yt* and *Yt-h* for *h = 1, 2...n*. Let's use R to create an *AR(1)* series and plot it:

```
> install.packages("forecast")

> set.seed(1966)

> ar1 <- arima.sim(list(order = c(1, 0, 0), ar = 0.5), n = 200)

> forecast::autoplot(ar1, main = "AR1")
```

The following is the output of the preceding command:

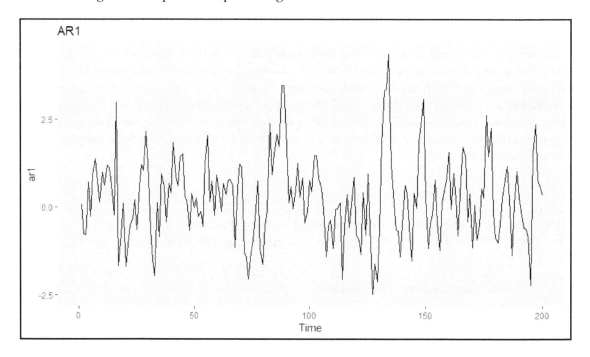

Now, let's examine ACF:

```
> forecast::autoplot(acf(ar1, plot = F), main = "ACF of simulated AR1")
```

The output of the preceding command is as follows:

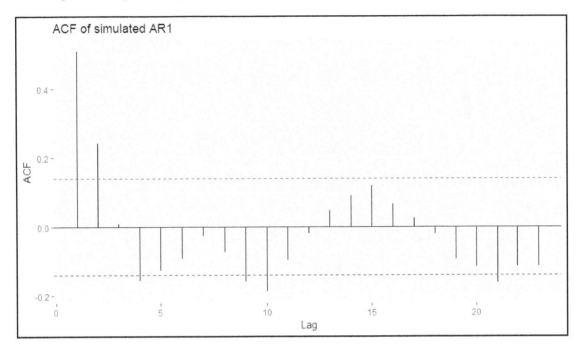

The **ACF** plot shows the correlations exponentially decreasing as the **Lag** increases. The dotted blue lines indicate the confidence bands of a significant correlation. Any line that extends above the high or below the low band is considered significant. In addition to ACF, we should also examine the **partial autocorrelation function (PACF)**. The PACF is a conditional correlation, which means that the correlation between Yt and $Yt-h$ is conditional on the observations that come between the two. One way to intuitively understand this is to think of a linear regression model and its coefficients. Let's assume that you have $Y = B0 + B1X1$ versus $Y = B0 + B1X1 + B2X2$. The relationship of X to Y in the first model is linear with a coefficient, but in the second model, the coefficient will be different because of the relationship between Y and $X2$ now being accounted for as well. Note that, in the following PACF plot, the partial autocorrelation value at lag-1 is identical to the autocorrelation value at lag-1, as this isn't a conditional correlation:

```
> forecast::autoplot(pacf(ar1, plot = F), main = "PACF of simulated AR1")
```

The following is the output of the preceding command:

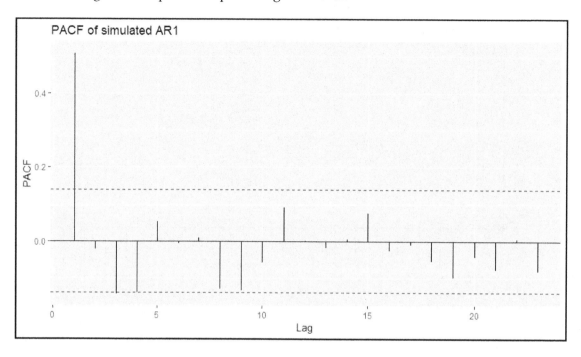

We can safely make the assumption that the series is stationary from the appearance of the preceding time series plot. We'll look at a couple of statistical tests in the practical exercise to ensure that the data is stationary but, on occasion, the eyeball test is sufficient. If the data isn't stationary, then it's possible to detrend the data by taking its differences. This is the Integrated (I) in ARIMA. After differencing, the new series becomes $\Delta Yt = Yt - Yt\text{-}1$. One should expect a first-order difference to achieve stationarity but, on some occasions, a second-order difference may be necessary. An ARIMA model with *AR(1)* and *I(1)* would be annotated as (1,1,0).

The **MA** stands for **Moving Average**. This isn't the simple moving average as the 50-day moving average of a stock price, it's rather a coefficient that is applied to the errors. The errors are, of course, identically and independently distributed with a mean zero and constant variance. The formula for an *MA(1)* model is $Yt = constant + Et + \Theta Et\text{-}1$. As we did with the *AR(1)* model, we can build an *MA(1)* in R, as follows:

```
> set.seed(123)
> ma1 <- arima.sim(list(order = c(0, 0, 1), ma = -0.5), n = 200)
> forecast::autoplot(ma1, main = "MA1")
```

The following is the output of the preceding command:

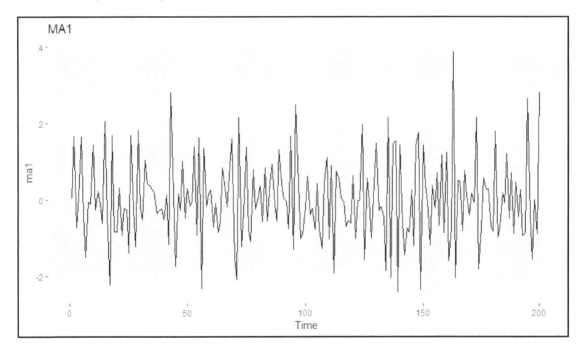

The ACF and PACF plots are a bit different from the *AR(1)* model. Note that there are some rules of thumb while looking at the plots in order to determine whether the model has AR and/or MA terms. They can be a bit subjective, so I'll leave it to you to learn these heuristics, but trust R to identify the proper model. In the following plots, we'll see a significant correlation at lag-1 and two significant partial correlations at lag-1 and lag-2:

```
> forecast::autoplot(acf(ma1, plot = F), main = "ACF of simulated MA1")
```

The output of the preceding command is as follows:

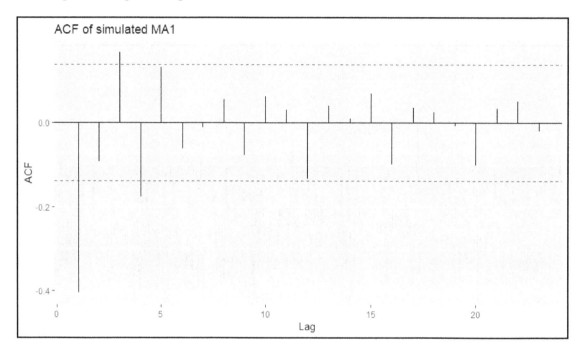

The preceding figure is the ACF plot, and now, we'll see the PACF plot:

```
> forecast::autoplot(pacf(ma1, plot = F), main = "PACF of simulated MA1")
```

The output of the preceding command is as follows:

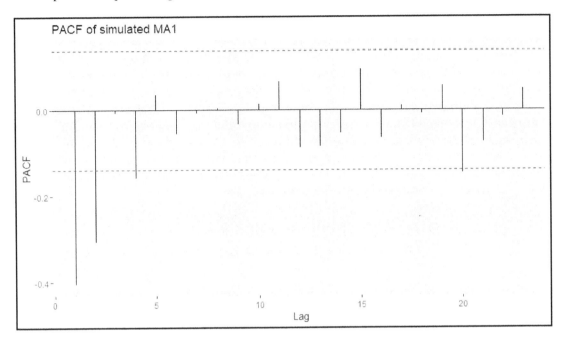

With the ARIMA models, it's possible to incorporate seasonality, including the autoregressive, integrated, and moving average terms. The non-seasonal ARIMA model notation is commonly *(p,d,q)*. With seasonal ARIMA, assume that the data is monthly, then the notation would be *(p,d,q) x (P,D,Q)12*, with the 12 in the notation taking the monthly seasonality into account. In the packages that we'll use, R can automatically identify whether the seasonality should be included; if so, the optimal terms will be included as well.

Understanding Granger causality

Imagine you're asked a question such as, *What's the relationship between the number of new prescriptions and total prescriptions for medicine X?* You know that these are measured monthly, so what could you do to understand that relationship, given that people believe that new scripts will drive up total scripts? Or how about testing the hypothesis that commodity prices—in particular, copper—is a leading indicator of stock market prices in the US? Well, with two sets of time series data, *x* and *y*, Granger causality is a method that attempts to determine whether one series is likely to influence a change in the other. This is done by taking different lags of one series and using this to model the change in the second series. To accomplish this, we'll create two models that will predict *y*, one with only the past values of *y* (Ω) and the other with the past values of *y* and *x* (π). The models are as follows, where *k* is the number of lags in the time series:

$$\text{Let } \Omega = yt = \beta0 + \beta1yt\text{-}1 + ... + \beta kyt\text{-}k + \in$$
$$\text{and let } \pi = yt = \beta0 + \beta1yt\text{-}1 + ... + \beta kyt\text{-}k + \alpha1yt\text{-}1 + ... + \alpha kyt\text{-}k + \in$$

The RSS is then compared and `F-test` is used to determine whether the nested model (Ω) is adequate enough to explain the future values of *y* or whether the full model (π) is better. `F-test` is used to test the following null and alternative hypotheses:

- *H0*: `αi = 0` for each *i* `∈[1,k]`, no Granger causality
- *H1*: `αi ≠ 0` for at least one *i* `∈[1,k]`, Granger causality

Essentially, we're trying to determine whether we can say that, statistically, *x* provides more information about the future values of *y* than the past values of *y* alone. In this definition, it's clear that we aren't trying to prove actual causation, only that the two values are related by some phenomenon. Along these lines, we must also run this model in reverse in order to verify that *y* doesn't provide information about the future values of *x*. If we find that this is the case, it's likely that there's some exogenous variable, say Z, that needs to be controlled or would possibly be a better candidate for the Granger causation. Originally, you had to apply the method to stationary time series to avoid spurious results. This is no longer the case as I will demonstrate.

Note that research papers are available that discuss the techniques nonlinear models use, but this is outside the scope of this book. I recommend reading an excellent introductory paper on Granger causality that revolves around the age-old conundrum of the chicken and the egg (Thurman, 1988).

There are a couple of different ways to identify the proper lag structure. Naturally, we can use brute force and ignorance to test all of the reasonable lags, one at a time. We may have a rational intuition based on domain expertise or perhaps prior research that exists to guide the lag selection. If not, then you can apply **vector autoregression (VAR)** to identify the lag structure with the lowest information criterion, such as **Aikake's information criterion (AIC)** or **final prediction error (FPE)**. For simplicity, here is the notation for the VAR models with two variables, and this incorporates only one lag for each variable. This notation can be extended for as many variables and lags as appropriate:

- $Y = constant_1 + B_{11}Y_{t-1} + B_{12}Y_{t-1} + e_1$
- $X = constant_1 + B2_1Y_{t-1} + B2_2Y_{t-1} + e2$

In R, this process is quite simple to implement as we'll see in the following practical problem.

Time series data

The planet isn't going anywhere. We are! We're goin' away.

- Philosopher and comedian, George Carlin

Climate change is happening. It always has and will, but the big question, at least from a political and economic standpoint, is the climate change man-made? I'll use this chapter to put econometric time series modeling to the test to try and learn whether carbon emissions cause, statistically speaking, climate change and, in particular, rising temperatures. Personally, I'd like to take a neutral stance on the issue, always keeping in mind the wise tenets that Mr. Carlin left for us in his teachings on the subject.

The first order of business is to find and gather the data. For temperature, I chose the **HadCRUT4** annual median temperature time series, which is probably the gold standard. This data is compiled by a cooperative effort of the Climate Research Unit of the University of East Anglia and the Hadley Centre at the UK Meteorological Office. A full discussion of how the data is compiled and modeled is available at
`http://www.metoffice.gov.uk/hadobs/index.html`.

The data that we'll use is provided as an annual anomaly, which is calculated as the difference of the median annual surface temperature for a given time period versus the average of the reference years (1961-1990). The annual surface temperature is an ensemble of the temperatures collected globally and blended from the **CRUTEM4** surface air temperature and **HadSST3** sea-surface datasets. Skeptics have attacked biased and unreliable: http://www.telegraph.co.uk/comment/11561629/Top-scientists-start-to-examine-fid dled-global-warming-figures.html. This is way outside of our scope of effort here, so we must accept and utilize this data as is, but I find it amusing nonetheless. I've pulled the data from 1919 through 2013 to match our CO2 data.

Global CO2 emission estimates can be found at the **Carbon Dioxide Information Analysis Center (CDIAC)** of the US Department of Energy at the following website: http://cdiac. ornl.gov/.

I've placed the data in a .csv file (climate.csv) for you to download and store in your working directory: https://github.com/datameister66/data/.

Let's install libraries as needed, load the data, and examine the structure:

```
> library(magrittr)

> install.packages("tidyverse")

> install.packages("ggplot2")

> install.packages("ggthemes")

> install.packages("tseries")

> climate <- readr::read_csv("climate.csv")

> str(climate)
Classes 'tbl_df', 'tbl' and 'data.frame':   95 obs. of 3 variables:
 $ Year: int  1919 1920 1921 1922 1923 1924 1925 1926 1927 1928 ...
 $ CO2 : int  806 932 803 845 970 963 975 983 1062 1065 ...
 $ Temp: num  -0.272 -0.241 -0.187 -0.301 -0.272 -0.292 -0.214 -0.105 -0.208
-0.206 ...
```

We'll put this in a time series structure, specifying the start and end years:

```
> climate_ts <- ts(climate[, 2:3],
    start = 1919,
    end = 2013)
```

With our data loaded and put in time series structures, we can now begin to understand and further prepare it for analysis.

Data exploration

Let's start out with a plot of the time series using base R:

```
> plot(climate_ts, main = "CO2 and Temperature Deviation")
```

The output of the preceding command is as follows:

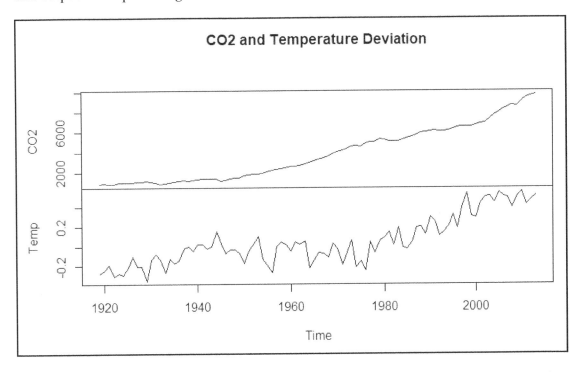

It appears that CO_2 levels really started to increase after World War II and there's a rapid rise in temperature anomalies in the mid-1970s. There doesn't appear to be any obvious outliers, and variation over time appears constant. Using the standard procedure, we can see that the two series are highly correlated, as follows:

```
> cor(climate_temp)
            CO2       Temp
CO2   1.0000000 0.8404215
Temp  0.8404215 1.0000000
```

As discussed earlier, this is nothing to jump for joy about as it proves absolutely nothing. We'll look for the structure by plotting ACF and PACF for both series:

```
> forecast::autoplot(acf(climate_ts[, 2], plot = F), main="Temperature
ACF")
```

The output of the preceding code snippet is as follows:

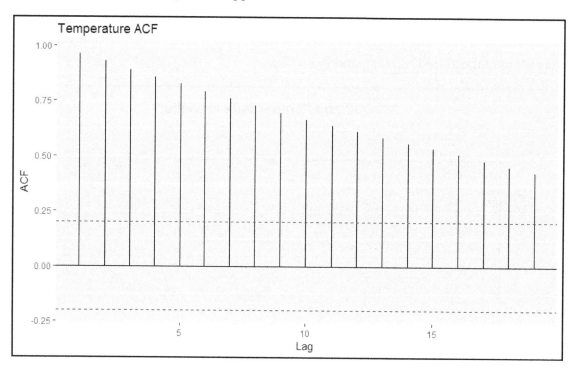

This code gives us the PACF plot for temperature:

```
> forecast::autoplot(pacf(climate_ts[, 2], plot = F), main = "Temperature
PACF")
```

The output of the preceding code snippet is as follows:

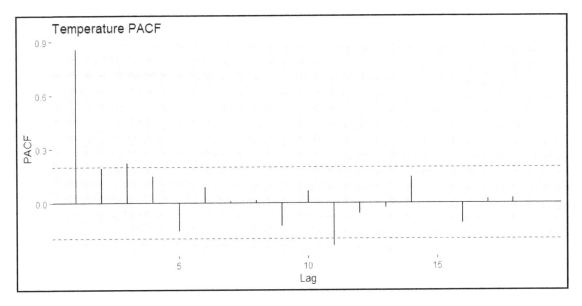

This code gives us the ACF plot for CO2:

```
> forecast::autoplot(acf(climate_ts[, 1], plot = F), main = "CO2 ACF")
```

The output of the preceding code snippet is as follows:

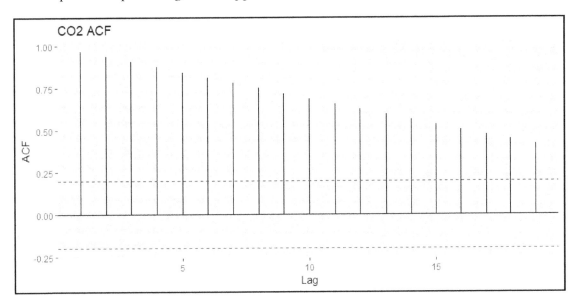

This code gives us the `PACF` plot for `CO2`:

```
> forecast::autoplot(acf(climate_ts[, 1], plot = F), main = "CO2 PACF")
```

The output of the preceding code snippet is as follows:

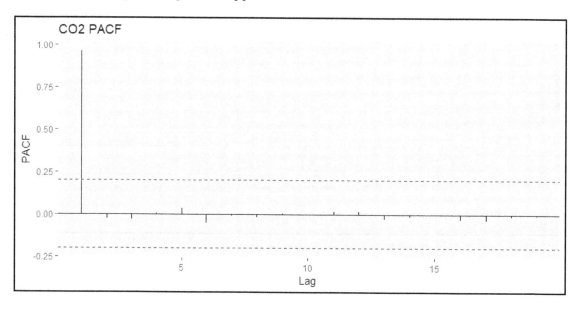

With the slowly decaying ACF patterns and rapidly decaying PACF patterns, we can assume that these series are both autoregressive, although `Temp` appears to have some significant MA terms. Next, let's have a look at the **Cross-Correlation Function (CCF)**. Note we put our x before our y in the function:

```
> forecast::autoplot(ccf(climate_ts[, 1], climate_ts[, 2], plot = F), main
= "CCF")
```

The output of the preceding code is as follows:

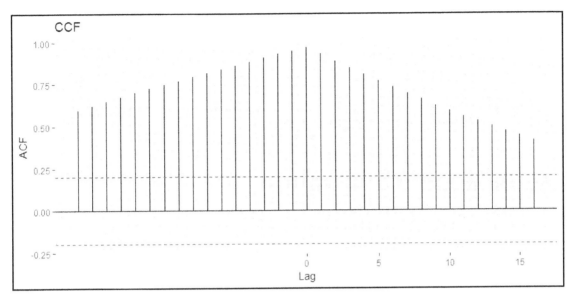

The **CCF** shows us the correlation between the temperature and lags of CO2. If the negative lags of the x variable have a high correlation, we can say that x leads y. If the positive lags of x have a high correlation, we say that x lags y. Here, we can see that CO2 is both a leading and lagging variable. For our analysis, it's encouraging that we see the former, but odd that we see the latter. We'll see during the VAR and Granger causality analysis whether this will matter or not.

Additionally, we need to test whether the data is stationary. We can prove this with the **Augmented Dickey-Fuller (ADF)** test available in the tseries package, using the adf.test() function, as follows:

```
> tseries::adf.test(climate_ts[, 1])

        Augmented Dickey-Fuller Test

data: climate_ts[, 1]
Dickey-Fuller = -1.1519, Lag order = 4, p-value =
0.9101
alternative hypothesis: stationary

> tseries::adf.test(climate_ts[, 2])

        Augmented Dickey-Fuller Test
```

```
data: climate_ts[, 2]
Dickey-Fuller = -1.8106, Lag order = 4, p-value =
0.6546
alternative hypothesis: stationary
```

For both series, we have insignificant `p-values`, so we cannot reject the null and conclude that they aren't stationary.

Having explored the data, let's begin the modeling process, starting with the application of univariate techniques to the temperature anomalies.

Modeling and evaluation

For the modeling and evaluation step, we'll focus on three tasks. The first is to produce a univariate forecast model applied to just the surface temperature. The second is to develop a vector autoregression model of the surface temperature and CO2 levels, using that output to inform our work on whether CO2 levels Granger-cause the surface temperature anomalies.

Univariate time series forecasting

With this task, the objective is to produce a univariate forecast for the surface temperature, focusing on choosing either an exponential smoothing model, an ARIMA model, or an ensemble of methods, including a neural net. We'll train the models and determine their predictive accuracy on an out-of-time test set, just like we've done in other learning endeavors. The following code creates the train and test sets:

```
> temp_ts <- ts(climate$Temp, start = 1919, frequency = 1)

> train <- window(temp_ts, end = 2007)

> test <- window(temp_ts, start = 2008)
```

To build our exponential smoothing model, we'll use the `ets()` function found in the `forecast` package. The function will find the best model with the lowest AIC:

```
> fit.ets <- forecast::ets(train)

> fit.ets
ETS(A,A,N)

Call:
 forecast::ets(y = train)

  Smoothing parameters:
    alpha = 0.3429
    beta = 1e-04

  Initial states:
    l = -0.2817
    b = 0.0095

  sigma: 0.1025

       AIC AICc BIC
 -0.1516906 0.5712010 12.2914912
```

The model object returns a number of parameters of interest. The first thing to check is what does (A,A,N) mean. It represents that the model selected is a simple exponential smoothing with additive errors. The first letter denotes the error type, the second letter the trend, and the third letter seasonality. The possible letters are as follows:

- *A = additive*
- *M = multiplicative*
- *N = none*

We also see the parameter estimates with alpha, the smoothing parameter, for error correction (the level), and beta for slope. Initial state values were used to initiate model selection; sigma is the variation of the residuals and model criteria values are provided. You can plot how the estimates change over time:

```
> forecast::autoplot(fit.ets)
```

The output of the preceding code is as follows:

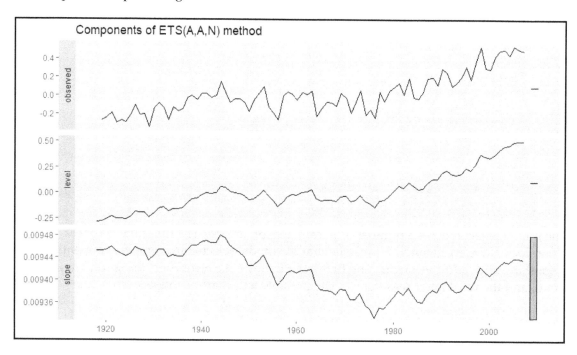

We'll now plot `forecast` and see how well it performed visually on the test data:

```
> plot(forecast::forecast(fit.ets, h = 6))

> lines(test, type = "o")
```

The output of the preceding code is as follows:

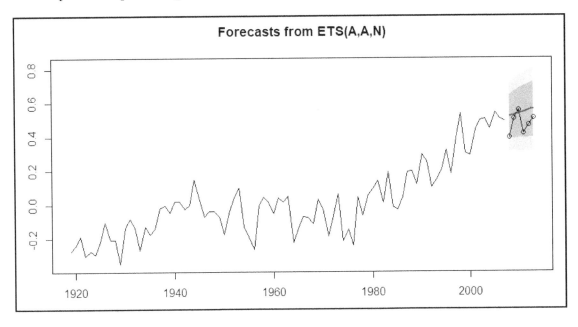

Looking at the plot, it seems that this forecast is showing a slight linear uptrend and is overestimating versus the actual values. We'll now look at the accuracy measures for the model:

```
> fit.ets %>% forecast::forecast(h = 6) %>%
    forecast::accuracy(temp_ts)
                         ME        RMSE         MAE        MPE     MAPE       MASE
Training set -0.00160570  0.10012357  0.08052241       -Inf      Inf  0.8752436
Test set      -0.06410776  0.08303044  0.07086704  -14.90784  16.12354  0.7702939
                  ACF1   Theil's U
Training set 0.1058923          NA
Test set     -0.1743445   0.7940449
```

There are eight measures for error. The one I believe we should focus on is Theil's U (actually U2 as the original Theil's U had some flaws), which is available only on the test data. Theil's U is an interesting statistic as it isn't dependent on scale, so you can compare multiple models. For instance, if in one model you transform the time series using a logarithmic scale, you can compare the statistic with a model that doesn't transform the data. You can think of it as the ratio that the forecast improves predictability over a naive forecast, or we can describe it at the **root mean square error** (**RMSE**) of the model divided by the RMSE of a naive model. Therefore, Theil's U statistics greater than 1 perform worse than a naive forecast, a value of 1 equals naive, and less than 1 indicates the model outperforms naive. Further discussion and how the statistic is derived is available at this link: http://www.forecastingprinciples.com/data/definitions/theil's%20u.html.

The smoothing model provided a statistic of 0.7940449. That isn't very impressive even though it's below one. We should strive for values at or below 0.5, in my opinion.

We'll now develop an ARIMA model, using auto.arima(), which is also from the forecast package. There are many options that you can specify in the function, or you can just include your time series data and it will find the best ARIMA fit. I recommend using the function with caution, as it can often return a model that violates assumptions for the residuals, as we shall see:

```
> fit.arima <- forecast::auto.arima(train)

> summary(fit.arima)
Series: train
ARIMA(1,1,1) with drift

Coefficients:
         ar1      ma1   drift
      0.2089  -0.7627  0.0087
s.e.  0.1372   0.0798  0.0033

sigma^2 estimated as 0.01021: log likelihood=78.09
AIC=-148.18 AICc=-147.7 BIC=-138.28

Training set error measures:
                       ME       RMSE        MAE MPE MAPE      MASE
Training set -8.396214e-05 0.09874311 0.07917484 Inf  Inf 0.8605961
                  ACF1
Training set 0.02010508
```

The abbreviated output shows that the model selected is an AR = 1, I = 1, and MA = 1, I = 1, or `ARIMA(1,1,1)` with drift (equivalent to an intercept term on differenced data and a slope term in undifferenced data). We can examine the plot of its performance on the `test` data in the same fashion as before:

```
> plot(forecast::forecast(fit.arima, h = 6))

> lines(test, type = "o")
```

The output of the preceding code is as follows:

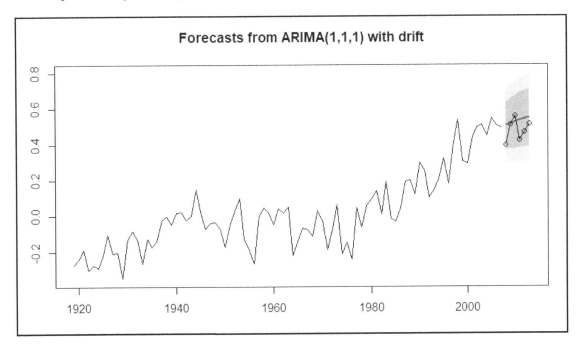

This is very similar to the prior method. Let's check those accuracy statistics, of course with a focus on Theil's U:

```
> fit.arima %>% forecast::forecast(h = 6) %>%
    forecast::accuracy(temperature)
                          ME        RMSE        MAE      MPE      MAPE
MASE
Training set -8.396214e-05 0.09874311 0.07917484      Inf      Inf
0.8605961
Test set      -4.971043e-02 0.07242892 0.06110011 -11.84965 13.89815
0.6641316
                    ACF1 Theil's U
Training set  0.02010508        NA
```

```
Test set      -0.18336583 0.6729521
```

The forecast error is slightly better with the ARIMA model. You should always review the residuals with your models and especially ARIMA, which relies on the assumption of no serial correlation in said residuals:

```
> forecast::checkresiduals(fit.arima)

    Ljung-Box test

data: Residuals from ARIMA(1,1,1) with drift
Q* = 18.071, df = 7, p-value = 0.01165

Model df: 3. Total lags used: 10
```

The output of the following code is as follows:

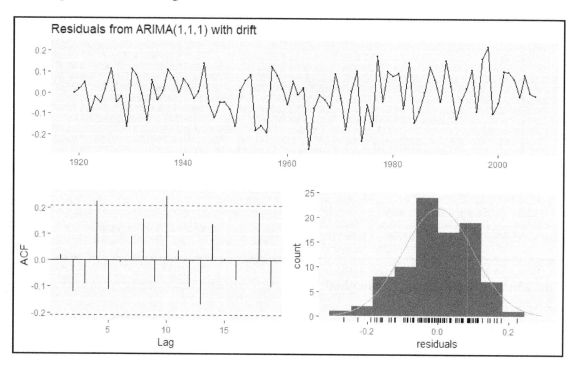

First of all, take a look at the Ljung-Box Q test. The null hypothesis is that the correlations in the residuals are zero, and the alternative is that the residuals exhibit serial correlation. We see a significant p-value so we can reject the null. This is confirmed visually in the ACF plot of the residuals where significant correlation exists at lag 4 and lag 10. With serial correlation present, the model coefficients are unbiased, but the standard errors and any statistics that rely on them are wrong. This fact may require you to manually select an appropriate ARIMA model manually through trial and error. To explain how to do that would require a separate chapter, so it's not in scope for this book.

With a couple of relatively weak models, we can try other methods, but let's look at creating an ensemble similar to what we produced in Chapter 8, *Creating Ensembles and Multiclass Methods*. We'll put together the two models just created and add a forward-feed neural network from the nnetar() function available in the forecast package. We won't stack the models, but simply take the average of the three models for comparison on the test data.

The first step in this process is to develop the forecasts for each of the models. This is straightforward:

```
> ETS <- forecast::forecast(forecast::ets(train), h = 6)

> ARIMA <- forecast::forecast(forecast::auto.arima(train), h = 6)

> NN <- forecast::forecast(forecast::nnetar(train), h = 6)
```

The next step is to create the ensemble values, which again is just a simple average:

```
> ensemble.fit <-
    (ETS[["mean"]] + ARIMA[["mean"]] + NN[["mean"]]) / 3
```

The comparison step is kind of an open canvas for you to produce the statistics you desire. Notice that I'm pulling the accuracy for only the test data and Theil's U. You can pull the necessary stats, such as RMSE or MAPE, should you so desire:

```
> c(ets = forecast::accuracy(ETS, temperature)["Test set", c("Theil's U")],
    arima = forecast::accuracy(ARIMA, temperature)["Test set", c("Theil's
U")],
    nn = forecast::accuracy(NN, temperature)["Test set", c("Theil's U")],
    ef = forecast::accuracy(ensemble.fit, temperature)["Test set",
c("Theil's U")])
      ets     arima        nn        ef
0.7940449 0.6729521 0.6794704 0.7104893
```

This is interesting, I think, as the exponential smoothing is dragging the ensemble performance down, and ARIMA and neural net are almost equal. Just for visual comparison, let's plot the neural network:

```
> plot(NN)

> lines(test, type = "o")
```

The output of the preceding code is as follows:

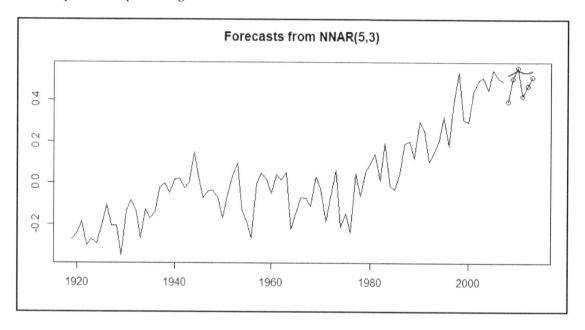

What are we to do with all of this? Here are a couple of thoughts. If you look at the time series pattern, you notice that it goes through what we could call different structural changes. There are a number of R packages to examine this structure and determine a point where it makes more sense to start the time series for forecasting. For example, there seems to be a discernible change in the slope of the time series in the mid-1960s. When you do this with your data, you're throwing away what may be valuable data points, so judgment comes into play. The implication is that if you want to totally automate your time series models, you'll need to take this into consideration.

You might try and transform the entire time series with log values (this doesn't work too well with negative values) or Box-Cox. In the `forecast` package, you can set `lambda` = `"auto"`, in your model function. I did this and the performance didn't improve. For the sake of example, let's try and detect structural changes and build an ARIMA model on a selected starting point. I'll demonstrate structural change with the `strucchange` package, which computationally determines changes in linear regression relationships. You can find a full discussion and vignette on the package at this link: `https://cran.r-project.org/web/packages/strucchange/vignettes/strucchange-intro.pdf`.

I find this method useful in discussions with stakeholders as it helps them to understand when and even why the underlying data generating process changed. Here goes:

```
> temp_struc <- strucchange::breakpoints(temp_ts ~ 1)

> summary(temp_struc)

    Optimal (m+1)-segment partition:

Call:
breakpoints.formula(formula = temp_ts ~ 1)

Breakpoints at observation number:
m = 1  68
m = 2  60  78
m = 3  18  60  78
m = 4  18  45  60  78
m = 5  17  31  45  60  78

Corresponding to breakdates:
m = 1  1986
m = 2  1978  1996
m = 3  1936  1978  1996
m = 4  1936  1963  1978  1996
m = 5  1935  1949  1963  1978  1996
```

The algorithm gave us five potential breakpoints in the time series, returning the information as an observation number and a year. Sure enough, 1963 indicates a structural change, but it tells us that 1978 and 1996 qualify also. Let's pursue the 1963 break as the start of our time series for an ARIMA model:

```
> train_bp <- window(temp_ts, start = 1963, end = 2007)

> fit.arima2 <- forecast::auto.arima(train_bp)

> fit.arima2 %>% forecast::forecast(h = 6) %>%
    forecast::accuracy(temperature)
```

```
                         ME      RMSE         MAE       MPE     MAPE
Training set -0.007696066 0.1034046 0.08505900  53.68130 99.93869
Test set      -0.086625082 0.1017767 0.08676477 -19.61829 19.64341
                    MASE        ACF1  Theil's U
Training set 0.7951128  0.09310454         NA
Test set     0.8110579 -0.08291170   1.057287
```

There you have it: much to my surprise performance, it's even worse than a naive forecast, but at least we've covered how to implement that methodology.

With this, we've completed the building of a univariate forecast model for the surface temperature anomalies, and now we'll move on to the next task of seeing whether CO2 levels cause these anomalies.

Examining the causality

For this chapter, this is where I think the rubber meets the road and we'll separate causality from mere correlation—well, statistically speaking, anyway. This isn't the first time that this technique has been applied to the problem. Triacca (2005) found no evidence to suggest that atmospheric CO2 Granger caused the surface temperature anomalies. On the other hand, Kodra (2010) concluded that there's a causal relationship, but put forth the caveat that their data wasn't stationary even after a second-order differencing. While this effort won't settle the debate, it'll hopefully inspire you to apply the methodology in your personal endeavors. The topic at hand certainly provides an effective training ground to demonstrate the Granger causality.

Our plan here is to first demonstrate spurious linear regression where the residuals suffer from autocorrelation, also known as serial correlation. Then, we'll examine two different approaches to Granger causality. The first will be the traditional methods, where both series are stationary. Then, we'll look at the method demonstrated by Toda and Yamamoto (1995), which applies the methodology to the raw data or, as it's sometimes called, the **levels**.

Linear regression

Let's get started with the spurious regression then, which I have seen implemented in the real world far too often. Here we simply build a linear model and examine the results:

```
> fit.lm <- lm(Temp ~ CO2, data = climate)

> summary(fit.lm)

Call:
lm(formula = Temp ~ CO2, data = climate)

Residuals:
     Min       1Q   Median       3Q      Max
-0.36411 -0.08986  0.00011  0.09475  0.28763

Coefficients:
              Estimate Std. Error t value Pr(>|t|)
(Intercept) -2.430e-01  2.357e-02  -10.31   <2e-16 ***
CO2          7.548e-05  5.047e-06   14.96   <2e-16 ***
---
Signif. codes:
0 '***' 0.001 '**' 0.01 '*' 0.05 '.' 0.1 ' ' 1

Residual standard error: 0.1299 on 93 degrees of freedom
Multiple R-squared: 0.7063, Adjusted R-squared: 0.7032
F-statistic: 223.7 on 1 and 93 DF, p-value: < 2.2e-16
```

Notice how everything is significant, and we have an adjusted R-squared of 0.7. OK, they're highly correlated but this is all meaningless as discussed by Granger and Newbold (1974). Again, I've seen results like these presented in meetings with many people with advanced degrees, and I had to be the bad guy and challenge the results.

We can plot the serial correlation, starting with a time series plot of the residuals, which produce a clear pattern:

```
> forecast::checkresiduals(fit.lm)

	Breusch-Godfrey test for serial correlation of order up to 10

data: Residuals
LM test = 46.193, df = 10, p-value = 1.323e-06
```

The output of the preceding code is as follows:

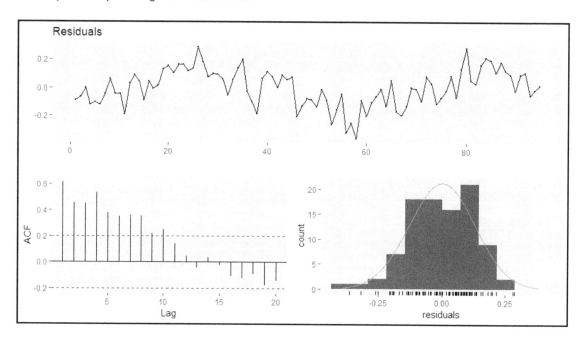

From examining the plots and the Breusch-Godfrey test, it comes as no surprise that we can safely reject the null hypothesis of no autocorrelation. The simple way to deal with autocorrelation is to incorporate lagged variables of the dependent time series and/or to make all of the data stationary. We'll do that next using vector autoregression to identify the appropriate lag structure to incorporate in our causality efforts. One of the structural change points was 1949, so we'll start there.

Vector autoregression

We've seen in the preceding section that temperature and CO2 require a first order difference. Another simple way to show this is with the `forecast` package's `ndiffs()` function. It provides an output that spells out the minimum number of differences needed to make the data stationary. In the function, you can specify which test out of the three available ones you would like to use: **Kwiatkowski, Philips, Schmidt & Shin (KPSS)**, **Augmented Dickey-Fuller (ADF)**, or **Philips-Peron (PP)**. I'll use ADF in the following code, which has a null hypothesis that the data isn't stationary:

```
> climate49 <- window(climate_ts, start = 1949)

> forecast::ndiffs(climate49[, 1], test = "adf")
```

```
    [1]  1

> forecast::ndiffs(climate49[, 2], test = "adf")
    [1]  1
```

We see that both require a first-order difference to become stationary. To get started, we'll create a difference. Then, we'll complete the traditional approach, where both series are stationary:

```
> climate_diff <- diff(climate49)
```

It's now a matter of determining the optimal lag structure based on the information criteria using vector autoregression. This is done with the VARselect function in the vars package. You only need to specify the data and number of lags in the model using lag.max = x in the function. Let's use a maximum of 12 lags:

```
> lag.select <- vars::VARselect(climate_diff, lag.max = 12)

> lag.select$selection
    AIC(n)  HQ(n)  SC(n)  FPE(n)
        5      1      1       5
```

We called the information criteria using lag$selection. Four different criteria are provided, including **AIC**, **Hannan-Quinn Criterion (HQ)**, **Schwarz-Bayes Criterion (SC)**, and **FPE**. Note that AIC and SC are covered in Chapter 2, *Linear Regression*, so I won't go over the criterion formulas or differences here. If you want to see the actual results for each lag, you can use lag$criteria. We can see that AIC and FPE have selected lag 5 and HQ and SC lag 1 as the optimal structure to a VAR model. It seems to make sense that the five-year lag is the one to use. We'll create that model using the var() function. I'll let you try it with lag 1:

```
> fit1 <- vars::VAR(climate_diff, p = 5)
```

The summary results are quite lengthy as it builds two separate models and would take up probably two whole pages. What I provide is the abbreviated output showing the results with temperature as the prediction:

```
> summary(fit1)
Residual standard error: 0.09877 on 48 degrees of freedom
Multiple R-Squared: 0.4692, Adjusted R-squared: 0.3586
F-statistic: 4.243 on 10 and 48 DF, p-value: 0.0002996
```

The model is significant with a resulting adjusted R-square of 0.36.

As we did in the previous section, we should check for serial correlation. Here, the VAR package provides the `serial.test()` function for multivariate autocorrelation. It offers several different tests, but let's focus on the `Portmanteau Test,` and please note that the popular Durbin-Watson test is for univariate series only. The null hypothesis is that autocorrelations are zero and the alternative is that they aren't zero:

```
> vars::serial.test(fit1, type = "PT.asymptotic")

  Portmanteau Test (asymptotic)

data: Residuals of VAR object fit1
Chi-squared = 33.332, df = 44, p-value = 0.8794
```

With `p-value` at 0.8794, we don't have evidence to reject the null and can say that the residuals aren't autocorrelated. What does the test say with 1 lag?

To do the Granger causality tests in R, you can use either the `lmtest` package and the `Grangertest()` function or the `causality()` function in the `vars` package. I'll demonstrate the technique using `causality()`. It's very easy as you just need to create two objects, one for x causing y and one for y causing x, utilizing the `fit1` object previously created:

```
> x2y <- vars::causality(fit1, cause = "CO2")

> y2x <- vars::causality(fit1, cause = "Temp")
```

It's now just a simple matter to call the Granger test results:

```
> x2y$Granger

  Granger causality H0: CO2 don't Granger-cause Temp

data: VAR object fit1
F-Test = 2.7907, df1 = 5, df2 = 96, p-value = 0.02133

> y2x$Granger

  Granger causality H0: Temp don't Granger-cause CO2

data: VAR object fit1
F-Test = 0.71623, df1 = 5, df2 = 96, p-value = 0.6128
```

The `p-value` value for CO2 differences of Granger causing temperature is 0.02133 and isn't significant in the other direction. So what does all of this mean? The first thing we can say is that Y doesn't cause X. As for X causing Y, we can reject the null at the 0.05 significance level and therefore conclude that X does Granger cause Y. However, is that the relevant conclusion here? Remember, the p-value evaluates how likely the effect is if the null hypothesis is true. Also, remember that the test was never designed to be some binary yea or nay. Since this study is based on observational data, I believe we can say that it's highly probable that *CO2 emissions Granger cause surface temperature anomalies*. But there's a lot of room for criticism on that conclusion. I mentioned upfront the controversy around the quality of the data.

However, we still need to model the original CO2 levels using the alternative Granger causality technique. The process to find the correct number of lags is the same as before, except we don't need to make the data stationary:

```
> level.select <- vars::VARselect(climate49, lag.max = 12)

> level.select$selection
AIC(n)  HQ(n)  SC(n)  FPE(n)
    10      1      1       6
```

Let's try the lag 6 structure and see whether we can achieve significance, remembering to add one extra lag to account for the integrated series. A discussion on the technique and why it needs to be done is available at `http://davegiles.blogspot.de/2011/04/testing-for-granger-causality.html`:

```
> fit2 <- vars::VAR(climate49, p = 7)

> vars::serial.test(fit2, type = "PT.asymptotic")

    Portmanteau Test (asymptotic)

data: Residuals of VAR object fit2
Chi-squared = 32.693, df = 36, p-value = 0.6267
```

Now, to determine Granger causality for X causing Y, you conduct a Wald test, where the coefficients of X and only X are 0 in the equation to predict Y, remembering not to include the extra coefficients that account for integration in the test.

The Wald test in R is available in the `aod` package we've already loaded. We need to specify the coefficients of the full model, its variance-covariance matrix, and the coefficients of the causative variable.

The coefficients for `Temp` that we need to test in the VAR object consist of a range of even numbers from 2 to 12, while the coefficients for CO2 are odd from 1 to 11. Instead of using c(2, 4, 6, and so on) in our function, let's create an object with base R's seq() function.

First, let's see how CO2 does Granger causing temperature:

```
> CO2terms <- seq(1, 11, 2)

> Tempterms <- seq(2, 12, 2)
```

We're now ready to run the `wald` test, described in the following code and abbreviated output:

```
> aod::wald.test(
    b = coef(fit2$varresult$Temp),
    Sigma = vcov(fit2$varresult$Temp),
    Terms = c(CO2terms)
 )

$result$`chi2`
      chi2           df           P
13.48661591  6.00000000  0.03592734
```

How about that? We have a significant p-value so let's test the other direction causality with the following code:

```
> aod::wald.test(
    b = coef(fit2$varresult$CO2),
    Sigma = vcov(fit2$varresult$CO2),
    Terms = c(Tempterms)
 )

$result$`chi2`
      chi2          df          P
4.7709016  6.0000000  0.5735146
```

Conversely, we can say that temperature doesn't Granger cause CO2. The last thing to show here is how to use a vector autoregression to produce a forecast. A `predict` function is available and we'll plot the forecast for 24 years:

```
> plot(predict(fit2, n.ahead = 24, ci = 0.95))
```

The output of the preceding code is as follows:

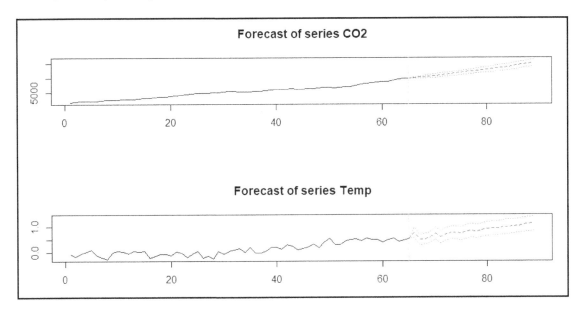

Looking out a couple of decades hence, we see temperature anomalies getting close to 1 degree. If nothing else, I hope this has stimulated your thinking on how to apply the technique to your own real-world problems or maybe even to examine the climate change data in more detail. There should be a high bar when it comes to demonstrating causality, and Granger causality is a great tool for assisting in that endeavor.

Summary

In this chapter, the goal was to discuss how important the element of time is in the field of machine learning and analytics, to identify the common traps when analyzing the time series, and to demonstrate the techniques and methods to work around these traps. We explored both the univariate and bivariate time series analysis for global temperature anomalies and human carbon dioxide emissions. Additionally, we looked at Granger causality to determine whether we can say, statistically speaking, that atmospheric CO_2 levels cause surface temperature anomalies. We discovered that the p-values are higher than 0.05 but less than 0.10 for Granger causality from CO_2 to temperature. It does show that Granger causality is an effective tool in investigating causality in machine learning problems. In the next chapter, we'll shift gears and take a look at how to apply learning methods to textual data.

Additionally, keep in mind that in time series analysis, we just skimmed the surface. I encourage you to explore other techniques around change point detection, decomposition of time series, nonlinear forecasting, and many others. Although not usually considered part of the machine learning toolbox, I believe you'll find it an invaluable addition to yours.

13
Text Mining

The world is awash with textual data. If you Google, Bing, or Yahoo! how much of that data is unstructured, that is, in a textual format, estimates would range from 80 to 90 percent. The real number doesn't matter. It matters that a large proportion of the data is in text format. The implication is that anyone seeking to find insights in that data must develop the capability to process and analyze text.

When I first started out as a market researcher, I used to manually pore through page after page of moderator-led focus group and interview transcripts with the hope of capturing some qualitative insight, an *aha moment* if you will, and then haggle with fellow team members over whether they had the same insight or not. Then, you would always have that one individual in a project who would swoop in and listen to two interviews—out of the 30 or 40 on the schedule—and, alas, they had their mind made up on what was really happening in the world. Contrast that with the techniques being used now, where an analyst can quickly distill data into meaningful quantitative results, support qualitative understanding, and maybe even sway the swooper.

Over the last few years, I've applied the techniques discussed here to mine physician-patient interactions, understand FDA fears on prescription drug advertising, capture patient concerns about rare cancer, and capture customer maintenance problems, to name just a few. Using R and the methods in this chapter, you too can extract the powerful information in textual data.

The following topics will be covered in this chapter:

- Text mining framework and methods
- Data overview
- Word frequency
- Sentiment analysis
- N-grams
- Topic models
- Classifying text
- Additional quantitative analysis

Text mining framework and methods

There are many different methods to use in text mining. The goal here is to provide a basic framework to apply to such an endeavor. This framework is not inclusive of all the possible methods, but will cover those that are probably the most important for the vast majority of projects that you will work on. Additionally, I will discuss the modeling methods in as succinct and clear a manner as possible, because they can get quite complicated. Gathering and compiling text data is a topic that could take up several chapters. One of the things I prefer and will put forward here is the use of the **tidy** framework. It will allow us to use **tibbles** and data frames for most of the steps, and the `tidytext` functions allow an easy transition to other types of text mining structures, such as a corpus.

The first task is to put the text files into a data frame. With that created, the data preparation can begin with the text transformation.

The following list is composed of probably some of the most common and useful transformations for text files:

- Change capital letters to lowercase
- Remove numbers
- Remove punctuation
- Remove stop words
- Remove excess whitespace characters
- Word stemming
- Word replacement

With these transformations, you are creating a more compact dataset and simplify the structure in order to facilitate relationships between the words, thereby leading to increased understanding. However, keep in mind that not all of these transformations are necessary all the time and judgment must be applied, or you can iterate to find the transformations that make the most sense.

By changing words to lowercase, you can prevent the improper counting of words. Say that you have a count for *hockey* three times and *Hockey* once, where it is the first word in a sentence. R will not give you a count of *hockey=4*, but *hockey=3* and *Hockey=1*.

Removing punctuation also achieves the same purpose, but in some cases, punctuation is important, especially if you want to tokenize your documents by sentences.

In removing stop words, you are getting rid of the common words that have no value; in fact, they are detrimental to the analysis, as their frequency masks important words. Examples of stop words are *and, is, the, not,* and *to*.

Removing whitespace makes data more compact by getting rid of things such as tabs, paragraph breaks, double-spacing, and so on.

The stemming of words can get tricky and might add to your confusion because it deletes word suffixes, creating the base word, or what is known as the **radical**. I personally am not a big fan of stemming and the analysts I've worked with agree with that sentiment. Recall that R would count this as two separate words. By running a stemming algorithm, the stemmed word for the two instances would become *famili*. This would prevent the incorrect count, but in some cases it can be odd to interpret and is not very visually appealing in a word cloud for presentation purposes. In some cases, it may make sense to run your analysis with both stemmed and unstemmed words in order to see which one facilitates understanding.

Probably the most optional of the transformations is to replace the words. The goal of replacement is to combine words with a similar meaning, for example, *management* and *leadership*. You can also use it in lieu of stemming. I once examined the outcome of stemmed and unstemmed words and concluded that I could achieve a more meaningful result by replacing about a dozen words instead of stemming. It can be important when you have manual data entry and different operators input data differently. For example, tech support person one types in the system *turbocharger*, while tech support person two types in *turbo charger* half the time, and *turbo-charger* the other half. All three versions are the same, so applying a replacement function such as `gsub()` or `grepl()` will solve the problem.

With transformations completed, one structure to create for topic modeling or classification is either a **document-term matrix** (**DTM**) or **term-document matrix** (**TDM**). What either of these matrices does is create a matrix of word counts for each individual document in the matrix. A DTM would have the documents as rows and the words as columns, while in a TDM, the reverse is true. We will be using a DTM for our example.

Topic models

Topic models are a powerful method to group documents by their main topics. Topic models allow probabilistic modeling of term frequency occurrence in documents. The fitted model can be used to estimate the similarity between documents, as well as between a set of specified keywords using an additional layer of latent variables, which are referred to as topics (Grun and Hornik, 2011). In essence, a document is assigned to a topic based on the distribution of the words in that document, and the other documents in that topic will have roughly the same frequency of words.

The algorithm that we will focus on is **Latent Dirichlet Allocation** (**LDA**) with Gibbs sampling, which is probably the most commonly used sampling algorithm. In building topic models, the number of topics must be determined before running the algorithm (k-dimensions). If no a priori reason for the number of topics exists, then you can build several and apply judgment and knowledge to the final selection. LDA with Gibbs sampling is quite complicated mathematically, but my intent is to provide an introduction so that you are at least able to describe how the algorithm learns to assign a document to a topic in layperson terms. If you are interested in mastering the math associated with the method, block out a couple of hours on your calendar and have a go at it. Excellent background material is available at `http://www.cs.columbia.edu/~blei/papers/Blei2012.pdf`.

LDA is a generative process, and so the following will iterate to a steady state:

1. For each document (j), there are 1 to j documents. We will randomly assign a multinomial distribution (**Dirichlet distribution**) to the topics (k) with 1 to k topics, for example, document A is 25 percent topic one, 25 percent topic two, and 50 percent topic three.
2. Probabilistically, for each word (i), there are 1 to i words to a topic (k); for example, the word *mean* has a probability of 0.25 for the topic statistics.
3. For each word (i) in document (j) and topic (k), calculate the proportion of words in that document assigned to that topic; note it as the probability of topic (k) with document (j), $p(k|j)$, and the proportion of word (i) in topic (k) from all the documents containing the word. Note it as the probability of word (i) with topic (k), $p(i|k)$.

4. Resample, that is, assign *w* a new *t* based on the probability that *t* contains *w*, which is based on *p(k|j)* times *p(i|k)*.

5. Rinse and repeat; over numerous iterations, the algorithm finally converges and a document is assigned a topic based on the proportion of words assigned to a topic in that document.

The LDA that we will be doing assumes that the order of words and documents does not matter. There has been work done to relax these assumptions in order to build models of language generation and sequence models over time (known as **dynamic topic modeling**).

Other quantitative analysis

We will now shift gears to analyze text semantically based on sentences and the tagging of words based on the parts of speech, such as noun, verb, pronoun, adjective, adverb, preposition, singular, plural, and so on. Often, just examining the frequency and latent topics in the text will suffice for your analysis. However, you may find occasions when a deeper understanding of the style is required in order to compare the speakers or writers.

There are many methods to accomplish this task, but we will focus on the following five:

- Polarity (sentiment analysis)
- Automated readability index (complexity)
- Formality
- Diversity
- Dispersion

Polarity is often referred to as sentiment analysis, which tells you how positive or negative the text is. By analyzing polarity in R , it will assign a score to each word and you can analyze the average and standard deviation of polarity by groups such as different authors, text, or topics. Different polarity dictionaries are available and we will explore them in more detail later. You can alter or change a dictionary according to your requirements.

The algorithm works by first tagging the words with a positive, negative, or neutral sentiment based on the dictionary. The tagged words are then clustered based on the four words prior and two words after a tagged word, and these clusters are tagged with what are known as **valence shifters** (neutral, negator, amplifier, and de-amplifier). A series of weights based on their number and position are applied to both the words and clusters. This is then summed and divided by the square root of the number of words in that sentence.

The automated readability index is a measure of the text complexity and a reader's ability to understand. A specific formula is used to calculate this index: *4.71(# of characters / #of words) + 0.5(# of words / # of sentences) - 21.43.*

The index produces a number, which is a rough estimate of a student's grade level to fully comprehend. If the number is 9, then a high school freshman, aged 13 to 15, should be able to grasp the meaning of the text.

The formality measure provides an understanding of how a text relates to the reader or speech relates to a listener. I like to think of it as a way to understand how comfortable the person producing the text is with the audience, or an understanding of the setting where this communication takes place. If you want to experience formal text, attend a medical conference or read a legal document. The informal text is said to be contextual in nature.

The formality measure is called **F-Measure**. This measure is calculated as follows:

- Formal words (*f*) are nouns, adjectives, prepositions, and articles
- Contextual words (*c*) are pronouns, verbs, adverbs, and interjections
- *N = sum of (f + c + conjunctions)*
- *Formality Index = 50((sum of f - sum of c / N) + 1)*

Diversity, as it relates to text mining, refers to the number of different words used in relation to the total number of words used. This can also mean the expanse of the text producer's vocabulary or lexicon richness. The `qdap` package provides five—that's right, five—different measures of diversity: `simpson`, `shannon`, `collision`, `bergen_parker`, and `brillouin`. I won't cover these five in detail but will only say that the algorithms are used not only for communication and information science retrieval but also for biodiversity in nature.

Finally, dispersion, or lexical dispersion, is a useful tool in order to understand how words are spread throughout a document and serve as an excellent way to explore text and identify patterns. The analysis is conducted by calling the specific word or words of interest, which are then produced in a plot showing when the word or words occurred in the text over time. As we will see, the `qdap` package has a built-in plotting function to analyze the text dispersion.

We have covered a framework on text mining about how to prepare the text, count words, and create topic models and, finally, dived deep into other lexical measures. Now, let's apply all this and do some real-world text mining.

Data overview

For this case study, we will take a look at the full text of State of the Union addresses. The State of the Union is an annual message that the President provides to Congress. The purpose is to provide an economic and diplomatic overview, as well as outline the legislative agenda. I would characterize it as your typical political feel-good propaganda, sprinkled with false hope and enthusiasm. I'm too old and too wise to consider it anything else.

The data is in an R package `sotu`. It consists of the text and metadata for 236 addresses, both oral and written.

> The data is technically not correct about State of the Union addresses. The proper definition for a first-term President's address in their first year in office is *address to a joint session*.

The learning goals for us are to explore work frequency, Abraham Lincoln's addresses, the sentiment of the addresses around the time of the US Civil War, topic models for the speeches from the time of the escalation of the Vietnam War to the present, political party classification modeling, and finally some of the advanced speech methods applied to two different Presidents.

Data frame creation

As per an old joke and bit of wisdom:

> *"How can you tell when a politician is lying? Their lips are moving!"*

If not already done, please install the following packages, and call the `magrittr` and `sotu` libraries:

```
> install.packages("ggplot2")

> install.packages("ggraph")

> install.packages("igraph")

> install.packages("quanteda")

> install.packages("qdap")

> install.packages("tidytext")
```

```
> install.packages("tidyverse")

> install.packages("sotu")

> install.packages("topicmodels")

> library(magrittr)

> library(sotu)
```

Since the data is located within the `sotu` package, we needed to call it to create the objects of the data like this:

```
> data(sotu_text)

> data(sotu_meta)
```

It is easy to turn this into a data frame with everything we need by adding the raw text to the metadata:

```
> sotu_meta$text <- sotu_text
```

Here are the column names. I recommend you spend a few minutes exploring this data on your own as well:

```
> colnames(sotu_meta)
[1] "president" "year" "years_active" "party" "sotu_type"
[6] "text"
```

The `text` column has the data of interest in a character string. Before we start analyzing the data, we need to tokenize the text and link it to each President. What does that mean? It means we put one token per row per document. A token can be a character, a word, an n-gram combination of words, or a sentence. This will set us up for applying tidy format procedures:

```
> sotu_meta %>%
    tidytext::unnest_tokens(word, text) -> sotu_unnest
```

All we did was just tell the `unnest_tokens()` function to take the column text and turn it into a column called `word`. The function we shall see accommodates n-grams but defaults to words. It also automatically removes all capitalization. When we tackle n-grams, we'll set that to false. Here is what the new `tibble` created looks like:

```
> sotu_unnest
# A tibble: 1,965,212 x 6
   president       year  years_active party      sotu_type word
   <chr>           <int> <chr>        <chr>      <chr>     <chr>
```

```
 1 George Washington 1790    1789-1793    Nonpartisan speech    fellow
 2 George Washington 1790    1789-1793    Nonpartisan speech    citizens
 3 George Washington 1790    1789-1793    Nonpartisan speech    of
 4 George Washington 1790    1789-1793    Nonpartisan speech    the
 5 George Washington 1790    1789-1793    Nonpartisan speech    senate
 6 George Washington 1790    1789-1793    Nonpartisan speech    and
 7 George Washington 1790    1789-1793    Nonpartisan speech    house
 8 George Washington 1790    1789-1793    Nonpartisan speech    of
 9 George Washington 1790    1789-1793    Nonpartisan speech
representatives
10 George Washington 1790    1789-1793    Nonpartisan speech    i
# ... with 1,965,202 more rows
```

With our data ready, let's get started.

Word frequency

With word frequency analysis, we want to clean this data by removing the stop words, which would just clutter our interpretation. We'll explore the top overall word frequencies, then take a look at President Lincoln's work.

Word frequency in all addresses

To get rid of stop words in a tidy format, you can use the `stop_words` data frame provided in the `tidytext` package. You call that `tibble` into the environment, then do an anti-join by word:

```
> library(tidytext)

> data(stop_words)

> sotu_tidy <- sotu_unnest %>%
    dplyr::anti_join(stop_words, by = "word")
```

Notice that the length of the data went from 1.97 million observations down to 778,161. Now, you can go ahead and see the top words. I don't do it in the following, but you can put this into a data frame if you so choose:

```
> sotu_tidy %>%
    dplyr::count(word, sort = TRUE)
# A tibble: 29,558 x 2
   word           n
   <chr>       <int>
```

```
 1 government    7573
 2 congress      5759
 3 united        5102
 4 people        4219
 5 country       3564
 6 public        3413
 7 time          3138
 8 war           2961
 9 american      2853
10 world         2581
# ... with 29,548 more rows
```

We can pass this data to `ggplot2`, in this case, words that occur more than 2,500 times:

```
> sotu_tidy %>%
    dplyr::count(word, sort = TRUE) %>%
    dplyr::filter(n > 2500) %>%
    dplyr::mutate(word = reorder(word, n)) %>%
    ggplot2::ggplot(ggplot2::aes(word, n)) +
    ggplot2::geom_col() +
    ggplot2::xlab(NULL) +
    ggplot2::coord_flip() +
    ggthemes::theme_igray()
```

The output of the preceding code is as follows:

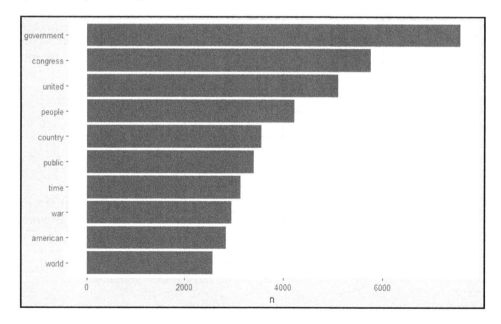

We can look at the addresses that contain the most total words:

```
> sotu_tidy %>%
    dplyr::group_by(year) %>%
    dplyr::summarise(totalWords = length(word)) %>%
    dplyr::arrange(desc(totalWords))
# A tibble: 225 x 2
    year totalWords
   <int>      <int>
 1 1981      18402
 2 1980      17553
 3 1946      12614
 4 1974      11813
 5 1979      11730
 6 1910      11178
 7 1907      10230
 8 1912      10215
 9 1911       9598
10 1899       9504
# ... with 215 more rows
```

How about that? The two longest speeches were given by Ronald Reagan, often called *The Great Communicator*. Moving on, we'll take a look at Lincoln's top word frequency, then create a word cloud for each of the separate addresses.

Lincoln's word frequency

In the same fashion as previously, we'll see the top 10 words Lincoln used. The filter to apply for Abe's addresses is 1861 through 1864:

```
> sotu_tidy %>%
    dplyr::filter(year > 1860 & year < 1865) %>%
    dplyr::count(word, sort = TRUE)
# A tibble: 3,562 x 2
   word           n
   <chr>      <int>
 1 congress      81
 2 united        81
 3 government    75
 4 people        70
 5 war           65
 6 country       62
 7 time          51
```

```
 8 union          50
 9 national       49
10 public         48
# ... with 3,552 more rows
```

No surprise that *war* is high on the list with the Civil War during that time period. One way to visualize how the addresses changed and stayed the same is to produce a word cloud for each address. A convenient way to do that is with the `qdap` package. We first need to filter out Lincoln's speeches from the tokenized data frame. Then, we produce a separate word cloud for each year. Notice that I specify a minimum frequency of seven words per year and specify no stemming. This produces the following four different plots:

```
> sotu_cloud <- sotu_tidy %>%
    dplyr::filter(year > 1860 & year < 1865)

> qdap::trans_cloud(
    text.var = sotu_cloud$word,
    grouping.var = sotu_cloud$year,
    stem = FALSE,
    min.freq = 7
  )
```

The output of the preceding code is as follows:

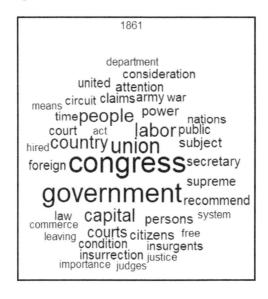

Output Frame 2:

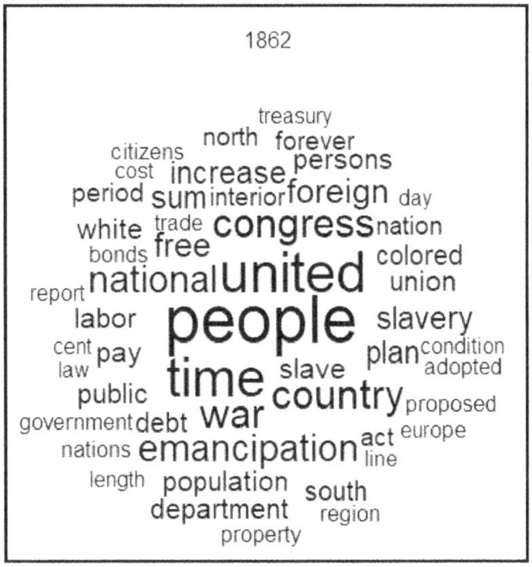

Output Frame 3:

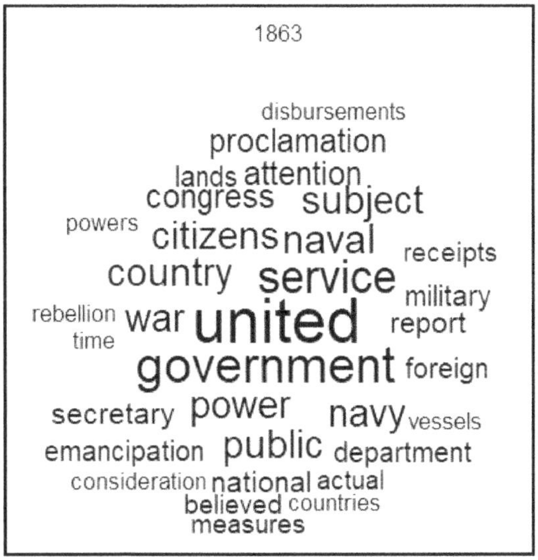

Output Frame 4:

1864

increase
public country
navy united service
session congress
condition election
people war union
government amount
naval national report
time
treasury department
secretary debt

Very similar themes throughout, but notice you have a clear focus on emancipation and slavery in 1862 and 1863. An interesting analytical method is to drill down on a term and put it in context, or what we can call keywords in context. However, to do that we need to transform our data. The `quanteda` package has a keyword in context function `kwic()`, but it requires the data be in a corpus, which demands that the text be back in one cell per document, and not one token per row per document. The implication to us is that we need to unnest the tidy data frame. This accomplishes that and just selects the year 1862:

```
> nested_1862 <- sotu_tidy %>%
    dplyr::filter(year == 1862) %>%
    dplyr::select(year, word) %>%
    tidyr::nest(word) %>%
    dplyr::mutate(
    text = purrr::map(data, unlist),
    text = purrr::map_chr(text, paste, collapse = " ")
  )
```

This gives us the text with stop words removed and back in one cell. To put this in a corpus structure, the `tm` package is useful:

```
> myCorpus <- tm::Corpus(tm::VectorSource(nested_1862$text))
```

For this example of keywords in context, we should look at where Lincoln discusses emancipation. An important specification in the function is how many words to the left and right of our keyword we want to see as the context of interest. Here is the abbreviated content:

```
> quanteda::kwic(x = myCorpus$content, pattern = "emancipation", window =
6)
 [text1, 1462] paper respectfully recall attention called compensated |
 [text1, 2076] plan mutual concessions plan adopted assumed |
 [text1, 2873] recommendation congress provide law compensating adopt |
 [text1, 2939] slave concurrence obtained assurance severally adopting |
 emancipation | nation consist territory people laws territory
 emancipation | follow article main emancipation length time
 emancipation | plan acted earnestly renewed advance plan
 emancipation | distant day constitutional terms assurance struggle
```

The output can be awkward to interpret at first. However, what it produces is the document number of the corpus the text is from, so with just one text cell, all output is text1. Then, it shows what character number our keyword starts with (1462). What we have left is the six words prior to our keyword and the six words after it. The first line of text would read like this: *paper respectfully recall attention called compensated emancipation nation consist territory people laws territory*. That might seem confusing, but the item of interest is the concept of compensating regions for emancipation. The full output, and including more context words, can help get a sense of Lincoln's problems and solutions for emancipation. As historical background, Lincoln delivered the address on December 1, 1862, and the political opposition in the Union was in an uproar over the Emancipation Proclamation he issued two and a half months before. Lincoln had to dance a political jig, in essence, moderating his stance by claiming that emancipation would be gradual and done with compensation. In short, looking at keywords in context can help in deriving an understanding for yourself and with your customers about how to interpret textual data.

We'll now take a look at implementing sentiment analysis in a tidyverse fashion.

Sentiment analysis

"We shall nobly save, or meanly lose, the last, best hope of earth."

– Abraham Lincoln

In this section, we'll take a look at the various sentiment options available in `tidytext`. Then, we'll apply that to a subset of the data before, during, and after the Civil War. To get started, let's explore the sentiments dataset that comes with `tidytext`:

```
> table(sentiments$lexicon)

  AFINN bing loughran    nrc
   2476 6788     4149 13901
```

The four sentiment options and researchers associated with them are as follows:

- `AFINN`: Finn, Arup, and Nielsen
- `bing`: Bing, Liu et al.
- `loughran`: Loughran and McDonald
- `nrc`: Mohammad and Turney

The `AFINN` sentiment categorizes words on a negative to positive scale from -5 to +5. The `bing` version has a simple binary negative or positive ranking; `loughran` provides six different categories including `negative`, `positive`, and such things as `superfluous`. With `nrc`, you get five categories such as `anger` or `trust`. Here is a glance at a few words and associated sentiment classification with `nrc`:

```
> get_sentiments("nrc")
# A tibble: 13,901 x 2
   word sentiment
   <chr> <chr>
 1 abacus      trust
 2 abandon     fear
 3 abandon     negative
 4 abandon     sadness
 5 abandoned   anger
 6 abandoned   fear
 7 abandoned   negative
 8 abandoned   sadness
 9 abandonment anger
10 abandonment fear
```

You see that a word can have multiple sentiment categories. Let's see whether Lincoln expressed `anger` in his 1862 attempt to mollify his political opponents:

```
> nrc_anger <- tidytext::get_sentiments("nrc") %>%
    dplyr::filter(sentiment == "anger")

> sotu_tidy %>%
    dplyr::filter(year == 1862) %>%
```

```
      dplyr::inner_join(nrc_anger) %>%
      dplyr::count(word, sort = TRUE)
Joining, by = "word"
# A tibble: 62 x 2
   word        n
   <chr>       <int>
 1 slavery     13
 2 slave       12
 3 demand       5
 4 force        5
 5 money        5
 6 abolish      4
 7 rebellion    4
 8 cash         3
 9 deportation  3
10 fugitive     3
# ... with 52 more rows
```

OK, that is interesting and might be an indication of the challenge of taking qualitative sentiment rankings developed recently and applying them to historical documents. We'll expand the analysis now by looking at addresses from 1853 to 1872 using the bing sentiment technique. We will build a data frame of the total positive and negative sentiment, using that to calculate an overall sentiment score for each year:

```
> sentiment <- sotu_tidy %>%
    dplyr::inner_join(tidytext::get_sentiments("bing")) %>%
    dplyr::filter(year > 1852 & year <1873) %>%
    dplyr::count(president, year, sentiment) %>%
    tidyr::spread(sentiment, n, fill = 0) %>%
    dplyr::mutate(sentiment = positive - negative) %>%
    dplyr::arrange(year)
Joining, by = "word"
```

You can explore that on your own, but in the meantime, here is a plot of sentiment by president and year:

```
> ggplot2::ggplot(sentiment, ggplot2::aes(year, sentiment, fill =
president)) +
    ggplot2::geom_col(show.legend = FALSE) +
    ggplot2::facet_wrap(~ president, ncol = 2, scales = "free_x") +
    ggthemes::theme_pander()
```

The output of the preceding code is as follows:

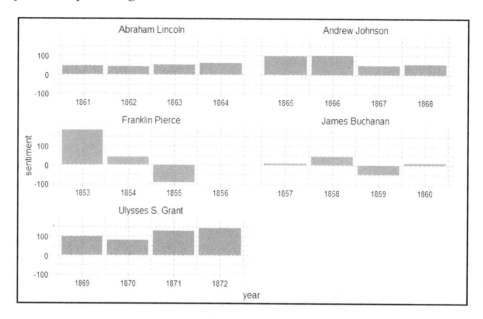

The pre-war Presidents had negative sentiment, I guess as things fell apart. Arguably, Buchanan was the worst President ever. Not even Jimmy Carter was as bad. It is interesting how positive Grant is, given, the difficulties of reconstruction, having to fight a near-guerrilla war in the south. He is as underrated a President as there is. Enough of my historical ruminations. It is an easy task to find and portray sentiment in text data using `tidytext`. Indeed, here is an example of most what words are driving `positive` or `negative` sentiment:

```
> sotu_tidy %>%
    dplyr::inner_join(tidytext::get_sentiments("bing")) %>%
    dplyr::count(word, sentiment, sort = TRUE) %>%
    dplyr::ungroup()
Joining, by = "word"
# A tibble: 3,592 x 3
   word sentiment n
        <chr> <chr>   <int>
 1      peace positive 2021
 2       free positive 1306
 3   progress positive 1157
 4    support positive  961
 5 protection positive  864
 6     proper positive  840
 7  recommend positive  836
```

```
 8       debt negative   795
 9    freedom positive   744
10     secure positive   724
# ... with 3,582 more rows
```

Peace is the number one positive word, despite its elusiveness, and the number one negative word is *debt*. Oh well, good luck with that!

One of the things to consider in processing text is what resolutions of it help facilitate learning. We've done just words up to this point, let's shift gears to word combinations or n-grams.

N-grams

Looking at combinations of words in, say, bigrams or trigrams can help you understand relationships between words. Using tidy methods again, we'll create bigrams and learn about those relationships to extract insights from the text. I will continue with the subject of President Lincoln as that will allow you to compare what you gain with n-grams versus just words. Getting started is easy, as you just specify the number of words to join. Notice in the following code that I maintain word capitalization:

```
> sotu_bigrams <- sotu_meta %>%
    dplyr::filter(year > 1860 & year < 1865) %>%
    tidytext::unnest_tokens(bigram, text, token = "ngrams", n = 2,
    to_lower =   FALSE)
```

Let's take a look at this:

```
> sotu_bigrams %>%
    dplyr::count(bigram, sort = TRUE)
# A tibble: 17,687 x 2
   bigram n
   <chr>         <int>
 1 of the          509
 2 to the          180
 3 in the          146
 4 by the           97
 5 for the          94
 6 have been        82
 7 United States    79
 8 and the          76
 9 has been         76
10 the United       73
# ... with 17,677 more rows
```

Those pesky stop words! Fear not, as we can deal with them in short order:

```
> bigrams_separated <- sotu_bigrams %>%
    tidyr::separate(bigram, c("word1", "word2"), sep = " ")

> bigrams_filtered <- bigrams_separated %>%
    dplyr::filter(!word1 %in% stop_words$word) %>%
    dplyr::filter(!word2 %in% stop_words$word)
```

Now, it makes sense to look at Lincoln's bigrams:

```
> bigram_counts <- bigrams_filtered %>%
    dplyr::count(word1, word2, sort = TRUE)

> bigram_counts
# A tibble: 3,488 x 3
   word1    word2        n
   <chr>    <chr>    <int>
 1 United   States      79
 2 public   debt        11
 3 public   lands       10
 4 Great    Britain      9
 5 civil    war          8
 6 I        recommend    8
 7 naval    service      8
 8 annual   message      7
 9 foreign  nations      7
10 free     colored      7
# ... with 3,478 more rows
```

This is interesting, I believe. I found it surprising that *Great Britain* was there nine times, but on reflection realized they were a political thorn in the Union's side. I'll spare you the details. You can create a visual representation of these word relationships via a network graph:

```
> bigram_graph <- bigram_counts %>%
 dplyr::filter(n > 4) %>%
 igraph::graph_from_data_frame()

> set.seed(1861) #

> ggraph::ggraph(bigram_graph, layout = "fr") +
 ggraph::geom_edge_link() +
 ggraph::geom_node_point() +
 ggraph::geom_node_text(ggplot2::aes(label = name), vjust = 1, hjust = 1)
```

The output of the preceding code is as follows:

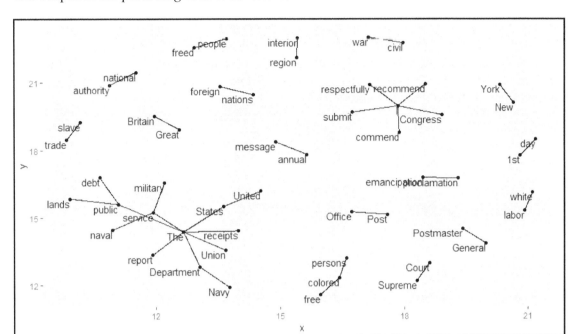

I think it is safe to say that the use of n-grams can help you learn from text. In combination with analysis by tokenizing words, we can start to see some patterns and themes. However, we can take our understanding to the next level by building topic models.

Topic models

We will leave behind the 19th century and look at these recent times of trial and tribulation (1965 through 2016). In looking at this data, I found something interesting and troubling. Let's take a look at the 1970s:

```
> sotu_meta[185:191, 1:4]
# A tibble: 7 x 4
  president        year  years_active party
  <chr>           <int> <chr>        <chr>
1 Richard M. Nixon 1970  1969-1973    Republican
2 Richard M. Nixon 1971  1969-1973    Republican
3 Richard M. Nixon 1972  1969-1973    Republican
4 Richard M. Nixon 1972  1969-1973    Republican
```

```
5 Richard M. Nixon 1974   1973-1974      Republican
6 Richard M. Nixon 1974   1973-1974      Republican
7 Gerald R.   Ford 1975   1974-1977      Republican
```

We see there are two 1972 and two 1974 addresses, but none for 1973. What? I went to the Nixon Foundation website, spent about 10 minutes trying to deconflict this, and finally threw my hands in the air and decided on implementing a quick fix. Be advised that there are a number of these conflicts to put in order:

```
> sotu_meta[188, 2] <- "1972_2"

> sotu_meta[190, 2] <- "1974_2"

> sotu_meta[157, 2] <- "1945_2"

> sotu_meta[166, 2] <- "1953_2"

> sotu_meta[170, 2] <- "1956_2"

> sotu_meta[176, 2] <- "1961_2"

> sotu_meta[195, 2] <- "1978_2"

> sotu_meta[197, 2] <- "1979_2"

> sotu_meta[199, 2] <- "1980_2"

> sotu_meta[201, 2] <- "1981_2"
```

An email to the author of this package is in order. I won't bother with that, but feel free to solve the issue yourself.

With this tragedy behind us, we'll go through tokenizing and removing stop words again for our relevant time frame:

```
> sotu_meta_recent <- sotu_meta %>%
    dplyr::filter(year > 1964)

> sotu_meta_recent %>%
    tidytext::unnest_tokens(word, text) -> sotu_unnest_recent

> sotu_recent <- sotu_unnest_recent %>%
    dplyr::anti_join(stop_words, by = "word")
```

As discussed previously, we need to put the data into a DTM before building a model. This is done by creating a word count grouped by year, then passing that to the `cast_dtm()` function:

```
> sotu_recent %>%
    dplyr::group_by(year) %>%
    dplyr::count(word) -> lda_words

> sotu_dtm <- tidytext::cast_dtm(lda_words, year, word, n)
```

Let's get our model built. I'm going to create six different topics using the `Gibbs` method, and I specified `verbose`. It should run 2,000 iterations:

```
> sotu_lda <-
  topicmodels::LDA(
  sotu_dtm,
  k = 6,
  method = "Gibbs",
  control = list(seed = 1965, verbose = 1)
  )

> sotu_lda
A LDA_Gibbs topic model with 6 topics.
```

The algorithm gives each topic a number. We can see what year is mapped to what topic. I abbreviate the output since 2002:

```
> topicmodels::topics(sotu_lda)
2002 2003 2004 2005 2006 2007 2008 2009 2010 2011 2012 2013 2014 2015 2016
   2    2    2    2    2    2    2    4    4    4    4    4    4    4    4
```

We see a clear transition between Bush and Obama from topic 2 to topic 4. Here is a table of the count of topics:

```
> table(topicmodels::topics(sotu_lda))

 1 2 3  4  5 6
 8 7 5 18 14 5
```

Topic 4 is the most prevalent, which is associated with Clinton's term also. This output gives us the top five words associated with each topic:

```
> topicmodels::terms(sotu_lda, 5)
     Topic 1       Topic 2      Topic 3
[1,] "future"      "america"    "administration"
[2,] "tax"         "security"   "congress"
[3,] "spending"    "country"    "economic"
[4,] "government"  "world"      "legislation"
[5,] "economic"    "iraq"       "energy"

     Topic 4       Topic 5      Topic 6
[1,] "people"      "world"      "federal"
[2,] "american"    "people"     "programs"
[3,] "jobs"        "american"   "government"
[4,] "america"     "congress"   "program"
[5,] "children"    "peace"      "act"
```

This all makes good sense, and topic 2 is spot on for the time. If you drill down further to, say, 10, 15, or 20 words, it is even more revealing, but I won't bore you further. What about an application in the tidy ecosystem and a visualization? Certainly! We'll turn the model object into a data frame first and in the process capture the per-topic-per-word probabilities called `beta`:

```
> lda_topics <- tidytext::tidy(sotu_lda, matrix = "beta")

> ap_top_terms <- lda_topics %>%
    dplyr::group_by(topic) %>%
    dplyr::top_n(10, beta) %>%
    dplyr::ungroup() %>%
    dplyr::arrange(topic, -beta)
```

We can explore that data further or just plot it as follows:

```
> ap_top_terms %>%
    dplyr::mutate(term = reorder(term, beta)) %>%
    ggplot2::ggplot(ggplot2::aes(term, beta, fill = factor(topic))) +
    ggplot2::geom_col(show.legend = FALSE) +
    ggplot2::facet_wrap(~ topic, scales = "free") +
    ggplot2::coord_flip() +
    ggthemes::theme_economist_white()
```

The output of the preceding code is as follows:

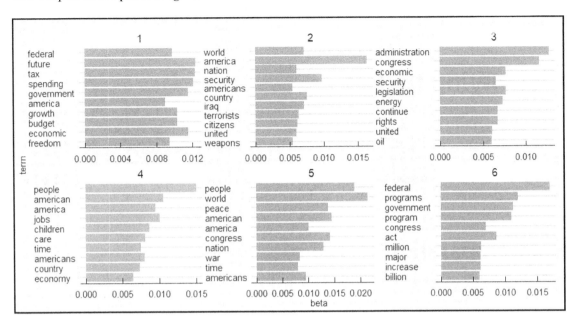

This is the top 10 words per topic based on the `beta` probability. Another thing we can do is look at the probability an address is related to a topic. This is referred to as `gamma` in the model and we can pull those in just like the `beta`:

```
> ap_documents <- tidytext::tidy(sotu_lda, matrix = "gamma")
```

We now have the probabilities of an address per topic. Let's look at the 1981 Ronald Reagan values:

```
> dplyr::filter(ap_documents, document == "1981")
# A tibble: 6 x 3
  document topic gamma
  <chr>    <int> <dbl>
1 1981         1  0.286
2 1981         2  0.0163
3 1981         3  0.0923
4 1981         4  0.118
5 1981         5  0.0777
6 1981         6  0.411
```

Topic 1 is a close second in the topic race. If you think about it, this means that more than six topics would help to create better separation in the probabilities. However, I like just six topics for this chapter for the purpose of demonstration.

Our next endeavor will consist of turning the DTM into input features for a simple classification model on predicting the political party, because partying is what politicians do best.

Classifying text

Our goal here is to build a classifier to predict Presidential party affiliation, either Democrat or Republican, since 1900. We will turn the word counts per year into features, create a DTM, create features using the **term frequency-inverse document frequency (tf-idf)**, and use them in our model. As you can imagine, we will have thousands of features, so we will change how the data is prepared versus what we covered in prior sections, and also use the `text2vec` package for feature creation and modeling.

Data preparation

We'll start by getting the pertinent data period. Then, we'll take a look at a table of the labels:

```
> sotu_party <- sotu_meta %>%
    dplyr::filter(year > 1899)

> table(sotu_party$party)

Democratic Republican
        61         64
```

The class is well balanced.

A few things can help in the modeling process. It is a good idea here to remove numbers, remove capitalization, remove stop words, stem the words, and remove punctuation. The built-in functions from the `tm` package are handy for this, and we can apply it to a column in the data frame:

```
> sotu_tidy_party$word <- tm::removeNumbers(sotu_tidy_party$word)

> sotu_tidy_party$word <- tm::removePunctuation(sotu_tidy_party$word)

> sotu_party$text <- tolower(sotu_party$text)

> sotu_tidy_party$word <- tm::stemDocument(sotu_tidy_party$word)

> sotu_party$text <- tm::removeWords(sotu_party$text, tm::stopwords("en"))
```

Now we can go ahead and create train and test datasets using `caret` as before:

```
> set.seed(222)

> index <- caret::createDataPartition(sotu_party$party, p = 0.8, list = F)

> train <- sotu_party[index, ]

> test <- sotu_party[-index, ]
```

The objective now is to create a word-based `tokenizer` function for the training data. It is also important to specify a document ID, which will be the column values for a year. We will apply this function to our test data as well:

```
> tok_fun = word_tokenizer

> it_train = text2vec::itoken(
    train$text,
    tokenizer = tok_fun,
    ids = train$year,
    progressbar = FALSE
  )
```

Now the `create_vocabulary()` function will create a data frame of the word, its total count, and the number of documents in which it appears:

```
> vocab = text2vec::create_vocabulary(it_train)
```

This produces data with 13,541 words. A consideration is to what extent you want to remove sparse words, even before doing anything else. In this example, if we remove any word that occurs less than four times, the number of words is reduced to 5,321:

```
> pruned <- text2vec::prune_vocabulary(vocab, term_count_min = 4)
```

Before creating the DTM, you must create an object of how to map the text to the indices. This is done with the `vocab_vectorizer()` function:

```
> vectorizer = text2vec::vocab_vectorizer(pruned)
```

We now create the DTM with the structure of a sparse matrix:

```
> dtm_train = text2vec::create_dtm(it_train, vectorizer)

> dim(dtm_train)
[1] 101 5321
```

You can see that the matrix has 101 observations corresponding to each year in training data and a column for each word. The final transformation prior to modeling is to turn the raw counts in the matrix to tf-idf values. This acts as a type of data normalization by identifying how important a word is in a specific document relative to its overall frequency in all documents. The calculation is to divide the frequency of a word in a document by the total number of words in that document (tf). Then this is multiplied by the log(number of documents/number of documents containing word), which is the idf. Said another way, it adjusts the frequency of a term in a document based on how rarely it is used overall.

We do this by defining the tf-idf model to use and apply that to the training data:

```
> tfidf = text2vec::TfIdf$new()

> dtm_train_tfidf = text2vec::fit_transform(dtm_train, tfidf)
```

You can apply this process to the test data in a similar fashion:

```
> it_test = text2vec::itoken(
 test$text,
 tokenizer = tok_fun,
 ids = test$year,
 progressbar = FALSE
 )

> dtm_test_tfidf = text2vec::create_dtm(it_test, vectorizer)

> dtm_test_tfidf = transform(dtm_test_tfidf, tfidf)
```

We now have our feature space created to begin classification modeling.

LASSO model

I'm going to provide limited commentary during this portion as we've done this before in Chapter 4, *Advanced Feature Selection in Linear Models*. We will create our model using LASSO and check the performance on the test data. Let's specify our x and y for the `cv.glmnet()` function:

```
> x <- dtm_train_tfidf

> y <- as.factor(train$party)
```

The minimum number of folds in cross-validation with `glmnet` is three, which we will use given the small number of observations:

```
> set.seed(123)
```

```
> lasso <- glmnet::cv.glmnet(
 x,
 y,
 nfolds = 3,
 type.measure = "class",
 alpha = 1,
 family = "binomial"
 )

> plot(lasso)
```

The output of the preceding code is as follows:

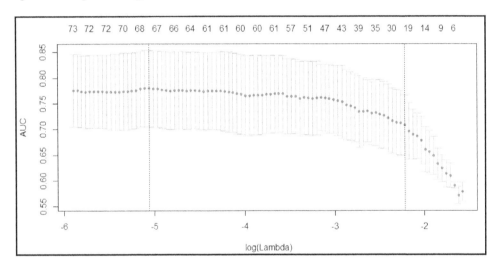

Wow! All those input features and just a handful are relevant, and the **area under the curve (AUC)** is around 0.75. Can that hold during validation?

```
> lasso_test <-
 data.frame(predict(lasso, newx = dtm_test_tfidf,
 type = 'response'), s = "lambda.1se")
> testY <- as.numeric(ifelse(test$party == "Republican", 1, 0))

> Metrics::auc(testY, lasso_test$X1)
[1] 0.8958333
```

It is a small dataset, observation-wise, but performance is OK. How could we improve this? Well, you may say we could add observations from the 19th century, but the party affiliation and political debate in that era were very different than today. You could possibly add principal components, or try ensembles. Those are just a few ideas. We'll transition now to looking at some other quantitative methods of interest.

Additional quantitative analysis

This portion of the analysis will focus on the power of the qdap package. It allows you to compare multiple documents over a wide array of measures. Our effort will be on comparing Teddy Roosevelt's 1908 written address and Ronald Reagan's 1982 speech. For starters, we will need to turn the text into data frames, perform sentence splitting, and then combine them to one data frame with a variable created that specifies the President. We will use this as our grouping variable in the analysis. Dealing with text data, even in R, can be tricky. The code that follows seemed to work the best, in this case, to get the data loaded and ready for analysis. I've created two text files of the addresses that I scraped off the internet. Help yourself to the files on GitHub at https://github.com/datameister66/ MMLR3rd.

The files are called tr.txt and reagan.txt.

We will use the readLines() function from base R, collapsing the results to eliminate unnecessary whitespace. I also recommend putting your text encoding to ASCII, otherwise you may run into some bizarre text that will mess up your analysis. That is done with the iconv() function:

```
> tr <- paste(readLines("~/corpus/tr.txt"), collapse=" ")

> tr <- iconv(tr, "latin1", "ASCII", "")
```

The warning message is not an issue, as it is just telling us that the final line of text is not the same length as the other lines in the .txt file. We now apply the qprep() function from qdap.

This function is a wrapper for a number of other replacement functions and using it will speed up preprocessing, but it should be used with caution if more detailed analysis is required. The functions it passes through are as follows:

- bracketX(): Applies bracket removal
- replace_abbreviation(): Replaces abbreviations
- replace_number(): Converts numbers to words, for example, *100* becomes *one hundred*
- replace_symbol(): Symbols become words, for example, @ becomes *at*

```
> prep_tr <- qdap::qprep(tr)
```

The other preprocessing we should do is to replace contractions (*can't* to *cannot*); remove stop words, in our case the top 100, and remove unwanted characters, with the exception of periods and question marks. They will come in handy shortly:

```
> prep_tr <  qdap::replace_contraction(prep_tr)

> prep_tr <- qdap::rm_stopwords(prep_tr, Top100Words, separate = F)

> prep_tr <- qdap::strip(prep_tr, char.keep = c("?", ".", "!"))
```

Critical to this analysis is to now split it into sentences and add what will be the grouping variable, the year of the speech. This also creates the `tot` variable, which stands for *turn of talk*, serving as an indicator of sentence order. This is especially helpful in a situation where you are analyzing dialogue, say in a debate or question and answer session:

```
> address_tr <- data.frame(speech = prep_tr)

> address_tr <- qdap::sentSplit(address_tr, "speech")

> address_tr$pres <- "TR"
```

Repeat the steps for the Ronald Reagan speech:

```
> reagan <-
paste(readLines("C:/Users/cory/Desktop/data/corpus/reagan.txt"), collapse="
")

> reagan <- iconv(reagan, "latin1", "ASCII", "")

> prep_reagan <- qdap::qprep(reagan)

> prep_reagan <- qdap::replace_contraction(prep_reagan)

> prep_reagan <- qdap::rm_stopwords(prep_reagan, Top100Words, separate = F)

> prep_reagan <- qdap::strip(prep_reagan, char.keep = c("?", ".", "!"))

> address_reagan <- data.frame(speech = prep_reagan)

> address_reagan <- qdap::sentSplit(address_reagan, "speech")

> address_reagan$pres <- "reagan"
```

Concatenate the separate years into one data frame:

```
> sentences <- dplyr::bind_rows(address_tr, address_reagan)
```

One of the great things about the qdap package is that it facilitates basic text exploration, as we did before. Let's see a plot of frequent terms:

```
> plot(qdap::freq_terms(sentences$speech))
```

The output of the preceding command is as follows:

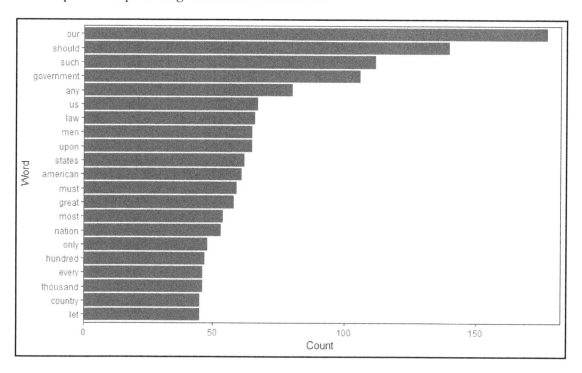

You can create a word frequency matrix that provides the counts for each word by speech:

```
> wordMat <- qdap::wfm(sentences$speech, sentences$pres)

> head(wordMat[order(wordMat[, 1], wordMat[, 2],decreasing = TRUE),])
            reagan   TR
our             69  107
us              44   17
let             33   12
government      18   77
years           17   20
america         17    7
```

This can also be converted into a DTM with the `as.dtm()` function, should you so desire.

Comprehensive word statistics are available. Here are tables of the statistics available in the package. A complete explanation of the statistics is available under `word_stats`:

```
> ws <- qdap::word_stats(sentences$speech, sentences$pres, rm.incomplete =
T)

> ws$word.elem
    pres    n.sent    n.words n.char n.syl n.poly      wps      cps
1     TR       667      12071  80780 25862   3786   18.097  121.109
2 reagan       222       2732  16935  5421    704   12.306   76.284
               sps       psps    cpw   spw    pspw n.hapax    n.dis
1     TR    38.774      5.676  6.692 2.142   0.314    1829      639
2 reagan    24.419      3.171  6.199 1.984   0.258     815      191
          grow.rate prop.dis
1     TR      0.152    0.053
2 reagan      0.298    0.070

> ws$sent.elem
  n.state n.quest p.state p.quest
1     667       0   1.000   0.000
2     217       5   0.977   0.023
```

Notice that Reagan's speech was much shorter than Roosevelt's written address, with a third of the total sentences. Also, he made use of asking questions five times as a rhetorical device while TR did not (`n.quest` 5 versus `n.quest` 0).

To compare the polarity (sentiment scores), use the `polarity()` function, specifying the text and grouping variables:

```
> pol = qdap::polarity(sentences$speech, sentences$pres)

> pol
    pres total.sentences total.words ave.polarity sd.polarity
stan.mean.polarity
1 reagan             222        2732        0.185       0.407
0.456
2 TR                 667       12071        0.028       0.501
0.056
```

The `stan.mean.polarity` value represents the standardized mean polarity, which is the average polarity divided by the standard deviation. We see that Reagan has slightly higher sentiment than TR. This seems expected as the address has evolved from a written document to Congress, to a televised speech. You can also plot the data. The plot produces two charts. The first shows the polarity by sentences over time and the second shows the distribution of the polarity:

```
> plot(pol)
```

The output of the preceding command is as follows:

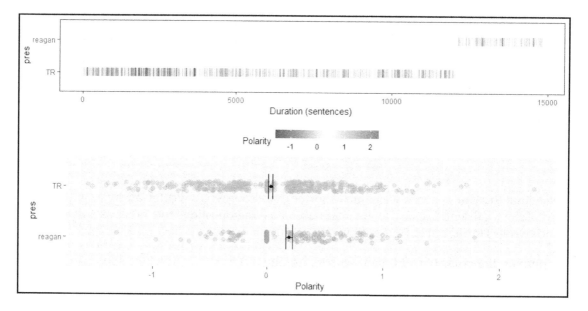

We can identify the most negative sentiment sentence by creating a data frame of the `pol` object, finding the sentence number, and producing it:

```
> pol.df <- pol$all

> which.min(pol.df$polarity)
[1] 86

> pol.df$text.var[86]
[1] "mobs frequently avenge commission crime themselves torturing death man
committing thus avenging bestial fashion bestial deed reducing themselves
level criminal."
```

Now that is negative sentiment! TR was actually quoting the Governor of Alabama about the horror of lynching. We will look at the readability index next:

```
> ari$Readability
    pres word.count sentence.count character.count
1 reagan      2732            222            16935
2     TR     12071            667            80780
  Automated_Readability_Index
1                    13.91929
2                    19.13838
```

Roosevelt's **Automated Readability Index (ARI)** is much higher than Reagan's ARI, a vestige of the language of his era. TR's sentences average 18 words. Formality analysis is next. This takes a couple of minutes to run in R, and you can overwhelm your memory if running it on a laptop or desktop computer. Therefore, we'll take a portion of TR's address, run it separately, then run it for Reagan:

```
> tr_sentences <- dplyr::filter(sentences, pres == "TR")

> tr_sentences <- tr_sentences[1:300, ]

> qdap::formality(tr_sentences$speech)
  all word.count formality
1 all       5726     72.08

> reagan_sentences <- dplyr::filter(sentences, pres == "reagan")

> formality(reagan_sentences$speech)
  all word.count formality
1 all       2732     67.15
```

TR is slightly more formal than Reagan.

Now, we will look at diversity measures. For most of the measures, TR is using a more diverse and richer lexicon than Reagan:

```
> diversity(sentences$speech, sentences$pres)
    pres    wc simpson shannon collision berger_parker brillouin
1 reagan  2732   0.998   6.653     5.896         0.025     6.104
2     TR 12071   0.999   7.491     6.659         0.011     7.101
```

One of my favorite plots is the dispersion plot. This shows the dispersion of a word throughout the text. Let's examine the dispersion of `"peace"`, `"government"`, and `"marksmanship"`:

```
> dispersion_plot(
    sentences$speech,
    rm.vars = sentences$pres,
    c("peace", "government", "marksmanship"),
    color = "black",
    bg.color = "white"
)
```

The output of the preceding command is as follows:

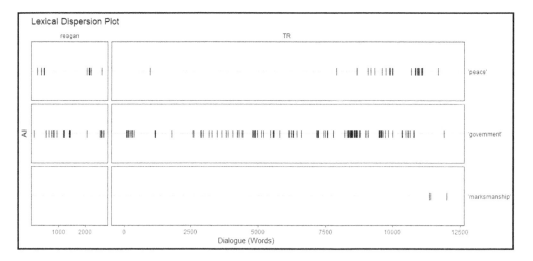

This is quite interesting as you can visualize how much longer TR's address is, as well as how he structured it to discuss foreign affairs later in the text. We can gain some insight into TR's mind with his discussion on marksmanship as he was looking at Switzerland as a shining example of how a populace could be armed and trained. You can see and understand how text analysis can provide insight into what someone is thinking, what their priorities are, and how they go about communicating them.

This completes our analysis of the two speeches. It provided some insight on to how the topics and speech formats have changed over time to accommodate political necessity. Keep in mind that this code can be adapted to text for dozens, if not hundreds, of documents and with multiple speakers, for example, screenplays, legal proceedings, interviews, social media, and so on. Indeed, text mining can bring quantitative order to what has been qualitative chaos.

Summary

In this chapter, we looked at how to address the massive volume of textual data that exists through text mining methods. We looked at a useful framework for text mining, including preparation, word frequency counts and visualization, and topic models using multiple packages in the `tidyverse`. Included in this framework were other quantitative techniques, such as polarity and formality, in order to provide a deeper lexical understanding, or what one could call style, with the `qdap` package. We applied the framework to the State of the Union addresses. Despite it not being practical to cover every possible text mining technique, those discussed in this chapter should be adequate for most problems that one might face.

In the next chapter, we are going to shift gears to reinforcement learning, where we train an algorithm to interactive with the environment to maximize rewards and minimize losses.

Creating a Package

"If you want something you never had, you have to do something you've never done."

– Thomas Jefferson

We are going to conclude this book by going through the process to create your own R package. If you are doing so, I recommend you start. I've put most of the functionality of data preparation from Chapter 1, *Preparing and Understanding Data*, into my own package. I'm not planning on putting it on CRAN, nor any package for that matter, with probably the exception of a package of American Civil War data like the Gettysburg file. So why bother with creating a package? If you are going to create code and put it into production, why would you not create a package with version control, examples, and other features? Plus, with RStudio, it is easy to do. So, we will use a simple example with one small function to show how easy it is.

Creating a new package

Before getting started, you will need to load two packages:

```
> install.packages("roxygen2")

> install.packages("devtools")
```

You now want to open **File** in RStudio and select **New Project**, which will put you at this point:

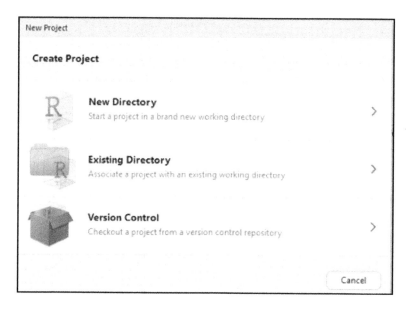

Select a new directory as desired, and specify **R Package**, as shown in the following screenshot:

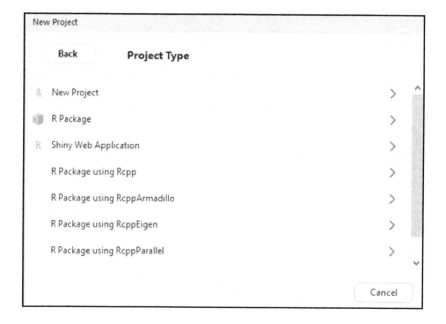

You will now name your package – I've innovatively called this one **package** – and select **Create Project**:

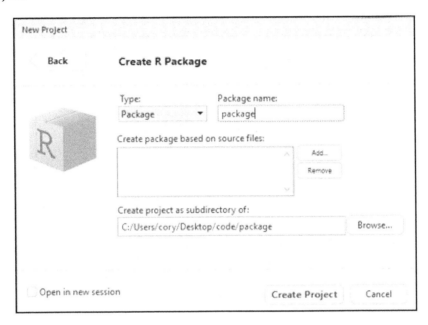

Go to your **Files** tab in RStudio and you should see several files populated like this:

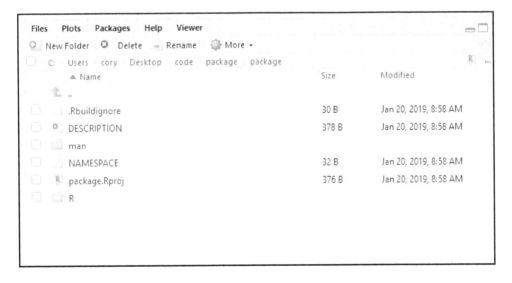

Notice the folder called R. That is where we will put the R functions for our package. But first, click on **Description** and fill it out accordingly, and save it. Here is my version, which will be a function to code all missing values in a dataframe to zero:

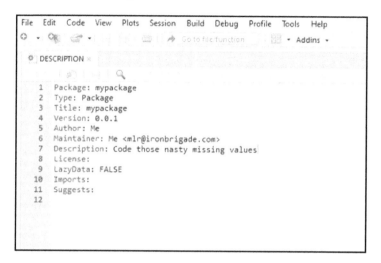

I've left imports and suggests blank. This is where you would load other packages, such as tidyverse or caret. Now, open up the hello.R function in the R folder, and delete all of it. The following format will work nicely:

- Title: Your package title of course
- Description: A brief description
- Param: The parameters for that function; the arguments
- Return: The values returned
- Examples: Provide any examples of how to use the function
- Export: Here, write the function you desire

Here is the function for our purposes, which just turns all NAs to zero:

```
#' @title package
#'
#' @description Turns NAs in a dataframe into zeroes
#'
#' @param dataframe
#'
#' @return dataframe
#'
#' @examples
#' dataset <- matrix(sample(c(NA, 1:5), 25, replace = TRUE), 5)
```

```
#' df <- as.data.frame(dataset)
#' package::na2zero(df)
#'
#' @export

na2zero <- function(dataframe)
{
 dataframe[is.na(dataframe)] <- 0
 return(dataframe)
}
```

You will now go to **Build** - **Configure Build Tools** and you should end up here:

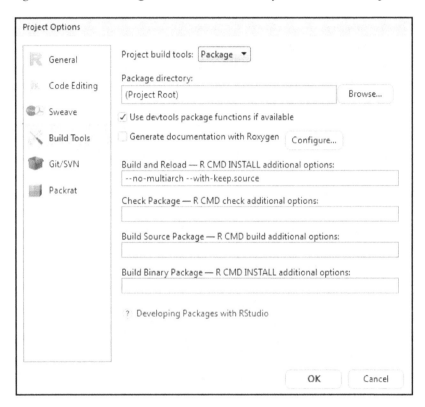

Click the checkmark for **Generate documentation with Roxygen**. Doing so will create this popup, which you can close and hit OK. You probably want to rename your function now from `hello.R` to something relevant. Now comes the moment of truth to build your package. Do this by clicking **Build** - **Clean and Rebuild**.

Now you can search for your package, and it should appear:

Click on it and go through the documentation:

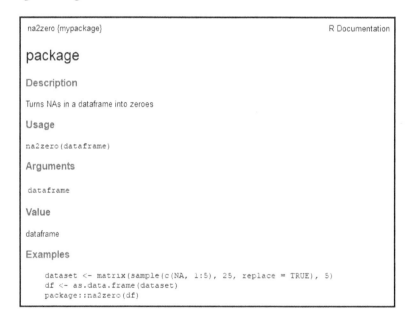

There you have it, a useless package, but think of what you can do by packaging your own or your favorite functions, and anyone who inherits your code will thank you.

Summary

In this final chapter, we went through the process of creating an R package, which can help you and your team put your code into production. We created one user-defined function for our package, but your only limit is your imagination. That concludes the primary chapters of the book. I hope you've enjoyed it and can implement the methods in here, as well as other methods you learn over time. Thank You!

Other Books You May Enjoy

If you enjoyed this book, you may be interested in these other books by Packt:

R Machine Learning Projects
Dr. Sunil Kumar Chinnamgari

ISBN: 9781789807943

- Explore deep neural networks and various frameworks that can be used in R
- Develop a joke recommendation engine to recommend jokes that match users' tastes
- Create powerful ML models with ensembles to predict employee attrition
- Build autoencoders for credit card fraud detection
- Work with image recognition and convolutional neural networks
- Make predictions for casino slot machine using reinforcement learning
- Implement NLP techniques for sentiment analysis and customer segmentation

R Deep Learning Essentials - Second Edition
Mark Hodnett, Joshua F. Wiley

ISBN: 9781788992893

- Build shallow neural network prediction models
- Prevent models from overfitting the data to improve generalizability
- Explore techniques for finding the best hyperparameters for deep learning models
- Create NLP models using Keras and TensorFlow in R
- Use deep learning for computer vision tasks
- Implement deep learning tasks, such as NLP, recommendation systems, and autoencoders

Leave a review - let other readers know what you think

Please share your thoughts on this book with others by leaving a review on the site that you bought it from. If you purchased the book from Amazon, please leave us an honest review on this book's Amazon page. This is vital so that other potential readers can see and use your unbiased opinion to make purchasing decisions, we can understand what our customers think about our products, and our authors can see your feedback on the title that they have worked with Packt to create. It will only take a few minutes of your time, but is valuable to other potential customers, our authors, and Packt. Thank you!

Index

overview 220, 221, 222
rotation 223, 224

Q

Quantile-Quantile (Q-Q) 36
quantitative analysis 295, 296, 320, 322, 325, 326
quartimax 223

R

R-squared 27
radical 293
random forest model
  evaluation process 187, 189, 190
  modeling process 187, 189, 190
random forest
  about 133, 136, 137, 200, 201
  used, for feature selection method 144, 146, 149, 151, 157, 159
Receiver Operating Characteristic (ROC) chart
  used, for model comparison 79, 80
recurrent neural networks (RNN) 170
Recursive Feature Elimination (RFE) 117
recursive partitioning 134
regression tree 134, 135
regularization
  about 167
  overview 84
Residual Sum of Squares (RSS) 28
restricted Boltzmann machine
  about 168
  reference 168
ridge regression
  about 85
  evaluation process 89, 91, 92, 93
  modeling process 89, 91, 92, 93
Root Mean Square Error (RMSE) 45

S

Schwarz-Bayes Criterion (SC) 285
sentiment analysis 306, 308
serial correlation 282
shrinkage penalty 84
sparse coding model
  about 168

reference 168
stacking 183
Subject Matter Experts (SMEs) 9
sum of squared error (SSE) 163, 256
supervised learning 193
support vector 109
support vector machines (SVM)
  about 105, 107, 108, 110, 133
  evolution process 125, 128, 130
  modeling process 125, 128, 130

T

TensorFlow 176, 177
term frequency-inverse document frequency (tf-idf) 316
term-document matrix (TDM) 294
text classification 316
text mining framework
  about 292, 293
  methods 292, 293
  quantitative analysis 295, 296
text2vec package
  used, for creating feature to classification model 316, 318
  used, for feature modeling for classification model 316
  used, for feature modeling to classification model 318
tidyverse
  reference 10
time series data
  about 265
  data exploration 267, 269, 271
topic models
  about 294
  building 311, 314, 316
tree-based learning 137
True Negative Rate 72
True Positive Rate (TPR) 72, 79

U

univariate linear regression
  about 28, 29, 30
  model assumptions, reviewing 34, 36
  model, building 31, 32, 34

72730775R00193

Made in the USA
Columbia, SC
31 August 2019